In the Days of Rain

In the Days of Rain

A DAUGHTER, A FATHER, A CULT

Rebecca Stott

Spiegel & Grau
New York

Published in the United States by Spiegel & Grau,
an imprint of Random House, a division of
Penguin Random House LLC, New York.

Spiegel & Grau and Design is a registered trademark
of Penguin Random House LLC.

Hardback ISBN 978-0-8129-8908-3
Ebook ISBN 978-0-8129-8909-0

Printed in the United States of America on acid-free paper

randomhousebooks.com
spiegelandgrau.com

987654321

First Edition

Photo credits and permissions can be found on pages 309–310.

Book design by Liz Cosgrove

Contents

In the Days of Rain

Reckoning

1

My father did the six weeks of his dying—raging, reciting poetry, and finally pacified by morphine—in a remote eighteenth-century windmill on the East Anglian fens. It was built to provide wind power to help drain the land, but by the time my father and stepmother bought it the sails and cogwheels were long gone. A previous owner had stripped out the rusting machinery, added a low nave with extra rooms, and painted it a dusky pink. From a distance and with the paint flaking off, it looked like a church washed up on the banks of a river. When the local farmer covered the black fields in every direction with plastic sheeting that miraged into floodwater in certain lights, the building always looked to me like a boat, or an ark, untethered from its moorings.

It was so far from civilization that it did not appear on GPS systems: The undertakers took four hours to reach us.

Since they'd moved into the mill six years earlier, my father had turned it into a pagan shrine, pasting its round, six-foot-thick walls with passages from Eliot's *Four Quartets* and Yeats's last poems, owl feathers, and Celtic symbols. He glued the lines of poetry onto the plaster, and when the damp made the paper curl off again he'd hammer in huge nails that made the plaster crack.

They bought the house on a whim a year after their wedding. They both wanted to live on flat land, he said. They both liked big skies.

"It's on the banks of a fen river," he said when he phoned to tell me they'd found the perfect house. "The Romans used it to ship building materials across the fens; during the war, a farmer plowed up a hoard of Roman silver plates covered in tritons and sea gods just a couple of fields away, and the local Baptists used to do their baptisms here. There's a mooring platform so we can buy a *boat*."

But you've got no money, I said to myself. *How exactly are you going to buy a boat?*

They drove me up to see it. We climbed through nettles and peered in through cobwebbed windows. It was beautiful, but it was also eerie and unsettling. All that sky. All that black soil. American bombers crossed the land on their flight path from the Mildenhall air base. Falcons hung low over the riverbank or scrutinized the fields from their posts on electricity cables.

Four months later my stepmother had turned the small circle of long-neglected riverside land into the beginnings of a garden. My father beat down the nettles with sticks. He borrowed a plow from a neighboring farmer and broke it within a few hours. The farmer patched up the worst parts of the road. My father planted beech hedges and supervised local lads in the laying out of a lawn. He ordered and planted a grove of white birches at the far end of the garden as a birthday present for my stepmother. Their white trunks were magnificent, luminous against the black soil of the fen fields, especially at dusk.

"He's always had a thing for silver birches," she told me. "I prefer willows."

My father was built on a different scale than the rest of us. In 2007, the year of his dying, he was sixty-eight, six foot four, and twenty stone. His long snow-white hair and beard would have made him look like an Old Testament prophet if it wasn't for the combat jacket he'd taken to wearing. He bought it from the Army and Navy Store to audition for the part of Mark Antony in a production of Shakespeare's *Antony and Cleopatra* and now wore it all the time. He thought of himself as an aging Mark Antony, but to me he was Sir Andrew Aguecheek, sometimes a Falstaff, occasionally a Lear. We called him Roger in our teens, and later on Rodge or Dodge or the Big Man, never Dad. He wasn't a dad, at least not in the way that most people mean it. I'd usually just refer to him as "my father"—Roger seemed an absurd name for a man built on his scale.

His head was twice the size of mine. When he had money he bought his clothes from an outsize shop called High and Mighty, but now that he was poor, most of his clothes—and my stepmother's—came from charity shops. When he split the seams in his trousers he'd staple them back together. It was far quicker and more efficient than sewing, he insisted when I asked what he was doing with the stapler in one hand and the washing basket in the other. My stepmother flashed me a look that meant hold your tongue. When he broke his glasses, he taped the arms back on. She flashed me a look about that too.

He had a set of dentures that replaced some of his back teeth, and sometimes he took them out when he was speaking fast or reciting poetry. He'd place them on the table between us. Sometimes he did this in restaurants or pubs. He belched too—at home and in public. His belches were loud, elongated, and cadenced like a long rumble of thunder. He belched, I think, as an act of defiance against all forms of gentility and because it made us laugh. My brothers—and then my son—competed to imitate those sounds. It became a tribal thing.

Through that final winter, increasingly lame, bilious, and irascible—his pancreas riddled with the still-undetected cancer—my father, the great limping bulk of him, walked the bank of the River Lark for hours every day, following the line of the river across the fens listening to Joyce's *Ulysses* through headphones for the seventh time. He and my stepmother had planted hundreds of bulbs— fritillaries and parrot tulips—on the path up to the mill door and in rows on the riverbank. By February they were pushing up shoots.

On Valentine's Day in a hospital in Bury St. Edmunds, doctors finally used the word "cancer" at the end of several weeks of euphemisms that had begun with "inflammation" and then progressed to "blockage," then "lump," and finally "tumor."

"Seems they manage bad news by drip-feeding it here," my father said. "It's exactly three centimeters by six centimeters," he added, indulging his obsession for numbers, tracing the edges of the shadow on the ultrasound printout. "They don't know how long I have. But they've given me a counselor. That's not good, is it?"

He'd have to finish his memoir now, he said, when he'd been allowed to go home and had stopped swearing, raving, and thumping walls and tables with his fist. He'd begun to think about what it might mean to put his affairs in order. When he told me he was going to need my help to finish that book of his, my heart sank.

He'd started writing a semi-fictionalized autobiography eight years earlier, shortly before meeting my stepmother. He called it *The Iron Room,* after the corrugated-iron meeting room where he and his parents and siblings worshipped five or six times a week when he was growing up. For the first three years, he talked about his memoir all the time. Every spare hour he took away from his paid work as a freelance copy editor he was at it: ten steps back into rewriting, one step forward into new writing. He sent me scores of drafts, each only slightly different from the last. I came to dread the sight of his emails in my inbox.

"I can't see the wood for the trees anymore," I pleaded. "Let me read it when it's finished. Then I'd be a fresh pair of eyes."

I was relieved when the emails stopped coming, when he was distracted by the mill, the garden, the broken plow, and the question of where to put the silver birches.

It was when he hit the 1960s, he said now, that he'd run into trouble. He hadn't been able to get any further. I did the calculations. That was a shortfall of forty-nine years. How long would that take him—or me—to write?

"The *Nazi* decade," he added, as if it was an explanation, and I nodded, telling myself the morphine was addling his head. Everything *after* 1960 had turned into a *thicket,* he whispered through tears and expletives while uncorking what was probably the third bottle of wine that afternoon. But he was going to finish it, he said. He *had* to. He wasn't going to let death win that sodding chess game. He thumped his huge fist down on the arm of his chair again. *Not anytime soon.* He gestured at the television, a forty-two-inch flat-screen, the only piece of equipment he kept within the cool damp interior of the mill tower, on which he'd paused a scene from Ingmar Bergman's *The Seventh Seal.* Within the black-and-white frame, two men dressed in medieval clothes sat playing chess against a wild sea.

"So long as the Knight keeps playing the game of chess," my father said, "Death can't take him."

He was going to keep death at bay by watching Ingmar Bergman films. He was damn well going to watch all fifty-eight of them again now, he declared.

Still from Bergman's *The Seventh Seal*

I could only remember seven Bergman films. My father had made me watch them when I was sixteen on afternoons when he persuaded me to skip school during my O levels: *Wild Strawberries, Autumn Sonata, Cries and Whispers, The Seventh Seal, Winter Light, The Silence,* and *Through a Glass Darkly.* He'd buy red wine, huge loaves of still-warm bread, and slabs of ham, and open a jar of his favorite whole-grain English mustard. We watched those films in his dusty, postdivorce flat, sitting on the floor amid piles of unpaid bills and documents and scatterings of poems. I'd go back to school—or to my mother's house—slightly drunk, my head spinning.

I started a list on the day he showed me Death playing chess on the TV screen. *Ingmar Bergman: 58*—I wrote at the top of the page in my notebook, thinking I'd order them online. I'd forgotten that my father had more than forty of them in a cupboard in the mill, that he'd been collecting them since he stole into the back row of a cinema to see *Wild Strawberries* at the age of eighteen.

Fifty-eight. How many films could you watch in a day?

My younger brother, traveling across New Zealand on sabbatical from work, flew home and moved into the mill. I stayed as often as I could, driving up from Cambridge every other day, leaving notes for my ex-husband and babysitters, managing a job and publishers with a phone and an Internet connection that rarely worked. My sister flew over from France. My two other brothers came as often as their jobs and young families allowed them. The five of us gathered around, steeled ourselves. My stepmother ordered in food and more cases of wine and turned the thermostat button to Constant.

In the crypt light of the mill tower, through late February and March, we watched Bergman films together, interspersed with long hours of cricket—the Cricket World Cup had just started. We played Mozart, drank wine, cooked, and ate together at a table that seated fifteen, only a few feet from my father's reclining chair, which was now permanently horizontal. It snowed. My son and I drove across fen dirt tracks in the dark to fetch foil boxes of Gressingham duck prepared for my father by the cooks at the White Pheasant pub at Fordham, but though he wanted to eat he had no appetite. He worked away at his memoir for several hours a day for the first week, propped up on pillows, but then, once the Macmillan nurse increased his daily doses of morphine, he was too tired to write.

Then there was the day he told me, tears in his eyes, that he didn't think he could finish his memoir after all. He'd gone back into the thicket, but he couldn't face it: *the muddle, the cruelty, the madness of it all.* And even if he *could* describe those years, he whispered, as if someone might be listening in, he'd never be able to close the great gap in time, get from 1960 to now, to *this*.

"Shandy's dilemma," I said, and he smiled darkly. For decades he'd been persuading me to read his favorite books. Many had become my household gods now too. A webwork of inside jokes and literary references had grown between us. We both read Laurence Sterne's mad fictional eighteenth-century memoir, *The Life and Opinions of Tristram Shandy, Gentleman.* But now that he had only weeks to live, the similarities between *Tristram Shandy* and my father's own unfinished fictional memoir struck me as both tragic and ridiculous.

Poor Tristram finds he's written several hundred pages before he's even been born. Convinced that the oddities of his personality were caused by the fact that his father was interrupted while having sex with his mother on the night of his conception by his mother asking if he'd forgotten to wind the clock, Tristram then has to explain about the clock, and to do that he has to explain about Uncle Toby, his father's brother . . . and while he is trying to explain all of this, and as the pages are clocking up, there's a knock at the door and Death is there on the threshold—cloak, scythe, and all. Tristram leaps from the window and gallops to Dover to take a boat to Calais. Death takes up pursuit.

I took the bus from my house into town to buy a portable tape recorder.

"If I ask you questions," I said to him as he disappeared into another cricket match, "it might be easier. You wouldn't get so tired. Then I could transcribe it later. We could do short bursts, when you felt like it."

The tape recorder was black. Out in the mill, dust coated everything within hours and I had to keep wiping the machine down. The dust bothered me. I'd never noticed it before. Dust and, even in March, fruit flies. The house was full of them. My father had started to keep a tally of the number he found in his wineglass. The fruit-fly count joined all his other reckonings in his notebooks: daily calorie count, his gambling winnings and losings, the daily diabetes count, the cricket scores. My stepmother just put an old beer mat over her glass. She didn't much like wine.

But although the tape recorder had been easy enough to choose in the department store that day, I hadn't anticipated that the tapes would stupefy me. How many did I need? They came in packs of four or eight or twelve. Each of them could hold a recording of eight hours. How long did he have? How far would he get? I stood in front of the display case in the shop for twenty minutes trying to do multiplication sums in my head. I picked up three packets of twelve: thirty-six tapes. That was 288 hours; 17,280 minutes.

I now have two tapes in my study drawer next to the old recorder. One is full, the other only partly full. I gave the unused ones away. My father got from 1960 to 1966, two years after my birth. He ran out of time. Like Tristram Shandy, like the Knight in *The Seventh Seal,* he didn't get to finish his story once Death had gotten into the house.

What he had to tell me was far worse than I could have imagined. No wonder he got stuck.

When we began, I imagined my father and me in that forest together with scythes, torches, and protective clothing, and then, triumphant, finally scaling the castle walls. We'd do whatever was needed—slay the dragon, cut down the thorns, rescue the princess—*together.* But we didn't make it.

Day by day he grew quieter. His reclining chair remained horizontal, and his morphine-induced sleeps lasted longer. I slipped the tape recorder and the pack of tapes into the back of the cupboard where he kept his dusty film collection and his store of Spanish reds.

In the fourth week of his six weeks of dying, my father, laid out at the center of the mill tower, opened his eyes and summoned my brother and me, his executors. He had already given me instructions about what to do about his memorial stone, the funeral, and his extensive debts. He was struggling hard to surface from his morphine-heightened dreams, to keep his eyes open, to sit up. We moved in closer.

"This is very important," he stressed, raising a finger from the bed and jabbing it into the air with all the strength he had, his white beard and hair wild, his jaundice-yellowed eyes bloodshot.

"You can't leave any of those bastards alone with me when I'm asleep, you understand? You know what they're like. They'll take advantage. They're like vultures."

He knew all too well from his fifteen years as a ministering brother in the Exclusive Brethren that the distant family members who were now visiting every day as the end grew nearer would want to pray over him, help him find his way back to the Lord. He was having none of that.

Dutifully we warned the cousins who came carrying Bibles and hymn books. How do you tell a Christian not to pray? What else were they supposed to do? Leave the dying man to the tortures of hellfire?

We asked them to respect his wishes. They were offended and baffled. They'd driven a long way. Many had gotten lost once GPS began to tell them to turn around and make for the nearest road. They drank tea and examined the strange pagan grotto of the mill and its many false idols. I watched a distant cousin run her eyes down the lines from *Four Quartets* that he'd pasted above the door, her brow furrowed.

He was right to warn us to be vigilant. Despite our requests, there were two or three times when we dropped our guard. On one occasion we saw the lips of one of the visiting cousins, a kind elderly woman, pressed up against my father's ear, while he lay commanding the room even in sleep, like a fallen tree or an oversize, dusty, and yellowing tomb effigy. She was whispering to him.

"Excuse me," my brother said, glancing anxiously at me, embarrassed, "please don't do that."

The promise we'd made had probably already been broken.

We never left him alone with visitors again. His eyes flickered open once to tell me as I leaned across him that I was *so beautiful.* He woke another time to implore me to keep the scale of his gambling debts secret from my stepmother. On the night before the equinox, I left the house for the first time in weeks. I'd been invited to interview for a job I applied for months before at the University of East Anglia. The nurse had taken me aside.

"I'm sure he'd want you to go," she said. "He'd want you to have a good shot at it."

From a building on the Norfolk campus, surrounded by lush green hummocks overrun with rabbits, I rang my brother every two hours. I stood in the empty toilet trying to apply makeup to my swollen face minutes before the interview, talking to my father in the mirror.

"You've never been arrogant enough," I heard him say to me as he'd so often done. "Be arrogant. Nail it."

When I got back late that night, my brother told me my father was still alive, although the nurse had said he probably wouldn't last to the morning. I volunteered to take the night watch. No one argued; they were all exhausted. My father's breaths rattled, paused, rattled, gasped, and began again.

"Get him to *let go*," my brother whispered after my stepmother had left the room. "He'll listen to you." He helped me drag the sofa across the room so that I could sleep next to my father's reclining chair, and then my brother was gone, the lights in the house out.

The wind rattled the windows. It was snowing again. I steadied my breathing in the darkness to match my father's breaths; I held my breath when his stopped. I told him about the interview. I told him I'd been arrogant, that I'd done a good job. Then I told him he could let go. Immediately I wished I hadn't said it.

My mobile rang. It was an old friend. He was walking home from a pub through the snow along a riverbank in the southern fens, and he'd called because he'd had a strange feeling about me and wanted to know if I was all right. I hadn't heard from him for more than two years. Startled by the sound of my sobs and my father's labored breathing, he stayed on the phone talking softly about anything that came into his head until the first birds began to sing, when I finally fell asleep.

When the vice chancellor rang in the morning to offer me the job, I asked if I could have a few days to get back to him. My father was about to die, I said. "About to die" struck me as an odd phrase. I wanted to tell him how strange it was to watch death fighting to take possession of a body, of how my father's body and the blackening ridges of his fingernails made me think of the color and texture of a felled oak tree I'd once seen out on the fens, but instead I said *thank you*. I told him that I was, of course, *delighted*. I would get back to him. I just needed to attend to this particular day. Take your time, he said. Take as much time as you need.

My brother and I played Chopin in the late afternoon. At around five, the light began to fade. My stepmother and sister-in-law set out to drive the six miles across the fens to buy milk. The phone rang. I walked from my father's chair through the nave of the mill to the sitting room at the far end of the building to take the call. It was an old friend of my father's asking how he was.

Across the fields in the half-light I could just make out something moving in the distance, a flash of white against the darkening trees. It was a barn owl, flying low through the dusk, following the path of the river, heading straight for the mill, heading straight for us. I walked back down the long corridor to where my father lay breathing in rasps, my brother reading the newspaper beside him.

"It's coming," I said.

I have no idea what I thought the "it" was. My brother put his newspaper down, I opened the window, and we each picked up one of my father's great gnarled hands, just as the owl passed by the front door, just as my father took his last breath, just as my stepmother opened the door with the milk, just as a great congregation of crows, lapwings, and blackbirds took up their positions in rows along the electrical cables and pylons. The owl circled the house for twenty minutes and then disappeared.

Twilight on the equinox, with an owl, by a river. It was just as he would have conjured it.

2

No one would guess that I was raised in a Christian fundamentalist cult or that my father and grandfather were ministering brothers in one of the most reclusive and savage Protestant sects in British history. So it was always my fault if the subject came up. It might be because I'd dropped my guard, gotten bored, or told a story from my childhood. Of course once it did come up, it was always difficult to make it go away. People were interested; they asked questions. I never learned how to shut the discussion down again.

You can't tell just bits of it, I'd remind myself. Once you get started, the whole thing begins unraveling, like a stitch in a scarf or a story that has no beginning or end. Best not to start at all. Best to keep quiet.

No matter how many times I tried to tell it, in pieces or at length, I always ended up baffled, feeling as though there was a part I'd left out or forgotten, a lost moral or a punch line.

"I was raised in a cult," I'd say, and then recoil, embarrassed by the melodrama of the words. Were the Brethren a cult? I didn't know. What was the difference between a sect and a cult? Was there a point on a spectrum where a sect became a cult?

"We wore headscarves," I'd say. "We weren't allowed to cut our hair. We weren't allowed television, newspapers, radios, cinemas, holidays, pets, wristwatches."

The list of prohibitions always seemed endless. I watched people's eyes open wider. They'd compete to ask questions, and look at me askance, and I'd think, *Oh no, not this again.*

"We weren't allowed to talk to the other children at school," I'd say. "They told us that everyone outside the Brethren was part of Satan's army and they were all out to get us. If you didn't do exactly what they said, they'd expel you, and then your family wouldn't be allowed to speak to you ever again. People committed suicide. People went mad. Yes, this was Brighton. Yes, this was Brighton in the sixties. Yes, during flower power. In the suburbs. During the sexual revolution. Yes. It's hard to explain."

"You were raised *Plymouth Brethren*?" people would say. They would have heard about the Plymouth Brethren. Some might even have read *Father and Son,* Edmund Gosse's beautiful memoir about growing up in a nineteenth-century Plymouth Brethren assembly. And I'd hear myself reply with a hint of superiority, "We weren't *Plymouth* Brethren. We were *Exclusive* Brethren.

"My people were the hard-liners," I'd say. "Gosse was in the *Open* Brethren. That was nothing. They were virtually *Baptist.* They had pulpits and priests and adult baptisms. They were allowed to talk to worldly people, even eat with them."

My people? Had I really just said "my people"?

But even if the subject didn't come up, my Brethren childhood would rear up like Banquo's ghost at the dinner table, refusing to be buried. At university, when I made new friends and confidantes, I couldn't explain how I became a teenage mother—or why I shoplifted books for years, or why I was reckless, impatient, afraid of the dark, and had a compulsion to rescue people—without explaining the Brethren, the God they made for us, and the Rapture they told us was coming.

But then I couldn't really talk about the Brethren without explaining about my father, how he'd been a ministering brother and then become addicted to roulette when he left the sect and stopped believing in God. I'd have to explain how he'd gone to prison for embezzlement and fraud and then ended up making films for the BBC, and that on his deathbed he'd talked about a "Nazi decade" and made us promise not to let anyone pray over his sleeping body.

And I could never really tell my father's story without telling my grandfather's—how the Scottish ship chandler had migrated south to supply food to the hotels of Brighton and ended up one of the ruling members of the Brethren and running the publishing house that printed Brethren ministries.

And to explain Brethren women, I'd have to tell the story of how my great-grandmother had been sent to an asylum in Australia for forty years by her Brethren husband not just because she had epilepsy but because she was considered too *willful*. Willfulness isn't allowed in Brethren women, I'd say, and then realize that I didn't really know what kind of willful she'd been.

My family, I'd tell them, had been caught up in the Brethren for a hundred years. And then I'd notice I just used that funny old-fashioned phrase my mother always used: *caught up in*.

"But back then, of course," she'd say when she was remembering something about rationing or the air raids, "we were caught up in the Brethren."

My family hadn't *belonged to* the Brethren, we'd been *caught up in* them. Caught up like a coat catching on thorns. Caught up in a scandal. Caught up in the arms of the Lord. Whichever way you phrased it, it meant you didn't get to choose, and that there was no getting away.

And then I'd be five years old again, sitting in meeting, listening to my grandfather preaching that soon we'd all be *caught up in* the arms of the Lord because the Rapture was coming. The Lord Jesus was going to take us with him up into the air in the middle of the night. We'd be *caught up in* his arms. My grandfather's usually harsh Scottish preaching voice would go soft when he talked about the Rapture. And I'd be sitting there swinging my legs on the chair in the meeting room, wondering how the Lord Jesus was going to lift all of us up at the same time—there were some large and sweaty people in our fellowship. The Lord Jesus would have to be a giant to be strong enough to lift my father off the ground. I'd never seen anyone do that.

After we left the cult my father sometimes tried to explain about the Brethren to people who'd never heard of them. Though he was a man who seized any opportunity to hold the floor, his eyes always seemed to glaze over when anyone asked him about it, as if he was bored or reading from a script. He complained that when he tried to write an Exclusive Brethren–in-a-nutshell section into his memoir, it just came out as a lump of gawky exposition. My mother refused to talk about it at all. Best to draw a line through all of that, she'd say. No use going back in there. It won't do any good.

3

After the funeral and the wake and the speeches and the fire we burned his chair in, my brother and I ventured into my father's study, stacked high with papers. It all had to be cleared out, my stepmother said, if the mill was to be sold. We rescued anything that looked important from piles of unpaid bills, receipts, photographs, and instructions for long-dead appliances.

If I was going to finish his book, I told my brother, I was going to need everything that looked as if it had anything to do with the

Brethren. So we shoved stacks of letters and diaries and yellowed documents into boxes without sorting through them. My brother and my son helped me carry the six boxes up three flights of stairs in my Cambridge house and slip them into the dark and dusty space under my Victorian iron bed. I'd deal with them later, I told myself, when I was ready, when I had time.

A month after my father's funeral, my stepmother rang to say that she'd been to see the doctors about her stomach cramps. After a series of tests, they had diagnosed her with bowel cancer. She'd be fine, she said. She had her cousins nearby. There'd be a course of chemo. Her cousins would drive her back and forth from the mill to the chemo sessions. Friends would come in to help with the garden. She didn't need me to come out there. She didn't need anything from any of us for now. She'd let us know if she did.

How could two newlyweds, living out an Indian summer, planting a garden on the banks of a river, *both* have been incubating cancerous growths? Did his cancer explain the biliousness of his behavior, his rants and storms, the way he started to talk to her in those last years, his complaints about how she refused to sit and watch Shakespeare with him?

"Perhaps she just doesn't like Shakespeare," I'd said to him. "It's not a crime."

"*Midsomer Murders,*" he said. "*Midsomer bloody Murders.* That's the level of philistinism we are talking about here."

I'd watch *Midsomer Murders,* I thought, if the alternative was listening to you lecture me about Wilson Knight and the late plays of Shakespeare for the fourteenth time.

I wanted to help my stepmother. We all did. But though I drove up every few weeks, I now dreaded the sight of the mill. *Puddleglum,* the little secondhand cabin boat my father and I had bought together, moored on the river under the willow tree, was now covered in mildew and leaves. The lawn grass was running to seed, the birch trees wilting in the sun. The pyre where we'd burned my father's chair had left a scorch mark and stumps of charcoaled wood on the grass. Someone needed to rake it all in and put some grass seed down.

My stepmother was struggling not just with the chemo but also with the bank. My father had left her almost penniless. I printed out the bank statement from his computer a week after the funeral. He'd placed scores of online bets in those final days, most made in the middle of the night when we were all asleep. Just one big win, he would have told himself. Just one big win so that he could leave my stepmother money to pay off the debts.

I reckoned up the bets. He spent thousands of pounds in those last weeks by moving money from one credit card to another. It wasn't even his money; it was the last of my stepmother's small inheritance.

I volunteered to spend an afternoon at the mill when my step-mother was in the hospital and her cousins were away for their summer holidays. I'd mow the lawn and water the birches, I told her. It was the least I could do.

I drove slowly up the long lane that gave way to the dirt track that followed the course of the river, coal-black fen fields in one direction and rising corn in the other. I parked the car and let myself in, using the key she kept under a rock near the back door. I found the mower in the shed, the blades encrusted with dried grass.

When the mower started up, the sound seemed a rude imposition on the birdsong and silence, but the smell and stripes of mowed grass made me feel I was pushing the encroaching wilderness farther back a little, that I could make all of this tidy again, at least for now.

Somewhere in the heat of the day, amid the smell of cut grass and the roar of the machine, I strayed into a corner of a flower bed. On the edge of my vision a black cloud rose up and hummed low and close, smoke-dark against the white of the birch trunks. The first sharp sting of venom broke my concentration. The second made me release the handle of the mower. It wasn't until I'd run screaming through the empty garden, casting off my clothes, and taken refuge in the sitting room, shaking, hurt, and enraged, that I examined my skin in the mirror. I counted twenty-one wasp stings, raised hot mounds on my arms, neck, hands. I'd run over a wasps' nest in the dark fen soil of that garden, in the twilight of its grieving afternoon.

Can a dead man conjure wasps? Can an owl flying at dusk take a dying man's soul? Out there in that pagan fen landscape that disgorged Roman silver plates on the plowshare, anything seemed possible. Like the house in Alan Garner's *The Owl Service,* the mill had unaccountable scratchings in its eaves now, presences everywhere.

"Leave me alone," I said to the empty air. "Leave me a-*lone*. I'll finish your book when I'm ready. You can't *make* me."

The contents of those six boxes under the bed made me think of chaos, the spillage of my father's body after his death, the gritty cremation ashes we scattered on the river by the mill, the mess of his life, the impossibility of telling the Brethren story, and my own grief. They stayed down there—under the bed, gaffer-taped up.

There was so much else to do. A new job and a commute, teenagers to cook for, homework to supervise, deadlines to meet, students to teach, lectures to write, and a mortgage to pay. It was two years before the letters from debt collectors and credit card companies and court summonses stopped coming and before I stopped posting out the photocopies of my father's death certificate with the cover letters that explained that he'd died *without assets,* that his debts and bills could not be paid. By then the mill had been sold and my stepmother had gone to Australia to live near her family.

What had I actually promised him, I began to wonder. If I was going to finish his book, I'd have to describe what happened in the sixties, in that decade he couldn't bear to look at. No one would understand the recklessness of his behavior without understanding that. But I didn't want to revisit that decade any more than he had. No one in the family wanted to go back there. Sometimes my father's cousins would refer to the years we were "caught up in the Brethren," or "living in the Jims," or "living under the system." Most of them seemed ashamed that they hadn't seen through it at the time; some clearly felt angry and duped. Most wanted to tell me that they should have gotten out earlier, but no one knew, they said, no one knew how bad it was going to get. Then they changed the subject. Best not to dwell on the past. Better to focus on the future.

Even if I did get a book written, the Brethren were rich and pow-erful. They attacked people who criticized them. They employed legal teams. When I once wrote about growing up in the Brethren for a Sunday magazine, a ministering brother sent me a letter to say they were praying for me; that meant they knew where I lived. I'd moved house since then but knew they could track me down if they wanted to, wherever I lived. What would my family have to say if I started asking questions about that history now? And I'd have to find a way of not writing about my mother, of steering around her, because she wouldn't want me to make her remember any of that.

If I was going to finish my father's story, I'd have to write about the girl I'd been in the Brethren too, because we'd both lived in that thicket and we'd both gotten caught up in its cruel aftermath. I'd have to think about the days I spent listening for the sound of Satan's hooves on the paving stones of Brighton, for instance, or making deals with the Lord, or hoarding tins of corned beef and condensed milk in preparation for the Tribulations. I didn't want to think about that Brethren girl in her red cardigan with brass buttons, wearing her headscarf and clutching her Bible. I'd drawn a line between me and her. My mother was right. Perhaps it was all best left well alone.

4

Four years after my father died I won a place at a monthlong silent writers' retreat in a fifteenth-century castle just south of Edinburgh. I was supposed to be writing a novel set in nineteenth-century London, but after a week sitting at a desk staring down over the castle grounds I was deleting everything I wrote, and that wasn't much. Every paragraph felt hollowed out; every sentence threw me off.

When I walked the castle grounds at dusk, down through the bracken and the fallen and rotting trees to the peat-red river, up to the edge of the mown lawns and the flower beds and back round again, I heard my father reciting parts of Revelation or Ezekiel, or Yeats's "The Wild Swans at Coole," or talking about that thicket of his. His voice echoed through the east and west wings of the castle, through the woods, in the wind. These were just aural grief hallucinations, I told myself, just flickers in my neural pathways. They were nothing out of the ordinary, nothing to worry about.

In the final week of the retreat, I joined the other four writers at dusk to swim in the river that curled wide and red-brown over rocks and pebbles through the castle woods. After we'd climbed from the freezing water and pulled our towels and robes around us, we followed the path up the steep riverbank into the darkening woods. I fixed my eyes on the poet's feet ahead of me, now level with my head, as they pressed into the leaves and bracken. When his foot slipped and he stumbled slightly, I saw, or thought I saw, a plume of smoke rising slowly from a hole in the ground that he'd disturbed.

I felt the scratchings and rustlings in my hair. The first stings began. The poet behind me, dressed in a red robe, was also engulfed. We ran through the woods back to the castle, tripping over undergrowth in the darkness, shaking our hair and pulling off our clothes, until we were sure we'd outrun them.

We'd had a lucky escape, we told ourselves over dinner. The retreat director, baffled, said he'd never come across wasps nesting in the ground. Nor did wasps usually sting unless they were attacked. It was most unusual. Was it, someone asked, lemon juice or ice you were supposed to put on wasp stings? Someone passed me a tumbler of whiskey. I took myself to bed early. The whiskey must have addled my head, I thought, because I seemed to be hearing voices that weren't there.

At three in the morning I woke, my pulse drumming wildly in my ears, fireworks exploding behind my eyelids. When I stumbled to a mirror to pry open a single eye, my face and neck were so swollen, taut, and shiny that I staggered backward in shock. I was struggling to breathe.

Two days later it was all over: the early-morning drive through the dark to the emergency room in the director's car, the steroids, the dosage of antihistamines large enough to floor an elephant, the semi-coma I slipped into for twenty-four hours. The doctor had counted up the hard lumps on my scalp and neck. Twenty-five stings. Enough to kill someone with an allergy, almost enough to kill someone who'd been stung before in an empty garden when a smoky swarm rose like a ghost from a hole in the ground.

Not enough to kill, I thought, but enough to make a point.

A few years earlier, I'd discovered that the man dressed in a turquoise and pink Hawaiian shirt sitting opposite me at a Cambridge dinner party was a world expert on shamanism. I plagued him with questions, and if I failed to observe the to-and-fro turn-taking of dinner party etiquette, I was not the only one. None of us wanted to talk about anything else.

For fifteen summers he'd lived with a shamanic tribe on the Russian steppes, he told us, studying shamans as they talked their dead down.

"Talking down," I said, "what does that mean?" Death for me had been all about going *up there,* the transcendent sucking *up* into the air, into the arms of Jesus. I thought again of the impossibility of that body weight of my father's going *up there,* going up *anywhere.* Even in the blood-red plastic cremation jar his ashes had been a dead weight.

The shaman expert told us that the bereaved Sora used the shaman as an intermediary to persuade the dead person to go down into the next world.

"Like laying a ghost?" I said.

"Something like that," he said. "Though it works both ways for them. The dead and the living both have to convince the other to let them go. It takes a long time."

Until the relatives had talked down the dead person, he told us, their spirit would be hanging around the village doing bad things, provoking, making people sick, causing the crops to fail. They had to be talked down and into the ground.

In that moment I saw my huge father up on a cliff ledge some-where, slightly drunk, swaying close to the edge, holding forth, and my siblings and me talking him down. Or trying to. Hadn't we done that? I asked myself. Isn't that what we'd done out there at the mill with the Bergman and the cricket?

But I hadn't even started. My father was still roaming. Still talk-ing. There were swarms of wasps, acts of provocation. It would get worse. *Someone* was going to have to talk him down.

5

Six years after my father died, my daughter Kezia, nineteen and home from university for the summer, went looking for an electric fan that I told her had been dismantled and would be in a cupboard some-where. It was impossible to think, she'd complained the day before, up in my study with the summer sun beating at the closed shutters.

She texted me at the desk where I was working a mile away in the cool of the British Library.

"I found Grandpa's boxes," she wrote. "Can I open them?"

It took me a while to reply.

"It's a mess in there," I texted back. "But maybe you could sort the papers into some kind of order, if you've got time."

When I came back to the house several hours later, Kez was sitting in the top-floor study, shutters closed, among neat piles of papers. Knife-thin shafts of light, pouring in through the cracks in the shutters, lit up the dust. Orlando, my elderly marmalade-striped cat, tiptoed over and between the piles of papers, trying to get himself into the path of her intense attention. The fan parts lay discarded, unassembled, on the floor.

She'd gone to the store around the corner and bought Post-it notes and plastic filing sleeves and filing boxes.

"I started in 1953," she said, flushed. "There's letters from South Africa and Grandpa's prison diary in that file. There's this letter he wrote to Granny when he tells her he wants a divorce and he says he wants to discuss which of you stays with her and which one goes with him. There's all these lists of Brethren rules and pamphlets. Mad stuff. Weird. I didn't know half of this. You've never told me."

"You can't just tell it in bits," I said, though I knew I could have tried. Why hadn't I told my children about the Brethren? Because I didn't know how to begin to answer the questions that I knew would follow, questions that I'd avoided for years. How do cults work? How had our family gotten caught up in such an extreme Protestant sect in the first place? Why would anyone have wanted to join the Brethren? How did the men get such power over the women? Why didn't anyone rebel? What marks had that history left on me? What might I have passed on to my children?

And then the girl in the red cardigan and headscarf is in the room with me again. The girl I'd once been. She's furious. She's sitting in meeting listening to the men preach and she's trying to figure out what "heavenly citizenship" is, or what it means for a house to be "hallowed," or whether the Holy Spirit is male or female and how transparent it is. And she wants to know why the women are not allowed to speak. But she knows she can't ask questions about that be-cause she's a girl and she's not allowed to speak either. And she's wondering why none of the women are standing up and shouting and stamping their feet like she wants to do, telling the men to stop talking all that nonsense.

My father might have died before he was able to face his ques-tions, but I still had time. This was going to be *my* story as well as his. I might be afraid of those bullying men and their lawyers, but I'd face them down. *Let* them come and find me.

Kez agreed to be my research assistant for a few weeks that summer. She made an archive in a series of box files, labeled everything. While I began to piece a history together, Kez found a website.

"They've renamed themselves the Plymouth Brethren Christian Church," she said, passing me her laptop.

"You must have found the wrong Brethren," I told her. "Exclusive Brethren never go anywhere near the Internet; mobile phones and computers are all banned; Bruce Hales—that's their current leader—once described the Internet as 'pipelines of filth.' They'd *never* have their own website."

But Kez was right. This *was* the same Exclusive Brethren that three generations of my family and I had all been born into: same leaders, same values, same rules. There were, according to Wikipe-dia, forty-six thousand of them, living in fellowship across nineteen different countries, sixteen thousand in the U.K. Bruce Hales was the nephew of the man who'd been in charge when I was growing up. They'd turned it into a family dynasty and rebranded—expensively. They must have renamed themselves to throw off the bad publicity they'd been attracting for decades, I told Kez. By why would they have spent this much money? They'd never cared about public opin-ion before.

The website had photographs and videos of Brethren Rapid Re-sponse Teams—young people dressed in high-visibility jackets—

setting up traveling kitchens to feed people who'd lost their homes in bushfires in Australia or in flooding in the U.K., handing out brownies to baffled fire crews or bottles of water to commuters in King's Cross Station during a heat wave. There were photographs of choirs of Brethren girls in long skirts and headscarves singing hymns to old people in care homes. It made the hairs on the back of my neck stand up.

Family is at the heart of everything we believe and everything we do, one caption read, printed over a close-up photograph of a small girl running her hand through ears of corn. I felt a sudden flare of fury. How dare they? I thought of the suicides, the thousands of families that the Brethren had tortured and broken up over the decades, the scores of ex-Brethren I knew who would never see their parents or siblings again. Did the members of the PR company have any idea about the group they'd agreed to promote?

But when we looked at news archives, we found that the Brethren were still getting bad press. In 2009 an Australian investigative journalist published a best-selling book about Brethren tax avoidance schemes; he had exposed their aggressive political lobbying in Australia; he'd interviewed hundreds of ex-Brethren about suicides, excommunications, severed families, and post-traumatic stress. The former Australian prime minister Kevin Rudd had once described them as "an extremist cult that breaks up families and is bad for Australia."

British investigative journalists were on their backs too. Newspaper articles about Brethren-faith schools and tax avoidance schemes had dented their reputation. In 2012, Britain's charity watchdog denied charitable status to the Brethren for one of its trusts in Devon. They risked losing millions of pounds in tax breaks as a result. So they appealed the decision and started up that PR and lobbying campaign to get their charitable status reinstated. But, British journalists wrote, these were no little guys being picked on by the charity commission. These people preached hate.

"We have to get a hatred, an utter hatred of the world," Hales told a large Brethren audience in 2006. "Unless you've come to a hatred of the world you're likely to be sucked in by it, and seduced by it." British Brethren launched an aggressive campaign to get their charitable status reinstated. The two London *Times* journalists got hold of minutes from a meeting in which Hales had urged Brethren lobbyists to apply "extreme pressure" to William Shawcross, the head of the U.K. Charity Commission; "go for jugular," he told them, "go for the underbelly." It made me shiver.

"That's in hand," one British Brethren lobbyist replied.

For Hales and his followers, Shawcross was a non-Brethren "worldy," an agent of Satan's system and thus fair game.

When I read that the U.K. Charity Commission *had* renewed the Brethren's charitable status in 2014, I began to wonder what they'd done to William Shawcross's jugular. Then I began to wonder what they might do to mine. I could see Kez was thinking that thought too.

"Shit," she said. "This is scary."

Over the next few weeks Kez labeled the box files BEFORE, DURING, and AFTER.

"You can change it later," she said. "It's just a way of dividing up the time for now."

I nodded. The girl in the red cardigan was in the room again.

"You might prefer 'Aftermath,'" Kez said, "rather than 'After.' It gives more of a sense of consequence . . . you know—that what happens to you and your father after is a result of the screws gradually tightening in the 'Before' and 'During' parts."

"Of course," I said. I was remembering the feel of the headscarf knot pressing at the back of my neck and the weight of my uncut hair hanging down my back in braided ropes. "Yes. That's good."

I made a note to watch *Wild Strawberries* with Kez. She'd never watched any Bergman.

A month after we started, I dreamed Kez and I were lowering ourselves down into a dark network of caves on a long rope. She was ahead of me. She had the torch. She made me think of those old stories where a young girl has to slay a dragon to break a curse.

Her young handwriting was layered over my father's when she put his letters in order. *This one's interesting,* she wrote on a plastic sleeve's label. *He was preaching out in the black townships during apartheid.* On the letter that my father had written to my mother about divorce, Kez wrote: *This one might be hard to read.*

"Break bread?" Kez says. "What's that?" She's secular. I raised her that way.

"Transubstantiation," I tell her. "Jesus died on the cross and left instructions that people were to remember his death, his *sacrifice,* by eating bread and drinking wine. The bread was supposed to be his body and the wine his blood. We called it breaking bread."

"I'll look it up," she said.

I'm already back there kneading the tiny piece of warm bread in my fingers in the early hours of the morning. It's winter. It is the first meeting of the day and it is still dark outside. I'm in my headscarf and my Best Dress and I am holding my Bible in one hand and my doll in the other.

We called it breaking bread, I'd told Kez. Who, I wondered, was this *we* I kept slipping back into?

Before

1

I was born fourth-generation Brethren. Hanging up there on all the branches of the family trees are generations of Brethren on both my mother's side and my father's side, and before that several generations of French Huguenots, Calvinist émigrés who fled waves of Catholic persecution. If you've been born into a group like the Brethren and everyone you know—parents, friends, work colleagues, siblings, grandparents, great-grandparents, cousins—is living by Brethren rules, you assume it's completely normal. It's the people *outside* your assembly who seem strange.

That long Brethren inheritance was a badge of honor in our household. It was held in place by the stories we were told and the objects and keepsakes in our home. An enormous oil painting of my eminent great-great-grandfather Grandpa Mallalieu, my grandmother's grandfather, hung over the fireplace in our sitting room. It would have reminded the Brethren guests who came for tea between meetings of our distinguished bloodline. Arthur Lee Mallalieu had "taken the ministry" across Australia, set up tent meetings and tin tabernacles, and helped to establish the first Brethren assemblies in

Adelaide, Canberra, Melbourne, and Sydney. When my mother toasted crumpets on the fire for us on cold winter days I'd look up and he'd be looking straight back down at me.

It was not an especially stern portrait. Grandpa Mallalieu was tall and handsome. In the painting he seems to have just looked up from reading his Bible, his head resting on his hand thoughtfully. But you could never escape Grandpa Mallalieu's eyes. Growing up I tried standing in every corner of our sitting room to find a spot where I might avoid them. There wasn't one.

Grandpa Mallalieu

There was always someone watching: God from above and Grandpa Mallalieu from the sitting room wall.

The portrait had been painted over another painting, my mother said, but she could not remember what it was. As a small child I imagined there was a ship under Grandpa Mallalieu, battling high waves, riding the wind.

In the kitchen my mother had hung a large framed print of Vermeer's *The Milkmaid*. She loved the cobalt blue of the milkmaid's apron, she said. It was her favorite color.

The milkmaid stood at a window, pouring milk at a table piled high with freshly baked bread. She didn't watch me like Grandpa Mallalieu did. Her eyes were down; she was rapt in her own daydreams, just as my mother often was. I watched the milkmaid from the kitchen table when my father was giving thanks before dinner, when my siblings and I were supposed to be praying with our eyes closed. Her milk poured from the mouth of her jug into that terracotta bowl below, *without end*. Because her head was covered like that and her table was full of freshly made bread, I always assumed she was a Brethren sister, just like my mother and aunts, busy preparing the bread for the Lord's Day meeting. While the men were discussing ministries or disciplinary decisions in the adjoining room as they did in our house, she was snatching a private moment, secret and off in her dreams.

But there was a wooden box in the lower-right corner of that picture that filled me with dread. Recently I read that it was probably a seventeenth-century foot warmer, but back then I imagined it was a trap or an instrument of torture. It meant that this dreaming, fleshy, cobalt-blue-wrapped girl was going to get caught.

Brethren were proud of their roots. My father would defend the radical Puritanism of the very first Brethren, sometimes passionately, long after he'd left the Brethren and given up his belief in God.

"It started out right-minded," he'd say. "But it went wrong. They weren't intending to start their own church. They were just good men walking in the Lord together, trying to find a way of living according to Paul's Gospel."

If I had any chance of understanding what my father had called the Nazi decade and its aftermath—the turbulence we lived through as a family in the 1960s, 1970s, and 1980s, the separations, the suicides, the scandal, the schisms, the gambling, my father's addictions, embezzlement, and prison sentence—I was going to have to understand how the Brethren crossed the line from being right-minded, as my father had put it, to being wrong-minded. I needed to find out how they had turned into a cult.

The handful of Brethren history books I consulted all confirmed my father's story. In the late 1820s a few young men, repelled by the corruption, decadence, and infighting they saw in the Anglican and Catholic churches, came together to break bread in sitting rooms and hired halls in Dublin. Certain that the world was fast approaching its end, they decided to return to the principles of the early Christian church as laid out by Paul's epistles, adapted, as they sought fit, for nineteenth-century believers:

No priests.
No ritual.
No intermediaries.
No incense.
No hierarchy.
No sacred ground.
No altars or pulpits.

They were not a denomination, they insisted. They were simply following the Spirit, and preparing for the End Times.

A charismatic ex-barrister and ex-curate, John Nelson Darby, eventually took the lead. They'd only be saved, he told his followers, if they separated completely from the rest of the world. They had to prepare a clean house for the Lord's coming.

When I was growing up there were framed photographs of Darby on the walls of most Brethren sitting rooms. Two elderly Brethren sisters called the Miss Ellimans used to give us sweets on the Lord's Day from a drawer under a glass-fronted cabinet in their front room where they kept their framed photograph of Darby. Though Brethren talked about him as a kind of saint, he always looked to me, glowering out from behind the glass door of the cabinet, like the kind of man who'd shout at you if he opened his mouth.

Darby is famous for having "invented" the idea of the Rapture. He'd had a vision, Darby told his followers, that there'd be *two* Second Comings, not just one. First, Christ would arrive and take the Breth-

John Nelson Darby

ren off the planet in a sudden, secret, exodus to heaven. It was all there in the Scriptures; hadn't the apostle Paul told the Thessalonians that the Lord's people would be "caught up" into the air? As soon as the Rapture took place, all the people left behind, the worldly people, would suffer the Great Tribulation. The Bible didn't specify what this was, exactly, but we all understood there'd be terrible storms, earthquakes, plagues, and famines.

Christ would return a second time, Darby wrote, for the Judgment Day reckonings, and there'd be people saved at that point, of course, but they'd be in the second ranking. The most privileged of the residents of heaven would be the Rapture people, the ones who'd gone in the first exodus: the elite, the first-class travelers, the emigrants.

That was *us,* my people, the Brethren.

They told us children that all we had to do was take the Lord Jesus into our hearts and "withdraw from iniquity" to be certain of a place in the much-longed-for upward rush of the Rapture. But despite my most strenuous efforts, I never managed to withdraw from iniquity for very long, and that meant, of course, that I knew I'd be left behind.

The Brethren visitors who came to our house for tea between meetings came from all over the world. Once people like Grandpa Mallalieu started the missionary work back in the nineteenth century, Brethrenism went everywhere. By 1845 there were 1,200 Brethren breaking bread together in a hall in Plymouth. By the end of the nineteenth century there were assemblies right across Europe, in Australia, New Zealand, America, Jamaica, and Canada, Brethren breaking bread in tents or assembling in corrugated-iron churches built from kits, in fields and jungles and the outback.

There were quarrels and schisms right from the start. When Darby returned from preaching in Europe in 1845 and found that the Brethren at Plymouth had reintroduced priests, he first denounced them, and then withdrew from them. This was the first withdrawal of many. The religious-tract war that followed, with Darby accusing their leader, Benjamin Newton, of being "a blind instrument of Satan," led to new rifts. When the Brethren of the Bethesda assembly in Bristol broke bread with some of Newton's followers, Darby withdrew from all of them. He wrote to the rest of the Brethren assemblies around the world, telling them that "to receive anyone from Bethesda is opening the door now to the infection of the abominable evil from which at so much painful cost we have been delivered."

Abominable evil. Infection. That was the way they talked. When we left the Brethren I was surprised to discover the rest of the world didn't talk like we did. Darby's way of seeing the world was absolute. He was certain he was right. Evil was real, he told his followers. It was everywhere.

The Brethren tract wars drew newspaper attention from the start. In 1869 the newspaper editor James Grant described Brethren as living in "a state of constant antagonism" with one another and the world. He reported the violent behavior he'd seen at Brethren conferences, but it was, he wrote, "the effect of Darbyism on family life" that was "perhaps its most awful feature." He reported numerous cases of families broken up by Brethren rules.

Brethrenism has always devastated families. It's a measure of their faith, they say, that they are prepared to put the Lord before "natural ties." When they say "natural ties," they mean family bonds, those complex threads of affection and loyalty that weave between siblings and parents and children. Those threads are good, they believe, but not if they lead to Brethren rules being broken. That's when you have to take a knife to them.

My father always had a bit of a thing for Darby's black-and-white, brooking-no-compromise asceticism. I was impressed by it too in my teens; it reminds me now of the excitement I felt when I later read Ralph Waldo Emerson or Henry David Thoreau on civil disobedience. There was something brave and bold, I thought, about these people refusing to kowtow to the church authorities, rejecting the incense, the idolatry, the angels-on-a-pinhead high church nonsense of it all. They'd gone their own way; they'd done their own thing. I liked that.

But the trouble is that if you persuade people that this world is a mere waiting room for the next, they'll come to despise it; if you teach people to believe that Satan is using all of the people outside your meeting room to try to stop you from going up in the Rapture, they'll come to think that all those people are tricksters and devils, or infected with evil, and if the promised Rapture doesn't come, pretty soon they'll become paranoid, impatient, and obsessive, and they'll be looking for ways to separate *harder*.

2

I found the Dublin auction house—one of the places where those first Brethren met together in the 1830s—on Google Street View; it had become a shop. I scrolled in close but couldn't get past the shop door. I would have liked to go inside to find the room where the Brethren brothers and sisters had laid out a circle of chairs around a table, shaken out a white cloth, and placed a freshly baked loaf and a cup of wine in the center, *just as we had done*. Afterward, I knew, they'd have stepped out into the noisy street, clutching their Bibles, feeling purged and clean, steeling themselves against Satan's world out there, the dirt and the devil of it, just as we had done.

My father grew up a hundred or so years later among Brethren who broke bread in the Iron Room in Kenilworth, a corrugated-iron shed assembled down on wasteland by the river, one of many Brethren tin tabernacles assembled across the world, either purpose-built or requisitioned from other dissenting groups who'd traded up or shut down. At the center of all that corrugated iron there was always a table with a white cloth, a freshly baked loaf, and a collection box inside a circle of chairs.

The Iron Room in Kenilworth had once stood at the end of a terrace of Victorian houses called The Close, overlooking waste ground near the brook, but had been demolished in 1982. When I drove to Kenilworth to try to find it, the man who worked the adjoining land on an allotment full of sweet peas and cabbages a few yards from the plot told me he kept pulling up sections of corrugated iron from his soil, even the occasional window frame. It had mystified him. He had no idea that he had the remains of a church underneath his dahlias. A local historian found a photograph for me.

The Iron Room, Kenilworth

The corrugated iron of Brethren meeting rooms testified to their indifference to the world and its materialism. Their God didn't need fan vaulting or gold leaf. He came because of *them*. Nor did they need to consider longevity when they built these rooms—they didn't think about rust, mold, leaks, heating, or frozen pipes—because they were certain the Rapture was only weeks or months away. Eventually, of course, the pipes froze, the windows leaked, the iron rusted, paint flaked, mold spread; journalists came and angled their long-distance lenses to peer in through those high windows. To keep them out, the Brethren frosted their glass, fitted curtain rails inside and railings and razor wire outside.

Satan was abroad, Darby told Brethren. Satan was stalking the streets of Dublin, Paris, London, New York. He'd gotten into the churches, he was in the pubs, the law courts, the pulpits, the theaters. "Satan is the god of this world," he wrote, "the prince of the power of the air, and the manager of this stupendous system." And Brethren, he preached, had to separate themselves completely from all this. They had to separate from "business, politics, education, governments, science, inventions, railroads, telegraphs, social arrangements, charitable institutions, reforms, religion." Telegraphs, invented in the 1830s, were a particular obsession for Darby, certain proof that Satan had gotten hold of the air.

There were so many things to separate from. Even the air. It all required so much vigilance.

Splitting, withdrawing—sometimes Brethren called it "circumcision"—became the Brethren way. They did it dramatically, defiantly, over and over again. It happened all the time in our meeting when I was growing up. There were always people my grandparents would be tutting about or praying over, sometimes people I knew or people in other meetings I'd heard about. If my grandparents were praying for someone it meant they were in big trouble. It almost always meant they'd be withdrawn from and then we wouldn't see them again.

After Darby and his followers split from the large Brethren assemblies in Plymouth and Bristol in 1848, people began to call them the Darbyite Brethren, the Exclusive, or the Close (or Closed) Brethren.

When I think of the word "close," I hear *Keep close. Come close. Be close. We're close.* There's a hushed, whispered sanctuary to it, something intimate, protective, and secretive, warm, perhaps with a hint of stale air. When I think of the word "closed," I hear doors banging, gates slamming, drawbridges shuddering into place, keys turning. *Closed room. Closed shop.* Closed is not the same as private or keep out. It means *We were open once but now we're closed. We might once have let you in, but now we won't.*

The Exclusive Brethren went from close to closed. They went from drawing close to shutting out. In or around 1848 this strict, close community began to *shun*.

I'm stepping gingerly here because I hear Brethren women—cousins, aunts, ancestors—gathering in the wings. They have something to say. They're whispering that Darby was right; they're telling me why my educated, skeptical, secular way of seeing things is so impoverished. They want to tell me that God loves me, that he wants to make everything right in the world, that he suffers with us, with me, that he died for my sins. They remind me that everything and everybody in this world, including me, is riddled with sin, and only Jesus can redeem us from that. They tell me to look at the pornography, the Internet, the self-harm, the levels of depression, and the empty churches. These are all signs of Satan's dominion, sure signs of his evil working in the world.

These women have my big bones and wild hair; they are serene, gracious, dignified. My grandmother is in the room. I can hear the swish of her silk skirts, smell her lily-of-the-valley talcum powder, I can hear her talking about the Lord Jesus as I stand on a chair at her kitchen sink blowing bubbles through my tiny fingers. They'd tell a different story if I let them. But I have to tell my father's story. And mine.

3

The Rapture was coming. It might come next week or next year, but it was always coming. I was sure I wouldn't be the only one left behind. I was pretty certain that my brothers and most of the Brethren children in our assembly wouldn't make it either.

Once all those thousands of Brethren grown-ups around the world had disappeared up into the clouds with their Bibles, I knew my brothers and I would have to get through the Tribulation as best we could. The trouble was that the not-good-enough Brethren and all those dangerous worldly people outside the Brethren would be left behind too. We'd have to find a way of hiding from them and getting to high ground so we wouldn't drown when the tidal waves came. I thought about that almost every day.

I knew my brothers wouldn't be much good in an emergency. I'd have to take charge when the time came, find a place for us to hide. I'd gone to look at the coal bunker in our house but decided against it. It was too dark and dirty. There were spiders. It would flood too when the tidal waves came. The garage at my grandparents' house was a much better proposition. Their house was halfway up a hill. There'd be less chance of it flooding. My grandmother kept crates of boxes of strawberry pop in little glass bottles there; there were candles and boxes of jam tarts from the Stott and Sons warehouse. I knew where she kept the garage key. We'd be fine there for a few weeks, I thought.

Because I knew I'd be left behind, I spent much of my childhood preparing for the Tribulation. My dreams were full of floods and lightning and earthquakes. Most of the games I played had boats in them. They were thrilling.

When I was growing up in the 1960s, my father and grandfather ran a Brethren wholesale grocery business called Stott and Sons from a cavernous and labyrinthine old warehouse on Shirley Street in Hove. If my father had sole charge of me and my brothers for a few hours, he would sometimes leave us to play unsupervised in the darkened storerooms while he did something "important" in the office next door. We were not to tell our mother.

Though the Stott and Sons warehouse drivers who came and went would protest about our safety, we scrambled up the cliffs made by stacks of rice and flour sacks, slipped over the top and down into the inner chambers we found or made there. We squeezed down rock faces made by piled-high boxes of tinned asparagus or tomatoes and hoisted ourselves up on the chain winches that ran through the trap-doors in the wooden ceiling to the upper rooms where the boxes of sweets and crisps were kept. We hid under crates in dusty back rooms we found up tiny staircases that seemed to appear from nowhere. There were no eyes on us in the warehouse.

Before we went to school, my brothers and I had no children's stories or fairy tales or cartoons to shape our play. They were banned. Instead we made up games based on mixed-up Bible stories from the Old and New Testaments. We transformed the darkened rice mountains and valleys and walls of boxes of the warehouse into the landscapes of the Holy Land. We marched around the walls of Jericho, waded across the Jordan, rescued Jonah from the whale, and then raised Lazarus so that he could fight alongside David when he took on Goliath.

While my brothers were fencing with swords that they'd made from sticks of wood, I was scrambling up those rice sack mountains, scraping my knees raw on the rough hessian, fleeing lashing rain and rising floodwater. I made arks from any inner chamber I found, pulling over old sacks across the top to keep out the relentless rain and lightning. As the smells of muscovado sugar or paprika or brown rice rose up around me, I was pressed into the ark's hold, feeling the swell of the waves or easing a white dove through an imaginary porthole. Or I was Jonah inside the belly of the whale, listening out for the sound of gulls through the whale's flanks, sounds that would tell me we were near land.

That boat ark was mine. I unfurled the sails. I stood on the deck at the helm. I got to decide which way we sailed.

Sometimes beautiful and incomprehensible lines from the Bible drifted into my daydreams or play: "Hast thou entered into the store-houses of the snow," the Lord asked Job as he and Satan took turns to torment him, "and hast thou seen the treasuries of the hail? . . . By what way is the light parted, [and] the east wind scattered upon the earth?" Or I repeated my favorite sentence of the Bible, four words that followed verse after verse of flooding, wind and rain, destruction and desolation:

"And-God-re-mem-bered-No-ah."

During those long hours spent listening to biblical exegeses in meeting, I could take myself to the imaginary salty, spice-scented hold of my boat or into the whale's belly as if they were parallel worlds. I can still smell the inside of that ark-boat nearly fifty years later, the feel of the hessian sacks against my knees.

It came as no surprise to me, then, to discover that those Brethren ancestors of mine were fishing folk, that they'd lived on the edge of the sea and land since 1800. Boats and fish were in my bloodline too, then, not just in my Tribulation-survival dreams.

I was the fourth generation of the Brethren Stotts. Unlike the rest of us, who had been born into the Brethren, my great-grandfather David Fairbairn Stott, a Scottish sailmaker, had chosen to join. He was the first. He'd made a choice that would shape the lives of all his children, grandchildren, and great-grandchildren because, due to the severity of Brethren rules, if you were born into the cult you'd have to be steel-willed to be able—or allowed—to leave it.

Could that austere Protestantism stay in the blood, linger as a kind of tribal consciousness generations later, I'd begun to wonder, like my boat imaginings, long after I'd left the Brethren? If I avoided friends who'd said something that had offended me, if I neglected to return their emails, would that be a Brethren thing or just a human thing?

I found David Fairbairn Stott on the 1890 census return, where he was listed as an apprentice sailmaker in Eyemouth, a fishing village on the coast fifty miles southeast of Edinburgh, located at the point

Herring gutters at Eyemouth

on the border between England and Scotland where the River Eye joins the sea—hence the Eye and the Mouth.

As far as I could trace from the records, in the nineteenth century these Eyemouth Stotts had either fished or made barrels or sails. When they were not at sea following the herring, they scanned the ocean and sky for signs of changes in the weather; they tapped barometers, they mended nets; they baited lines, hauled barrels, and dragged nets.

For weeks I sat at a desk in the British Library behind a pile of books—sailmaking manuals, books about witchcraft and smuggling and Scottish dissenting groups—reading about the Lowland Clearances and how sails were made and how the herring were gutted and preserved in barrels of salt. When I looked at my hands scribbling notes, I thought about the women I descended from who'd gutted fish for ten hours a day in the fish yard, hands cut and bleeding from their sharp knives. They must have been in pain every hour of the day from plunging those raw hands in and out of salt.

Why would someone—anyone—from an already hard life like this have *wanted* to join the Brethren? The nineteenth-century Eyemouth I was reading about didn't seem to be a particularly religious place. It was a frontier town, a hard-drinking, law-defying town. There were Primitive Methodists here in the 1830s; Baptists and Presbyterians too. But most of the fishermen and fisherwomen in Eyemouth were in constant battle with the church because the Kirk—that's the Church of Scotland—collected large tithes or taxes from all their profits. The minister patroled the harbor when the boats came in to make sure no one tried to cheat him of his tithes.

Eyemouth people seemed to be more superstitious than devout. The local history books included lists of things that sailors avoided before the boats sailed. Women were bad luck. So were pigs, hares, white cats, and apples. It was unlucky to give away salt. It was unlucky to give your mother change from your pocket. If a sailor said the wrong thing, an unlucky thing, he had to touch cold iron.

The devil could snatch you. The sea could swallow you. Staying alive seemed to be more a matter of luck in Eyemouth, and making sure you didn't test it.

4

It's easy to be romantic about lives lived out on the edge of the sea. The history books told me something darker. In the seventeenth century, several Eyemouth residents, almost all women, were tortured, tried, condemned, and burned as witches, or torn limb from limb because someone had testified to seeing them consorting with the devil. Local ministers ran the witch hunts, it seemed, not just to drive out the devil but also to sustain their power, just as Brethren leaders would do with their own witch hunts and expulsions generations later.

These were closed communities; people covered for one another. In the seventeenth century, villagers smuggled contraband lace or brandy and hid it in passageways dug through the rock, or stowed it inside hidden chambers they'd made in their chimneys or under floorboards. They'd be hanged if they were caught. The town had its own Masonic lodge too, established in the mid–eighteenth century; its members included both smugglers and excisemen, all committed, just as the Closed Brethren were later, not just to religious worship but to sustaining close, secret, and lucrative business networks.

But the nineteenth-century census returns told me nothing about my family's religious affiliations. The census officers who'd visited the Eyemouth fishermen and fisherwomen had asked them about parents, children, birthplace, birth date, even about blindness or madness, but they hadn't asked about God. So though I found David Fairbairn Stott on the census returns, I was still no wiser about what he thought about the Tribulation or the Rapture, where he went on Sunday mornings, or whether he called Sunday Sunday or the Lord's Day.

I would have to drive north, I realized, to find out what took David Fairbairn Stott across the threshold of a Brethren meeting room for the first time. The books and historical records weren't going to tell me.

I found his grandmother listed as the widowed innkeeper of the Whale Inn on Eyemouth's harborfront, a ten-bedroom inn with a bar. How—and why—had the grandson of an innkeeper in a rough town like Eyemouth become a leading member of the Brethren? I'd found scores of Brethren meeting rooms farther north along the coast but none in Eyemouth. Perhaps if I went to the town, it would give me something to go on.

I followed the coast road from Edinburgh east and then south through the border towns and villages where I'd found Stotts in the library records: Haddington, East Linton, Dunbar, Dunglass, Cockburnspath, and Coldingham. The road wound through high moorland and wooded dells, past the high walls and gatehouses of great estates, down to sandy coves and inlets—where fishing villages huddled against the sides of black cliffs studded with nesting seabirds—and back up again to high moor and big sky. The sea came in and out of view as I drove; the low sun gilded mudflats or dunes or black rocks down below.

On the outskirts of Eyemouth, the road passed through gray pebble dash suburbs and caravan parks. Along the harbor road the fishing sheds and warehouses gave way to a row of old pubs and inns facing the sea. Among them was The Whale, its windows and doors boarded up, one of three semi-derelict public houses still standing on the harborfront.

I parked the car and stepped out into a cold sea wind laced with the harbor smells of engine oil, petrol, and fish from the fish yards. I walked around the perimeter of the inn, looking for gaps in the boarding, wading through the rubbish piled up around its walls, under the gaze of a group of fishermen smoking outside the adjacent pub. How had a forty-year-old widow, my ancestor, raised five children, managed the drunken sailors and the brawls, and run a ten-bedroom inn here single-handedly?

I ordered a glass of beer from the landlord in the pub next door. Inside, half a dozen local fishermen and construction workers sat hunched over crosswords or watched football on a screen. The Whale had been closed for twenty years or more, the landlord told me. A developer from Hull owned the building now. It was a listed building, he said, protected by law, so the owner was probably waiting for it to become derelict enough for the council to allow him to knock it down. Then he'd build something that would make him some *real* money. He laughed.

When I asked for the name of this Hull developer, four or five men lifted their heads from their newspapers and looked in my direction. Was I a journalist? the landlord asked, looking away. I had planned to tell him how Margaret Stott, my great-great-grandmother, had run the Whale in the 1850s, but now I thought better of it. I was just doing some family history research, I said, and changed the subject.

Eyemouth would have been packed with people at the height of the herring season, I reminded myself as I took pictures of the now almost empty harbor outside: There would have been carts coming and going, clusters of young women working against the clock to gut the fish and get them barreled up and onto the backs of the waiting carts. During the 1850s, David Fairbairn's father, Robert Stott, an apprentice barrel maker—a cooper—would have presided over those herring-packing girls, the ones with the cut and salted hands.

It was difficult to imagine this sleepy town as a once-dangerous and violent place, the site of political protests and demonstrations. In the 1850s and 1860s, after years of struggle, the Eyemouth fishermen and fisherwomen had finally refused to pay the tithe that the Kirk demanded from them. Robert Stott—the apprentice cooper—and his fishing cousins had marched with the two thousand protesters along this harborfront behind an enormous green banner embroidered with the words PAY NO TITHE. Robert would have been just fifteen when the local men stoned the policemen who came to arrest the charismatic leader of the protest, William "the Kingfisher" Stearnes.

At the age of nineteen, when the police standoffs, protests, and demonstrations were still playing out in Eyemouth, Robert had been courting one of the girls of the gutting yards, Lizzie Fairbairn, the eldest daughter of one of the largest fishing families in town. She was eighteen and seven months pregnant when they married. Her own mother was also pregnant, with her twelfth child, so with no room left at home Lizzie moved into the Whale with her husband's mother and his three siblings. She gave birth to Agnes there in 1862, behind one of those boarded-up windows I stood beneath. I could see her now walking out from the inn with her baby strapped to her back, swaddled against the wind, her much younger siblings running from all directions to cluster around her skirts.

I reached for the phone to call my father and tell him about Agnes and David before I remembered: I couldn't call my father anymore. He was dead. I couldn't tell him about the Whale Inn or his great-grandfather's run-ins with the Kirk, or how—when I'd seen that old inn all boarded up—I'd wanted to find a way to buy it and rescue it from the Hull developer, replace the glass in the windows, and get the roof fixed. I couldn't tell him that for a moment I thought I saw Lizzie as if she were still alive and striding along the harbor wall.

My father had always been proud of this Scottish ship chandler inheritance of ours. When he and I bought the little cabin boat for the mill and moored it on the river a few yards from the mill door, he drove me across the fens to the ship chandler's in Ely. We needed stocking up, he told my stepmother. He was in one of his extreme spending moods; she and I both knew there was no reasoning with him when he was like that. I followed him through the narrow aisles of the Ely ship chandler's as he selected objects that interested him, regardless of price or usefulness: a stove, a ladder, spare buoys, a captain's hat, an extra-large waterproof coat.

"Stott and Sons," he said when the shop owner took his credit card. "Scottish ship chandlers," he added, as if he'd expected the shopkeeper to doff his cap or give him a discount. I winced but the shopkeeper was charmed. They had already begun to exchange stories.

What would my father have thought of this messy and scattered older family history I'd now found in Eyemouth? What would he have made of the Eyemouth riots and his intemperate great-grandfather Robert? Would he have seen himself in Robert's reflection as I was beginning to do?

At twenty-one years old, Robert, most likely in trouble with the police for his part in the anti-Kirk protests and stonings, or in debt to the local moneylender, decided it was time to leave town. According to the census returns he moved Lizzie and baby Agnes into one of the upper floors of a tenement in Edinburgh where he'd taken a job as a cooper in a large brewery. By the time Lizzie was twenty-nine years

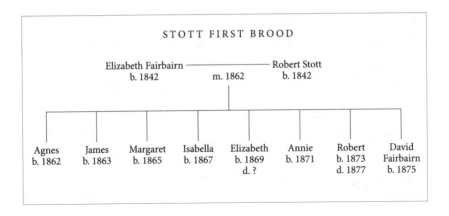

old, she was managing six children under the age of eight, carrying water and small infants up and down the steep stairs of the tenement, and sharing an outside toilet with several neighboring families. Then, after nine years in Edinburgh, Robert moved his family three hundred miles south to Grimsby, one of the biggest new dockyards in the world. The Stotts moved into one of the hundreds of small terraces newly built to house the two thousand new workers. Lizzie gave birth to two more boys here, Robert and David Fairbairn Stott. Then, in January 1876, at the age of thirty-four, she died in the Grimsby terrace giving birth to her ninth child. The baby did not survive.

For a year, Agnes, now thirteen, and her sisters, eleven-year-old Margaret and nine-year-old Isabella, must have cleaned and fed and cared for their younger brothers and sisters in that overcrowded terrace in Grimsby, doing laundry, keeping house, making ends meet as best they could while their father made barrels down in the dockyard. Their grandmother Margaret had died that summer back in Eyemouth. Unmarried Aunt Isabella took over the management of the Whale from her mother, but running the inn on her own, she would not have been in a position to take in any of her older brother's city-born children.

Back in the Grimsby terrace, baby Robert died that winter, only three years old. Eight-year-old Elizabeth slips off the records around this time, probably a victim of one of the epidemics that swept the town. Remarkably, David Fairbairn Stott, the youngest, survived. Having buried two of their siblings that winter, and their mother a year before that, Agnes and her sisters must have been tending to their baby brother with special care. What would they have made of the heavily pregnant stepmother their father brought home to live with them, another Elizabeth, a twenty-nine-year-old Lincolnshire woman who'd been working as a scullery maid since she was fourteen? Her first baby, born in December 1877 and christened Mary, did not survive the winter.

Now Aunt Isabella sent for her brother's four oldest children—Agnes, James, Margaret, and Isabella. The next census, taken in April 1881, looks better for all of them. Margaret and Isabella are listed as living at the Whale Inn working as domestic servants. James, the eldest boy, had joined an Eyemouth fishing crew. Agnes, eighteen, had married a sailmaker named John Wilson and had a baby son. The couple were living in their own house down near Eyemouth market-place. Annie and David Fairbairn, the two youngest surviving members of the first brood of Stotts, stayed on down in Grimsby with their father and stepmother and two new siblings. They were both attending school.

Might those older Stott children, I wondered, have finally found some solid ground after all those years of poverty, migration, and loss? But I'd forgotten about the storm.

When the hurricane hit the east coast six months later, one of the most violent storms in British history, Agnes, nineteen and pregnant with her second child, would have been among the crowd of Eyemouth women standing on the harbor wall outside the Whale Inn as the fleet of battered fishing boats tried to make it back into the harbor through the towering waves. One hundred twenty-nine husbands, brothers, uncles, cousins, sons, and fathers were killed in a few hours that afternoon in 1881, thrown from boats, drowned, or smashed against the rocks or the harbor wall. They included Agnes's three

Eyemouth harbor. The Whale Inn can be seen between the boat and the car.

young Stott cousins and three of her Fairbairn uncles. For weeks afterward, the bodies of those Eyemouth men washed up in coves and on beaches, limbs missing, faces unrecognizable.

I did the math. That was ten, perhaps eleven, family members Agnes had lost: mother Lizzie, grandmother Margaret, baby brother Robert, sister Eliza, baby half sister Mary, three Stott cousins, and three Fairbairn uncles, and she was still only nineteen.

5

Agnes must have considered herself lucky to have married a sailmaker and not a sailor, lucky that her sisters hadn't married sailors, that they'd been spared the fate of the eighty-two widows of Eyemouth.

According to the records I found in the Eyemouth fishing museum, many of those women were, like Agnes, pregnant when they buried their husbands. They named their newborn babies after their dead fathers. Now I understood why Robert had named his new daughter, his twelfth child, born just after the disaster, Adelina Purves Spouse Stott. It had always struck me as an odd name. James Purves and Thomas Spouse had been Robert's childhood friends, and they'd died in the storm. Adelina Purves Spouse Stott was Robert's twelfth child.

Few Eyemouth families escaped the long aftermath of the storm. With the fishing fleet largely destroyed, John Wilson's sailmaking business, like all the businesses in Eyemouth, was soon on a knife-edge. Within four years he'd be listed in the Glasgow *Herald* as a "Scotch Bankrupt." He was one of many from the town. If they'd built a new harbor instead of having to fight the Kirk all those years, historians say, those fishermen would probably have lived. They'd only gone out in that storm because they had to, because they had children to feed and the Kirk tithe to pay.

John and Agnes moved forty miles north along the coast to start up a new sailmaking business in Port Seton, a small fishing village just south of Edinburgh. Since its new harbor had opened in 1880, thirty-five boats had been registered there. The population had tripled in twenty years. It was an industrious town, the history books claim, and, compared to Eyemouth, a God-fearing town. New churches were going up everywhere.

But things just kept getting worse for them. Agnes and John and their two small children had only been in Port Seton for four years when news came from Agnes's younger sister Annie down in Grimsby that their father had died, at only forty-six years old. Robert Stott died, his son David always told people, *a drinker's death.* Five months later, his widow died in childbirth, leaving seven orphaned children in the Grimsby terrace.

Within weeks all seven had all been taken in—adopted—by their older brothers or sisters, or put to work. Agnes took her fourteen-

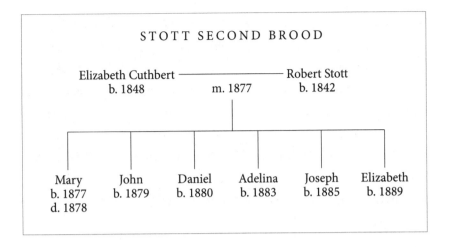

year-old brother, David, and her four-year-old half brother, Joseph, to live with her in Port Seton. Her husband would take David on as an apprentice in the Wilson sail sheds.

Could any of these Stott children read? If the older ones had been taught their letters, it would have been at one of the many Grimsby Sunday schools, like the one the Primitive Methodists opened in 1867 just a few streets away from the Stott house. The younger children were luckier. Annie and David had just enough time between their mother's death in 1876 and their father's and stepmother's deaths in 1889 to attend the new public-funded school. They had learned to read, write, and do sums.

I was the oldest girl in a family of five children, with an absent father and a hardworking, sleep-deprived mother. I knew that Agnes and her young sisters would have been carrying those babies around in Grimsby, mashing up food, wiping noses, cleaning up cuts, singing songs, telling stories, just as I did. I helped my mother feed my adored twin brother and sister, born when I was nearly six, and I read to them and listened to them read when they were old enough.

But there were older Brethren "sisters" who helped my mother; shadowy, kind women who baked and stitched, who took us out for picnics or to the beach. My mother had electricity, a washing machine, a sewing machine, and a food mixer; she had powdered mashed potato mix, tins of Spam and sliced pineapples in her kitchen cupboards, and her own car parked outside. She taught me to read long before I went to school. I'd like to think that at least some of those Grimsby Stott children had books stowed under their pillows as I did.

But though they'd suffered through those early years, Agnes and David must have considered themselves on safe and solid ground in their new house in bustling Port Seton, with its brand-new harbor and all those boats out there bringing in trade to the Wilson sailmaking sheds.

6

The disorder of Agnes and David's life in Grimsby was determined in part by the alcoholism of their father and the worn-down compliance of their mother and stepmother. But now that I'd been to the Eyemouth fishing museum and read the local history books, I was beginning to see a bigger picture. The chaos and bereavement the Stotts had lived through was also caused, at least to some extent, by the Lowland Clearances that propelled so many Scots from their farms into a migrant life in search of work or toward one of the emigration ships sailing to New Zealand, Canada, or America. The destiny of the Stotts, like millions of their fellow Scots, had been driven by violent historical forces.

From the eighteenth century, as part of what historians call the Clearances, the owners of large Scottish estates began to clear the "peasants" off the land and put sheep in their place to maximize profits. In the Lowlands of Scotland, down near the borders where my family lived, small tenant or landowning farmers were forced off their farms not by violent eviction, as happened in the later Highland Clearances, but by *stealth*. Landowners hiked rents, and eventually farms and businesses went bankrupt. Tens of thousands of Lowland cottars moved to newly built villages or to cities in search of work, or to the coast to fish, and thousands emigrated.

The Stotts had once been tenant farmers too. I found Robert's grandfather James Stott listed as a tenant cattle farmer living in Gairmuir near Lauder on the Borders in the 1790s, a hundred miles inland from Eyemouth. He was declared bankrupt in 1799, five years after the Earl of Lauderdale's agents decided to hike the rents. Like thousands of other bankrupt laborers and tenants, James Stott gave up his farm and went to the city to look for work. He set up as a butcher in Edinburgh. His three sons went south to Eyemouth to look for work as fishermen and drovers. The family had stayed put until the storm of 1881 forced them to migrate again.

I stood on the edge of the remote drovers' road etched into the hills in the rough high moor at Gairmuir, watching it undulate through the heather and gorse and disappear into the mist. This was the road my drover ancestors walked alongside their cattle to the Edinburgh cattle market. They'd called it the Thieves Road, a farmer told me. Robbers attacked the drovers at night when they returned from the city carrying the money they'd made at market. The rain began, lashing diagonally in great lines, bringing the night down with it. Up on the hill on the edge of the drovers' road a mile away, lights glowed in the windows of a remote farmhouse. You'd be glad to see the light from your farmhouse, I thought, if you were a young drover out here alone in the rain with the dark closing in on you. You'd be glad to get home and bolt the door against the robbers and the night.

Of course the displaced laborers and tenant farmers weren't just looking for security when they joined the Presbyterians, the Baptists, the Free Church, or the Open or Closed Brethren in their thousands in the religious revivals of the 1880s. Joining a nonconformist church must also have been a way of rebelling, *closing their doors* on all outside authority, refusing to rent a seat in a pew or to pay tithes to a corrupt church or to kowtow to a landowner who had cleared them off their land. What looked like an act of extreme religious dissent was also a political one.

By the time Agnes and John Wilson arrived in Port Seton in 1885, five years after the new harbor had been built there and at a time when migrants from all over Scotland were flocking to the town, there were hymns being sung out of *six* buildings on Sunday mornings, including two Brethren meeting rooms, a Methodist hall, and a Mission hall. Around the corner local builders were digging the foundations for a fishermen's bethel.

Brethren were kin; they were in fellowship together. They shut out the rest of the world, but they looked after one another. Brethren married other Brethren and had large numbers of children. They worked hard. They prospered. They kept themselves apart. After the chaos Agnes and David had lived through, they must have been looking for not just stability and faith but also a door to close defiantly against the world. Of all the religious groups in Port Seton they might have joined, the Closed Brethren offered them the greatest degree of separation from the world.

7

"Were your folk Red-Tilers or Blue-Tilers?" the Port Seton fishmonger enquired when I asked directions to the Brethren meeting room. He looked up from the parcel of crab he was wrapping for me and raised an eyebrow. "Brethren meeting rooms are ten-a-penny round here. Red-Tilers don't talk to Blue-Tilers. No one knows what that's all about. Queer folk."

He pointed in one direction to a building with a red-tiled roof and in the other to one with a blue-tiled roof. Despite all the detective work I'd done, I had no idea which one my family had belonged to.

Where had Agnes and David Fairbairn Stott broken bread? It proved easier to figure out than I feared. The board outside the red-tiled meeting room did not welcome visitors, so I knew it must belong to the Closed Brethren. The blue-tiled meeting room did welcome visitors, so these must be Plymouth—or Open—Brethren. My folk, then, had been Red-Tilers.

It must have been difficult to live in Port Seton in the 1880s, I thought, without attending one of these churches and chapels. Agnes and her husband were probably breaking bread with the Red-Tilers before her two orphaned brothers stepped off the boat. The Port Seton Brethren most likely helped John set up his new sailmaking business. Even if they hadn't helped out financially, they would have told the family that if they were prepared to give up their will to the Lord, they'd find a better life to come once he took them skyward in the Rapture. Agnes would see her mother and grandmother in heaven, and all those siblings and cousins she'd lost.

If Agnes had taken David and four-year-old Joseph along to the Red-Tiled Meeting Room, the boys would have been treated kindly, helped along, listened to, given a seat in the center circle. Eventually they'd be asked to break bread and then to preach. It would have given them a strong sense of belonging, safety, and purpose, a conviction that they were the chosen ones and that the Rapture was coming soon.

From the census returns of 1901, I could see that David Fairbairn Stott married Lizzie Durham, the eldest daughter of a prosperous fishing family. They were Brethren too. The census officers recorded that David was running both his own sailmaking shed on the harborfront and a shop that sold shipping tackle. He'd become well-to-do. When he bought the first car in Port Seton, cousins told me, Lizzie wouldn't get into it in front of the house. She was afraid that the neighbors would think she was putting on airs, so her husband and children had to pick her up from the edge of the village. It was the Protestant way. Work hard, save money, do well, but don't flaunt your wealth.

Though David now had security, prosperity, community, wife, and family, I knew he'd still have had to watch his back. He lived with the knowledge that the Brethren assembly might withdraw from him at any moment if he didn't comply with the rules. Brethren used the verb "withdraw" to mean "to separate from someone unclean," but really withdrawal meant expulsion. If you were withdrawn from you couldn't break bread, you were out of fellowship, you'd lose everyone you trusted, everyone you knew, immediately and for always, and you would be forced to live "out there" with all the wicked people. Sometimes a single individual might be withdrawn from; sometimes whole assemblies.

So, in 1905, when Lizzie and David Stott and the other Port Seton Red-Tilers heard about an acrimonious Brethren rift in a small Northumberland market town called Alnwick, just seventy miles south, they'd have talked and prayed about little else. They'd seen it happen before; they knew that rifts like these could get out of hand and spread, engulfing neighboring assemblies. It never ended well.

According to Brethren pamphlets I found, the trouble in the Alnwick assembly was caused, as usual, by disagreements about degrees of separation. One group of Brethren believed they should be out in the world saving souls; the other insisted that they withdraw from iniquity and prepare for the Rapture. Thomas Pringle, one of the older ministering brothers who supported the harder-line separatist approach, locked the nineteen dissenters out of Green Batt Hall, their meeting room, and issued a letter excommunicating them.

The distressed "outs" followed Brethren rules and wrote to the neighboring Brethren in the tiny village of Glanton eight miles away asking for guidance about what to do. The Glantons, also following Brethren rules, urged them to seek reconciliation but would not break bread with them.

Three years passed. Thomas Pringle would not retract his excommunication. Most of the remaining Brethren in Alnwick left to join the defectors. Soon Pringle was breaking bread with only one or two other Brethren in Green Batt Hall, but he was still certain he was right.

Although David and Lizzie Stott and the other Port Seton Red-Tilers were sympathetic to the Alnwick "outs" and frustrated by the way Pringle was behaving, Brethren rules stipulated that they were not to get involved. If they did, they might find themselves withdrawn from too.

In 1908, Brethren leaders in London took Alnwick off the list of approved assemblies. With so few Brethren left breaking bread together there, it was no longer viable. When this happened, the Glantons decided they could now break bread with the Alnwick "outs." It proved to be a disastrous decision. Other Brethren in neighboring assemblies declared that the Glantons had broken Brethren rules; they were now unclean too.

Once Brethren assemblies across the north of England and southern Scotland started taking sides, the trouble spread south. A Brethren woman who belonged to an Edinburgh assembly that had taken a fierce anti-Glanton stand visited in Stoke Newington in North London. The Stoke Newington Brethren appealed to Brethren leaders in the Park Street, Islington, assembly. Was it safe to break bread with her or would they also be excommunicated?

The London Brethren patriarchs consulted, prayed, and debated. Thomas Pringle, they finally ruled, had been right to pull up the drawbridge on the Alnwick defectors; the outs had been dangerously "intercommunional." The Glantons, they agreed, had broken Brethren rules.

The London Brethren excommunicated not just the entire Glanton assembly but also all the Brethren up and down the country who'd supported them, including, of course, the Red-Tilers in Port Seton and Lizzie and David and their little growing family.

In this new, large-scale rift, the Glanton sympathizers in Port Seton held on to the red-tiled meeting room. The smaller number of hard-liners, now calling themselves the London Brethren, took over the former fishermen's bethel on South Doors, a six-minute walk west. From the satellite view on Google Maps it seems the building had a *gray-tiled* roof. So now there were three Brethren meeting rooms in Port Seton: with blue-, red-, and gray-tiled roofs.

All this excommunication was not just chillingly familiar—I'd watched the ministering brothers in our assembly suddenly turn on and expel once-respectable members of our fellowship—it was beginning to look to me like some kind of collective psychosis. The fact that there were three Brethren meeting rooms in this tiny fishing village was not just absurd, it was shameful. The crab parcel in my rucksack had leaked in my bag. It had seeped through the pages of my copy of Haruki Murakami's *The Wind-Up Bird Chronicle* and stained them brown. It felt appropriate. The intense and small-minded sectarianism of these people turned my stomach like the crab juice stains on the pages of my book.

The Glanton rift must have affected the whole village in those years before the Great War. There would have been trouble among the newly divided fishing crews; daily tensions in the Stott store on the harborfront, and tight lips on Main Street on the Lord's Day as

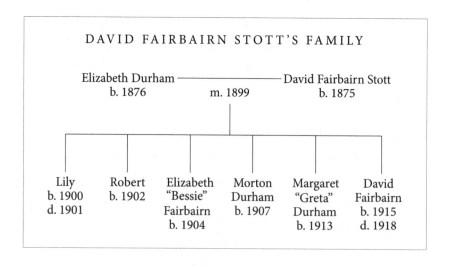

DAVID FAIRBAIRN STOTT'S FAMILY

Elizabeth Durham ———————— David Fairbairn Stott
b. 1876   m. 1899   b. 1875

Lily	Robert	Elizabeth "Bessie" Fairbairn	Morton Durham	Margaret "Greta" Durham	David Fairbairn
b. 1900	b. 1902	b. 1904	b. 1907	b. 1913	b. 1915
d. 1901					d. 1918

three Brethren groups made their way to the Plymouth, Glanton, and London Brethren meeting rooms: red, blue, and now gray. Didn't these people have enough on their plates just surviving the winters and feeding their children without having to engage in religious feuds as well?

Lizzie and David and their children, my cousin tells me, were "in the Glantons" for only four years.

Increasingly uncomfortable with the intercommunional ways of the Glanton Brethren, David and Lizzie rejoined the hard-liners over on South Doors. My great-aunt Greta, their fourth surviving child, born in 1913, would tell people proudly that she was the only one of the family who'd *never* been "in Glanton Brethren." By this she meant that she'd never breathed the "liberal" Glanton air; she was born after the family returned to the hard-line Brethren. She was pure Brethren, pure *Exclusive* Brethren. During the later years of extreme separation, that pure blood would matter.

8

When the Great War began in 1914, David Fairbairn Stott, as an older man, now almost forty, wasn't called up until 1916. Once he refused to fight, following the biblical injunction "Thou shalt not kill," he was one of hundreds of Plymouth and Closed Brethren sent south to Wormwood Scrubs to await military tribunal. He served out his sentence of hard labor in Dartmoor Prison along with hundreds of other religious and political conscientious objectors.

Sixty-three years later my own father would be sent to Wormwood Scrubs, sentenced not for conscientious objection but for embezzling money to feed his roulette habit. I was sixteen when my father went to "the Scrubs," as they called it; my grandfather Robert was fourteen when his father was sent there. Robert was forced to leave school to take care of the shop because his mother had three-year-old Greta and one-year-old David to mind. Our household had suffered too. While I was studying for my A levels my mother had bailiffs and debt collectors calling at our door.

My father did not like his father, Robert, but in his dying days he talked about him tenderly. He empathized with him.

"It must have been hard being the son of a conscientious objector in a fishing village like Port Seton," he said, looking at the photographs I'd found of his father as a young man in a suit, his hair slicked back with oil, trying to look older than his years. "Before the war he'd written poetry and hymns," he said. "He was learning fine lettering so he could paint signs for local shops; but when the war came he had to stop all that and mind the shop. Customers gave him a hard time; many of the villagers boycotted the shop. He was only fourteen. My auntie Bessie used to say that sometimes he'd lose his temper and hurl tins like missiles across the shop."

My father smiled.

Like father like son, I thought.

"Things got worse," he said, trying to sit up so that he could rummage through the shoe box of photographs. "While my grandfather was in prison, Morton—he was only ten then—contracted a bacterial infection in his leg; the doctors rushed him to the hospital in Edinburgh. My grandmother had to travel back and forth to visit him every day with baby David in his pram. The doctors had to cut out a chunk of Morton's leg to drain the poison. They said he wouldn't recover. When they sent him home they expected him to die."

There was a little white coffin in this story, I remembered. A little white coffin and a Brethren procession. I'd heard my father tell this story before. But now that he was dying I realized this would be the last time.

"The prison warden allowed my grandfather to go home," he continued, lost in a photograph of Lizzie pushing the pram along the seafront at Port Seton during the war, "so that he could see his son one last time. But by the time he got all the way from Dartmoor to Scotland, and it must have taken days in wartime, baby David had died instead."

"Meningitis," I say, remembering, thinking about how poor Lizzie must have had to break the news to her husband.

"The Brethren," he went on, "carried the little white coffin along the coast to the graveyard in the next village. Then David had to go all the way back to Dartmoor, leaving Lizzie to teach Morton to walk again."

I thought about Robert trapped behind that shop counter, an open target for the taunts of local lads. Did those boys say the words that all the village must have been thinking—that David's death and Morton's leg had been a punishment for his father's cowardice? That it served those nose-in-the-air Stotts right? Robert must have hurled a fair few more tins then, perhaps even cursed his father. But there would have been older Brethren men looking out for him, I reminded myself, and the Brethren sisters would have been helping Lizzie. That's what Brethren did. At least the Stotts knew they weren't on their own.

The social stigma would have lasted for a long time after the war ended. Conscientious objectors describe being ostracized for decades: People wouldn't shake your hand; you couldn't get a job with a prison record; if you ran a business, people wouldn't buy from you.

The Stotts decided to move the family business south. It wasn't just the stigma of David's having been a conscientious objector that was making life difficult in Port Seton, my father said. The great herring gold rush was over, the fish stocks depleted. Neighbors were shutting up shop, selling their boats when they could find people to buy them, moving away. Lizzie's youngest brother decided to emi-

The Stotts, 1925. From the left: Lizzie, Morton, Greta, Bessie, Robert, and David Fairbairn Stott.

grate to Australia. One of her cousins moved to Hastings on the south coast of England.

"My father knew he and his siblings would never find Brethren to marry in Port Seton," my father said. "There were just not enough young Brethren left. If they wanted families they'd *have* to go south. My father had been taking the train down to London several times a year for the big London Brethren meetings," he added. "He'd even started seeing a Brethren girl in London, but he kept that secret from his parents. He got his sisters to cover for him."

I found a photograph of the family taken a year or so before they left Port Seton to go south. They'd dressed up, I guess, for the picture, gone out into the garden behind the shop to get the best of the light. They look nervous and awkward, unsure where to put their hands. Except for my grandfather. He's standing behind his father, looking straight at the camera. He's carefully dressed and groomed, sure of himself. He looks like a man who wants to impress. He looks like a man who might have a secret romance.

The Stotts moved to Brighton in 1927, a seaside town a hundred times bigger and worldlier than Port Seton. Lizzie had cousins along the coast in Hastings, but a Brighton Brethren builder had offered the Stott brothers work on a site and found them somewhere to live. I imagine the four young Stotts walking among day-trippers, both fascinated and shocked by street-gang fights, piers, parks, and a royal palace. Their Scottish accents would have singled them out among Brighton Brethren as well as in local shops. They'd have caused a stir in the Brighton meeting room.

While Robert and Morton worked on the building site, Greta and Bessie enrolled in Pitman's College to study secretarial skills and accountancy. After a year, Hastings Brethren helped David buy a wholesale chemist's business in the town. The family moved into a flat above the shop and joined the Hastings Brethren assembly. The two Stott brothers, by now in their twenties, would have been looking for potential Brethren wives. Brethren fathers would have been sizing them up too.

In 1930 a well-known Australian ministering brother named Hugh Wasson arrived in Hastings with his two pretty daughters, Kathleen and Betty. He'd grown up in a big family in Northern Ireland before emigrating to Australia, and he'd promised his daughters a grand tour of Great Britain and Ireland. Robert and Morton offered to accompany the Wassons when they visited the Highlands. Two years later Kathleen sailed halfway around the world again from Adelaide to Tilbury Docks to marry Robert. Betty followed two years later to marry Morton.

My father's memoir began here, with my grandmother's sea voyage. Kathleen Wasson, exotic, elegantly but demurely dressed, the daughter of an eminent Australian Brethren brother, the granddaughter of a Brethren missionary, had sailed across the world to marry my Scottish grandfather.

9

He had painted signs and sold rope, sailcloth, and groceries in Port Seton, worked on building sites in Brighton; now Brighton Brethren helped my grandfather secure a job as a traveling salesman for Dubarry, the perfumers. He was going up in the world. During the week he drove hundreds of miles in his company car to peddle fancy perfumes and soaps with French names that promised Compelling Loveliness, Soft White Hands, or a Matte, Velvety Complexion. On the weekends and in the evenings he preached.

Three years later, when he took a sales job at Roger & Gallet, the French soap makers, he virtually tripled his salary. He and Kathleen bought a detached house in Kenilworth in the Midlands, far from the sea, at the center point of Robert's new sales territory. They painted a nursery for the new baby, David, employed a nursery maid, and parked the shiny family Austin outside. Robert stacked the perfume, talc, and soap samples in all the spare cupboards and the attic. Three times a week, sometimes more, they put on their best clothes and hats and pushed the pram the short distance to worship with the Kenilworth assembly in the Iron Room down on the allotment land by the brook.

Brethren were expected to live in detached houses as close to the local meeting room as possible, because detached houses minimized contact with worldly people and kept the local fellowship *close* and in sight. Robert Stott was now head of his detached household; he was a respected ministering brother of the Iron Room and at the center of a commercial sales network that stretched beyond the border between England and Scotland.

My father was born in June 1938. Although my grandparents gave their other children biblical names, they must have named my father, Roger, after the fancy French perfume company that paid my grandfather's wages. There's no other explanation for this worldly name. Was it a curse or a blessing? Did it set him at odds from the start? Did that account for him being the rule-breaking, hedonistic cuckoo in the nest, the aesthete born among puritans? Was it an ill omen or the best kind of one?

10

My Australian grandmother, Kathleen, had cadences in her voice that were different from everyone else I'd heard. Her father was Northern Irish. Her mother's father, the man in the portrait on our sitting room wall, the man we called Grandpa Mallalieu, was born in Leeds and emigrated in the 1880s to Australia, where he established all those Brethren tent assemblies. People sometimes stop me and ask where I'm from: South Africa? Australia? My voice has my grandmother's mongrel tones too.

She showed me on the atlas where she'd been born and all the places where she'd lived. She talked to me about the Lord Jesus and about her mother, who'd been taken away to an asylum. She lifted me onto a chair so I could blow bubbles between my fingers at the kitchen sink. She taught me how to cut crosses into the base of brussels sprouts. She showed me how to use her hostess trolley, the one she used for entertaining Brethren guests and Brethren visitors from overseas. Her house was always full of guests. She was, other Brethren women told me, an especially spiritual woman.

When she was eighty-eight years old she sent me a transcript of an interview she'd just given to the local oral history group. Now that she was very old, she told me when I visited, her memory was doing strange things. When she sat in her room at the back of my aunts' house looking out over the garden, watching the birds fly between the feeders, she'd suddenly find that she was looking out over the grounds of one of the houses she'd lived in as a child in Melbourne or Adelaide. Or she'd wake up staring at the patterned wallpaper of her bedroom in the Adelaide house. When she closed her eyes she saw giant redwoods, she told me. She could smell eucalyptus.

My grandmother had told the interviewer that when her mother was sent almost a hundred miles away from their home in Melbourne to a mental asylum in Ballarat in 1914, she and her sister, then nine and six years old, were sent to live with Aunt Marguerite, their mother's sister, who ran a school in a tiny timber mill town called Beech Forest on Cape Otway, two hundred miles south, in a redwood forest right at the tip of one of the southernmost peninsulas in Australia.

I liked the sound of Aunt Marguerite. She'd lost a leg in her childhood—no one knew how—but, my grandmother said, that never stopped her from doing anything. The two Mallalieu sisters—Ada Louise and Marguerite—were raised among the Box Hill Brethren in a suburb of Melbourne. Marguerite studied hard, became a schoolteacher, and then in her early twenties married a young laborer who wasn't in the Brethren and already had a prison record. She had her first and only child, a daughter, a year later, and when her husband disappeared, she took a job in a school as far from her father's preaching territory as she could. She never remarried.

Brethren relatives called Aunt Marguerite "the man hater," but she seemed like a pirate adventurer to me. I imagined her striding out to school in that remote town along the railway sidings between the tall trees, her wooden leg hidden under her long skirts, her daughter running along beside her.

Aunt Marguerite's school had fourteen pupils; most of them traveled long distances from outlying farms every day on horseback through the forest to reach it. My grandmother told the interviewer about the bullock wagon that came to meet her and her sister at the station and the journey across what she called "corduroyed roads"— muddy tracks with wooden slats laid across them—through giant redwoods and past waterfalls. Kathleen and Betty spent the summers with their young cousin, wandering the forests between the scattered farms on horseback: "There were big bushfires sometimes," she told the interviewer. "At night we saw showers of sparks where branches suddenly broke off in the fires on the hills."

My grandmother might have remembered those bushfires when, decades later, she and her husband and sons crouched under the kitchen table during the air raids on nearby Coventry, their eyes fixed on the explosions in the sky beyond the window. Robert, her husband, was at home in Kenilworth through World War II, working as a fire watcher, too old to be drafted into the army or to register as a conscientious objector. When the planes came, she told my father, Robert read from the Psalms by the light of his torch under the kitchen table.

My father made up a prayer for his memoir to illustrate the kind of Brethren prayer his father might have given under that Kenilworth table where the family took shelter during the bombing raids. "Our God and Father we cry to Thee," he wrote, imitating his father. "We cry to Thee that Thy protecting hand may be over us in this house tonight. We pray that Thou wilt use this fear and our sense of danger to make us more dependent on Thee. Help us to realize Thy power as well as Thy love and mercy. We think of all the saints who love Thee and we ask Thee to have them especially in Thy care. And that men and women who do not know Thee may repent and turn to Thee in their hour of need."

My father must have learned to speak—or mimic—this language long before he could read. He would have heard so much of it, just as I had. All the Brethren men made those strange singsong noises when they preached, pausing for long periods, tuning in so that the Lord could guide the direction they were taking, then starting up the zigzag cadences again. Ministry was impromptu. That was the Brethren way, though some of the longer addresses must have been scripted. In the circles of seats, Brethren brothers and sisters said amen or made assenting noises that sounded like half-awake hums or quiet moans or almost a kind of singing. You were supposed to make those sounds, my father said, once you were "in the Spirit."

When I read the prayer my father put in his memoir, it's my father's voice I hear, that strange tremor that would appear occasionally when something in the Scriptures moved him and he seemed about to cry.

11

The Brethren childhood that my father described in his memoir was very similar to my own but much less circumscribed. Brethren rules were strict in the forties but nothing compared to the prohibitions introduced in the sixties, when I was born.

What had it been like to grow up as a boy in the Brethren? I'd always felt so cross as a small Brethren girl—not a sulky, smoldering kind of cross but a fire-out-of-control-sweeping-across-landscapes kind of cross. But I did not dare show it. I was supposed to like being subject. My grandmother did. She'd drop her head when my grandfather was having one of his rages, as if submitting to her bullying husband was a way of serving the Lord Jesus. Sometimes I'd have to bite my lip so I wouldn't howl with rage when I watched her. It was so unfair. Why did women have to do exactly as the men said? Just because Paul had said so? Who was Paul that he could say such things and have everyone follow his instructions blindly like that? Even thinking those thoughts was a terrible sin, my grandmother would have told me. It was against Scripture.

But what if I'd been a Brethren boy? My father grew up knowing he'd be head of his household one day, head of the family business, even an important ministering brother if he was good enough at talking about the Scriptures. He could preach in meeting. He could shout in his house. I didn't much like any of the Brethren boys I knew.

They called me "just a girl," and I grew up knowing that I'd be "just a girl" until I became "just a woman." Would I have liked the Brethren boy my father had been? I don't think so. He'd have probably called me "just a girl" too.

"If we were at home for the Lord's Day," my father wrote, "we set out on foot for the eleven o'clock meeting at the Iron Room. We were expected to walk quietly and sensibly: My brother and I usually walked ahead and my father and mother followed, pushing my baby sister in the pram. Each of us carried a hymnbook and a Bible. This was part of our testimony—*amongst whom ye shine as lights in the world.*

"But there weren't many people about to shine on," my father complained. "There'd have been Baptist and Methodist services in Kenilworth at the same time, and there was certainly a Holy Communion at St. John's Church in the other direction," he wrote, "but we only ever saw Mr. and Mrs. Bert Clayton and Mr. and Mrs. Foster, the two Brethren couples who also lived on Waverley Road. They were either ahead or behind walking on the other side of the road. We never walked with them," he added. "I have no idea why. Mr. Foster had a long neck and a very prominent Adam's apple. He was tall and thin and he walked quickly in a kind of stalking manner. His much shorter wife struggled to keep up with him. My father called them 'the long and the short of it.'"

In the forties and fifties, all the Brethren sisters wore hats. In the Scriptures, the apostle Paul stipulated that all women's heads should be covered when they were "in the temple," my father explained, but Paul also said that men were to have their heads uncovered. For a group of postwar fundamentalists living in the British suburbs two thousand years later, this injunction of Paul's proved to be difficult to follow. One of the early Brethren leaders made a rule that if men were supposed to have their heads *uncovered* in the temple, they should have their heads *covered* on their way *to* it. So the brothers wore hats to the meeting and hung them on the rows of hooks at the back of the Iron Room.

When my father was a child, the lack of symmetry in this hat rule vexed him. He asked my grandfather why the sisters weren't carrying their hats to the meeting and putting them on when they went in. His father laughed, my father wrote, but he didn't answer the question. He wasn't sure my grandfather knew the answer. He began to wonder if there were other things his father did not know.

"The morning meeting in the Iron Room," my father remembered, "lasted for just over an hour. Brethren boys had to make sure that all the sisters had any cushions they wanted before the meeting started and a hassock, or footstool. Hassocks were piled at the back of the room, fat and thick and stuffed with some kind of coarse material, some patterned, some plain. All the sisters had to have one to put their feet on. The chairs were arranged in a circle around a table covered in a white cloth. On the table there was a goblet, a loaf of freshly baked bread in a basket, and a collection box."

First, a brother "gave out the notices." These included the times of the following week's meetings, who was giving the address in the Iron Room that night, and what fellowship meetings were scheduled for the following Saturday. Next, the same brother would read out any letters of commendation for any Brethren visitors present that week. Then the morning meeting would start. There was no script or written plan, but there was "a general understanding," my father wrote, "that things moved in a particular order. Brothers gave out hymns or got to their feet to pray as they were moved by the Spirit to do so. Brethren sisters were not permitted to speak, though they could join in the hymns."

After the first hymn, a brother walked to the table, broke the bread into pieces, and passed it around, just as we did twenty years or so later. Everyone breaking bread took a piece and ate it slowly. When the basket of bread was back on the table, the brother prayed a second time before passing the goblet of wine around. Then the collection box was circulated, a small wicker basket with a green baize lining, which had a hole in the top for the money.

In the forties, Brethren children were expected to ask to start breaking bread at the age of around twelve. As soon as senior ministering brothers had interviewed the child and confirmed that a conversion had taken place, the child would be declared "in the Spirit." Teenage children who weren't "in the Spirit" were considered a disgrace to their parents.

If you hadn't been converted, my father wrote, or if you doubted any of the doctrine, it was better to pretend to be "in the Spirit" rather than shame your family or risk getting withdrawn from. Eventually you forgot how to put up any resistance. Or you were just too fearful.

Better to pretend. So my father had muddled through just as I did. He'd been baffled too, and he'd found ways to keep quiet and pretend he wasn't. If he and I had been Brethren kids sitting on a fence together outside the Iron Room, could we have found a way of saying how strange it all was? I doubt it. I would still have been "just a girl" to him. He wouldn't have told me about the secret games he played during the Scripture readings. I wouldn't have told him about the hold of the ark that I walked through inside my head when I was supposed to be praying.

"Unless you were 'in the Spirit,'" my father wrote, "the afternoon Bible reading was usually not very interesting." At the age of seven he worked out a game to make the time pass more quickly. He'd choose a letter of the alphabet and start counting all the times it appeared in the chapter of the Bible they were reading that day. Soon he discovered that there were more *E*'s than any other letter. So he'd give *E* a less popular partner, like *K* or *U,* to slow it down. The total score of these two paired letters in a chapter had to beat a combination of two other letters, usually *S* and *N.*

"When I completed the chapter," my father wrote, "I'd move on to neighboring chapters, noting the scores down in the back of my Bible. The results were often quite close. A word like 'possessions' at the end of the chapter could tip the balance just in time. For some reason, the *SN* team seemed to do better in the Old Testament.

"My mother," he added, "never worked out what I was doing, but as long as I was quiet and apparently reading my Bible she was content."

Was this game an early sign of his gambling? Did my father learn to gamble to stave off his boredom in Scripture meetings? Even as a seven-year-old, my father was racing letters and keeping scores. He was still keeping tallies on his deathbed—of calories, fruit flies, gambling winnings, and diabetes counts. My father was smart. When his teachers tested his IQ in grammar school several years later, his score was the highest they'd ever seen. I heard people describe him as having a photographic memory. He could memorize whole poems in a few minutes.

His obsession with numbers plagued me and my siblings. He was a compulsive keeper of scores. Later, when we had families of our own and he came to visit, the first thing he'd want to explain to everyone gathered at the dinner table—*every time*—was how he had shaved three or four minutes off his previous driving record for the distance he had just covered. He'd brandish tattered pieces of paper with dates and times and distances. My then-husband would meet my eye and raise an eyebrow.

"The preaching came at half past six on the Lord's Day," my father remembered. "It was always a familiar mixture of the tough and the mawkish: threats of Judgment and hell on the one hand and sentimental appeals on the other. The general idea was that all humans were hopelessly bad—*the heart of man is deceitful and desperately wicked*—and that unless we repented and believed in Jesus and the saving power of His blood we'd be judged at the Great White Throne and put into the Lake of Fire. There were variations, but the basic theme was always the same. To be fair," he added, "the Brethren didn't go on about hell as much as some people. They talked about the Day of Judgment more.

"Apart from the Lake of Fire," he wrote, "there was the certainty of being Eaten by Worms. There was also going to be a lot of Weeping and Gnashing of Teeth." He'd tried gnashing his teeth, he wrote, and it hurt. The image of hell that impressed him most was the Bottomless Pit. The idea of falling down a hole forever frightened him more than any of the other descriptions. "I used to imagine that endless lonely falling as I lay in bed at night," he wrote. "It made me feel dizzy."

Edmund Gosse, when he put together his notes for *Father and Son*, remembered something similar happening in his dreams as a boy—an intense sense of vertigo, of being spun through time and space, his heart racing. I didn't have falling dreams. Mine had rain and flood, earthquakes and tidal waves in them. It was, I suppose, just a different kind of vertigo.

"If a visiting ministering brother was preaching," my father remembered, "he'd corner you after the meeting to ask if you loved the Lord or if you'd put your faith in the blood of the lamb. I never knew what to say. I didn't blame the preachers, though," he added. "They were expected to do that. It was their job."

His empathy took me by surprise again, but then I remembered that later, of course, when my father began to preach, he had to corner children himself. I'd watch him rounding on a child after meeting and asking the same thing: "Have you put your faith in the Lord?" he'd ask, or "Have you taken the Lord into your heart?" I got asked those questions too as I stood in my Best Dress, clasping my stuffed rabbit. But, now that I think of it, I don't remember my father asking me about the Lord being in my heart. It was usually the Brethren sisters who asked about that.

I worried a lot about that taking-the-Lord-into-your-heart question when I was a very small child. Sometimes I was sure He was in there. I welcomed Him in. I could relax my efforts. I was glad He was there. Joyous, even. Mostly just relieved. Then a day or so later He'd be gone again. Sometimes His disappearance would coincide with me doing something naughty, sometimes not. I'd have to do the "taking-in ritual"—praying, confessing, subjecting myself—all over again. But those questions that vexed me—Was the Lord supposed to wander off like that? Was that normal?—were not the kinds of questions I'd dare to ask. I was supposed to take the Lord Jesus *in* and He was supposed to take me *up* when the Rapture came. I wasn't sure how all of that worked either. You had to make sense of it all in whatever way you could, without help from the grown-ups.

My father's closest friend in the Brethren—I'll call him William to protect his identity—now in his seventies, told me that it was often the little things that kept you obedient, that kept you from running away. William had an uncle who was withdrawn from for some misdemeanor or other. When, at the age of eight, he asked his father what had happened to the uncle he'd adored—why he'd disappeared, whether they'd ever see him again—his father simply said: "Outside those doors, son, there is *darkness*." William had developed an image in his head, he said, of his beloved uncle groping about in some "murky, dark horror.

"I grew up terrified of the dark," he added. Now I began to wonder if my fear of the dark came from the same place that William's had. We'd both grown up believing that the darkness beyond our small circle of light was full of scuttling monsters waiting to snatch us. Most children, I guess, feel a dread of what they can't see. Few children are told that they are right to be terrified, that their imaginary monsters are real devils sent by Satan to steal their souls, or that they might even be Satan himself.

12

In the 1940s my traveling salesman grandfather became one of the most important ministering brothers in the Iron Room in Kenilworth. At home he was strict, my father wrote. He'd make his children drop to their knees to pray at the slightest transgression. He was often angry or getting angry. His rages would come from nowhere.

His father had had a quick temper, my grandfather would tell people by way of apology or explanation, when he caught himself. David Fairbairn Stott had been a disciplinarian. He'd bullied his children. With Brethren women and children expected to show absolute compliance and subjection, Brethren men had absolute power in their homes. Their anger must have often gone unchecked. Bullying of women and children must have been common even among otherwise good men.

When my father wrote about my grandfather, he described him as a monster who raged and ranted.

"I was afraid of my father," he wrote. "He was prone to terrible rages. They came suddenly, like thunderstorms. 'Why on *airth* did you do that?' he'd say. 'What on *airth* were you thinking about?'

"Sometimes he'd lose control of himself for ten minutes or so, roaring at the top of his voice and beating his fists on the table. He wasn't roaring *at* anyone, he was just roaring. Once he roared on the lower part of the Kenilworth staircase, beating his fists against one of the steps. Afterward he was exhausted and tearful. It was as if he had been taken ill.

"He was never violent towards my mother," my father wrote. "That was something outside his range. He punished us, sometimes with a ruler across the palm of the hand, or if we'd been especially bad he'd use a belt. Sometimes he'd just slap us hard on the side of the head. 'By,' he would say heavily when he was angry, 'by.' Not 'by' anything, just 'by,' and he'd draw a deep breath. His anger was always much worse than the physical blows.

"My father's rage hung in the air as a dreadful possibility. 'You'll set me off,' he'd say when we tried to justify or explain. If one of us misbehaved when he was preaching in the Iron Room, he'd stop speaking and frown at us. Other Brethren would turn and look at us. 'I'll stop the meeting,' he'd say to us at home. 'If I see you doing that again, I'll stop the meeting.'"

My grandfather had a nervous tic when he was on edge, a kind of winking with his left eye that took the left-hand side of his mouth up with it. "When this started," my father wrote, "it was better to apologize and propitiate, even if the matter under investigation had been an accident. Even then you couldn't always stop the rage; sometimes there was no stopping it whatever one said. Justice did not come into it. If something had been broken or spilt, someone must be to blame. Anger hung in the air, waiting to discharge itself. It was like living on a fault line or the slopes of a volcano.

"When I read Shakespeare years later," he wrote, "I understood the final roarings and the stricken, exhausted peace at the end of *Hamlet, Othello, Macbeth,* and *Lear.* The only durable calm, I already knew, was the one that came after cataclysmic events. You braced yourself and braced yourself and then the terror came and

Ada Louise at the age of about twenty

you lived through it and then it blew itself out and you were exhausted and shaking but everything was all right again."

I thought of my grandmother, raised in a big house by her kindly aunt, playing out in the Australian backwoods with her sister and cousin, now living out a life of constant appeasement in suburban rainy Britain, stepping between her husband and her children, making peace or trying to keep it, praying for it, smoothing feathers.

The rage wasn't just in the men or only in the Stott branch of the family; my grandmother's mother, the hauntingly mournful-looking Ada Louise, had been a legendary fury. She'd once thrown one of her daughters across the room and broken her arm. I found that hard to believe when I looked at the picture my father had given me.

Ada Louise had a strong Huguenot jaw, the long family face. She looked like my two dark-haired brothers. She looked like me. She looked like my son. There are a few black-and-white photographs of Ada Louise in her twenties—striking, mournful, and laced up to the neck—and then photographs of her in her sixties, white-haired, blank-eyed, smiling, propped up by others. In those forty or so in-between years she lived in an asylum where they didn't take photographs.

My great-grandfather Hugh Wasson, the man who'd run away from his home in Northern Ireland to take a boat to Australia at the age of thirteen, sent his beautiful, troublesome wife away to an asylum soon after his two daughters started school. She wasn't mad, she had epilepsy. Grand mal seizures. And she was willful. Medical experts thought this was the best place for her. Epileptics were considered loose, untrustworthy, and maniacal in Australia around the turn of the century. In 1901 the country's most eminent epileptic specialist decided to gather all of Australia's epileptic women together in an asylum at Ballarat where they could look after one another and not breed or infect others. One third of those women died in the first seventeen years of the experiment.

When my grandmother talked about her mother, she usually described her as dressed in white. She remembered her mother having a seizure at the school gates wearing that white dress. A male stranger lifted her unconscious body up in his arms and carried her home, daughters in tow clutching schoolbooks. My grandmother remembered her mother disappearing to Ballarat, then brief visits to the grand asylum building. She remembered the upset and shame, the fear and grief of it all. She remembered seeing her mother in a white straitjacket in a padded cell.

"My mother was willful," my grandmother would say when I was ten or so, the two of us in the kitchen cutting those cross shapes into the stalks of brussels sprouts. Not just ill, but *willful*. And if there were other Brethren women around the kitchen table they'd nod when my grandmother told that story. Willful women needed locking up. Willful women had husbands who signed papers, doctors who prescribed lobotomies and ECT. They got sent away and they didn't return for forty years.

You didn't want anyone to be using the word "willful" about you.

Rage was in my father's blood too, but although he wrote about his father's temper in his memoir, he did not describe his own. We, his children, grew up under its shadow, the marks of it on the walls and doors. My first memories of my father are the walking-on-eggshells kind. He was big, he was volatile, and, though he was often affectionate and funny, his affection sometimes had a sharp edge.

We learned to avoid him when he was in certain moods. He'd warn my mother not to set him off. He'd warn us. When something did set him off, my mother would shepherd us quickly into the sitting room and lock the door behind her. Then the kicking and shouting would begin.

When I was three or four years old, I've been told, my father came home after a grilling from one of the senior ministering brothers to find me sitting in a corner of the kitchen taking great gasping breaths after a long sobbing spell. He shouted at me to be quiet. This made me start crying harder. All of a sudden he lost control, flew across the room, and hit me hard around the head and face. Disgusted at himself, he fled the house.

My face swelled up black and blue. Within hours I couldn't open my eyes. My face had to be covered in foundation and talcum powder to mask the bruises. I had to be hidden for a week from the eyes of visitors so that other Brethren wouldn't see what my father had done.

It was probably one of the reasons he doted on me later, I was told. He never forgave himself.

But I don't have any memory of the blows. And he never talked to me about it.

When I told my father's friend William this story, forty-five years after it happened, his eyes welled up with tears, not just for me but for my father, my mother, and himself.

"We were under terrible pressure," he said. "Those were the Jim Taylor, Jr., years. We were all sleepless, anxious, trapped. We were being watched all the time. We were all living on the edge of a volcano."

13

But I'm jumping ahead. All of that shouting and kicking of doors came later, in the 1960s. My father grew up in the 1940s, when the Brethren were strict—fanatical, even—but not yet maniacal. It was my grandfather who was doing the shouting back then. My father was still a child, adding up his *E* scores in his Bible and hoping no one could see what he was doing.

My father won the school English prize in 1946 and brought home Arthur Mee's *The Book of Everlasting Things,* an anthology of extracts from great literary works. He was seven. My grandfather must have been proud of the award but wary of the prize. Only certain books were allowed in Brethren homes. He examined the expensively bound heavy volume and pronounced it acceptable. "This was a serious mistake," my father recalled.

"I knew there was a world outside the Brethren," he wrote, "but I'd seen nothing like this. The Brethren line was that literature, sculpture, painting, and secular music—even human imagination itself— were all mischievous, frivolous, and seductive distractions from the Scriptures. When Paul came to Athens and saw all the ancient beauty there, he dismissed it as *idolatrous . . . the graven forms of man's art and imagination.* The only important thing to God, we were told, was your reborn self in the Spirit."

To my father's surprise, sin, repentance, and being born again weren't mentioned in *The Book of Everlasting Things.* "A gap began to open up in the wall that had been built between me and 'the world,'" he wrote. "I slipped through it."

My grandparents, seeing my father's pleasure in the book, bought him Mee's companion volumes for subsequent birthdays: *One Thousand Famous Things* and *One Thousand Beautiful Things.* They ordered a set of children's encyclopedias. When the crate containing the volumes arrived, my grandfather summoned the family to watch as he selected the *D* volume and with a sharp knife cut out the entry on Darwin's theory of evolution. He threw the excised pages into the fire. Darwin's ideas, he told them, were wrong and wicked and against Scripture.

I have my father's copies of Mee's books on my bookshelves. They smell musty and the pages have yellowed. *The Book of Everlasting Things* is 352 pages long. The American Declaration of Independence sits next to Matthew Arnold, Henry Vaughan next to George Eliot. Later in the book there's the best part of "The Rime of the Ancient Mariner," twelve pages of "In Memoriam," nine pages of *Samson Agonistes,* Gray's "Elegy," five pages of *Paradise Lost,* Shelley's "To a Skylark" and "Adonais"—"in which I almost drowned," my father wrote—a long passage from *Robinson Crusoe*, Keats's "Ode to a Nightingale," whole speeches by Demosthenes and Pericles, eight pages from *The Odyssey*, Cicero's essay on old age, Plato's account of the death of Socrates, Edward FitzGerald's translation of *The Rubái-yát of Omar Khayyám*, eleven of Shakespeare's sonnets, and several passages from his plays.

What was my Brethren grandfather thinking in allowing such "worldly" books into the house? My father, seven years old, was enthralled. He memorized the Shakespeare speeches anthologized there, rehearsing them in his bedroom when his parents were out—*Julius Caesar*'s "This was the noblest Roman of them all," *Twelfth Night*'s "Make me a willow cabin at your gate," "Tomorrow and to-morrow and tomorrow" from *Macbeth,* and "Come, let's away to prison" from *King Lear*. He fell in love with Emily Brontë, he told me, his eyes full of tears. He took his magnifying glass to the paintings in *The Book of Everlasting Things,* paintings by Raphael, Holbein, Bellini, Velázquez, and Rembrandt, and photographs of ancient sculptures from Egypt, Greece, and Rome.

"The words of remarkable men and women," he wrote, "began to swarm inside my head. Other feelings, other judgments, other passionate beliefs, a different seriousness, and an unfamiliar gaiety opened up to me as I read." And then he quoted the lines from Keats's "On First Looking into Chapman's Homer," as he would do again many years later to me during our car journeys, often weeping: *"Then felt I like some watcher of the skies / When a new planet swims into his ken."*

"Soon I had a small library of pieces in my head," he wrote. "I could go there at any time, even when I was in a meeting. I had a secret, non-Brethren compartment inside my head."

I thought of the salty ark I'd made for myself, the secret, non-Brethren room inside my own head. I wondered where all the other Brethren children went to in those long hours of meeting. Did they have private rooms too? Had the women daydreamed? What about

William? Had anyone—other than a small group of men—really been listening to all that angels-on-a-pinhead exegesis?

14

My father was ten when doctors found an abscess in his mother's womb and rushed her into the Queen Elizabeth Hospital in Birmingham. They did not expect her to survive. My father and his brother were sent to stay with Auntie Bessie and her husband on their farm in Kent. The prayers for her in the Kent meeting room were urgent and serious, my father remembered. His mother's father and grandfather were "famous" ministering brothers in Australia, so my grandmother's illness was much discussed, much whispered about. Weeks passed. The news was not good. The Kent Brethren redoubled their prayers; my father and his brother fended off the sympathetic embraces of the elderly Brethren sisters.

And then, just as the doctors and my grandfather had given up hope, the abscess suddenly burst. "A wave of relief and gratitude swept through the Brethren meeting rooms in Kenilworth and Kent," my father wrote. "In Brethren terms, my mother's recovery was a high-profile event. A miracle."

"To me," my father added, "it was proof that God existed."

When my grandmother returned home from the hospital, she told my father about a recurring vision she'd had through the last ten days of her illness. Sometimes, she said, she'd surfaced from her dreams to find doctors or nurses bending over her or my grandfather, sitting holding her hand; but most of the time, in her mind, she was walking across a winter landscape, looking up at a network of winter trees and branches silhouetted against a red and gold sky while a heavy bell tolled somewhere close.

She'd been in a prolonged struggle with the Lord, she told my ten-year-old father. She couldn't die, she told God. How would Robert manage? And the children needed her. In answer to her pleas a simple phrase repeated itself, remotely, impersonally, against the steady tolling of the bell: *"One will in the universe,"* the voice said, *"one will in the universe."*

My grandmother lived like this, slipping between the physical world and the metaphysical sunset, for more than a week. And then one day she capitulated, she told my father. She gave herself up to God's will. *"Thy will be done,"* she'd said finally. *"Thy will be done . . . not what I will but what Thou wilt."* Within twelve hours the poisonous abscess inside her broke and dissipated. My grandmother had summoned my father to tell him this story, I guess, because she wanted him to give up his will too. Give up everything, let the Lord direct your ways. That was the Brethren way.

For months after she returned home, my father's mother would walk to the back door of their Kenilworth house at sunset to look at the pattern of winter trees against the sky. "Sometimes," she said to my father years later, "I could hardly breathe when I looked up at them." He must have felt the same way when he looked at her.

15

In the year that my grandmother nearly died, 1948, James Taylor, the Brethren world leader, the man we called J.T., a Sligo, Ireland–born New York linen merchant, received "new light" from the Lord about worshipping the Holy Spirit.

"New light" was important. You could tell the Rapture was close because the Lord would start to send lots of it. New light meant new instructions, new truths, revealed only to the Brethren's leader, the Man of God. But this particular new light about the Spirit upset people. John Nelson Darby had always taught that Brethren should worship the Lord and the Father, not the Spirit by itself. Now J.T. was telling them that the Lord wanted them to worship the Spirit equally with God and the Lord. Was he right?

Some senior ministering brothers expressed their concern privately. There was, they said, too much emphasis being placed on the ministry of Brethren leaders—from Darby to James Taylor.

Some people were placing more emphasis on ministries than on the Scriptures. Surely that was wrong. Most of the doubters, however, were wary of saying such things publicly for fear of being withdrawn from. Most did as Brethren usually did—they decided to wait, keep their counsel, and see how things played out.

"The morning meeting now had to be changed," my father wrote. "Everything had to be rearranged. We worshipped the Lord at the beginning, then after the passing round of the bread and wine and the money box, everything was about Christ and the assembly. Then we worshipped the Spirit, then the Father, then the Trinity. There had to be a revision of the Brethren hymnbook so that there were hymns addressed to the Spirit. All the Brethren who fancied themselves as hymn writers got busy writing new hymns."

J.T.'s teaching was complex and increasingly esoteric in the late forties and early fifties. "We were the children of Israel fleeing from Egypt through the wilderness to the promised land," my father wrote, remembering the sense of adventure and risk that those stories excited in them all. "We thought of ourselves as a community of refugees, traveling across the Jordanian desert, exposed to danger from all directions."

"Egypt," he wrote, "was supposed to be the world system we'd left behind, where we'd been in bondage. We'd escaped all the way to the Red Sea. The Red Sea was supposed to be the Gospel, salvation through the death of Christ, God parting the waters and letting the Brethren through on dry land. That took us into the wilderness. We were following the Ark of the Covenant, which was Christ, through the wilderness, and we were being fed by the manna which was also Christ."

When my father talked or wrote about the manna—the mysterious food that God provided for the Israelites in the desert—he'd always quote the lines from the Bible: *And it was like coriander seed, white, and the taste of it was like cake with honey.* I imagined the boy in the meeting room thinking about honey cake and coriander seed just as I had pressed the bread between my four-year-old fingers to see if it tasted or smelled better squashed, relishing the yeasty aroma that lingered on my fingers.

"At the other end of the wilderness," my father wrote, "was the River Jordan. The Ark of the Covenant went ahead of you down into the riverbed, and we were supposed to follow it. This was Christ's death *in you*, a painful experience. Then you came up on the other side and began your life in the new land. On the other side we'd still have to fight encroaching tribes and get things built and established. But this landscape was heavenly—we were now on God's territory, not man's."

Just to make things more complicated, J.T. told them that all these things were happening at the same time. "Spiritually," my father wrote, "you'd be leaving Egypt through the Red Sea, learning the lessons of the wilderness, going down into the Jordan, and living your life in the land on the other side, *simultaneously*."

It was a lot to keep in mind, particularly if you were ten years old. My father seems to have struggled not just with the metaphysics of the flight-from-Jordan story but also with the geography. He was vexed by the fact that the children of Israel were supposed to have taken forty years to travel a distance that should have taken a few weeks. He asked his primary school teacher about the exact distance during a Scripture lesson. When he quoted the answer at home, his mother wrote to the school and had him "excused" from Scripture lessons. Enraged, he waited for his mother to go shopping, then took down his father's atlas and used the scale and a ruler to confirm the distance his teacher had given him. *Sixty-five miles.* Had it really taken them forty years to walk sixty-five miles? This meant that the average speed of the children of Israel through the wilderness was about twenty yards a day, he told me years later. "And they were supposed to be traveling *day and night*. It made no sense. How could people walk *that* slowly?"

16

The miracle of his mother's recovery in 1948 made my father resolve to try harder to be a better Brethren boy. He was deeply affected by the story she told him about giving up her will to God. But there was another event in my father's life in the same year that also changed everything.

My father's Australian grandfather, Hugh Wasson, arrived from

Central Hall, Westminster

Australia to spend that summer with his convalescent daughter. The Stott clan traveled together down to the great international gathering of Brethren clans that took place every summer at Central Hall, Westminster. They called it the "universal gathering." Although women, children, and non-ministering Brethren men were not allowed to go to the meetings during the day, they could attend the evening addresses. Admission was by numbered ticket, checked at the door.

For these meetings, the Brethren rented Central Hall from the Methodists. It was the only nonconformist religious hall in London big enough to seat all the thousands of Brethren who congregated from around the world. That it was just a few yards from the House of Commons must have added to the sense of occasion and dissenting power. Compared to Brethren meeting rooms, the décor, polished wood, and red damask must have seemed both disturbingly ornate and very impressive.

At the age of ten, my father had never seen so many people all in one place, nor seated in such a way that made the Brethren hierarchy so immediately visible. On a raised dais just below the huge organ there were about a hundred men seated around J.T.

"I could see that if you made it into that section of a hundred men," my father wrote, "you were getting somewhere. J.T. was in the front row. In the middle. It was a little bit like those May Day parades in Moscow," he wrote, "when the Soviet leaders stood in a particular order around Stalin and you could see at a glance who was in and who was out of favor that year. In the J.T. era, these placements only changed slowly. Later, it would be different. At this stage, in 1948, my father was still in the body of the hall, but he was in the part from which you took off into the top hundred. My grandfather sat in the second row just behind J.T. I looked on him with a new respect."

I was looking for excuses for him now. How could the ten-year-old Brethren boy, already nearly as tall as his own short and stocky father, indoctrinated by the patriarchal begats of the Bible and the family business, not have been moved by this visual display of male power? In that noisy red hall, he discovered that his father, the dictator of his domestic world, had little status and was seated only in the stalls. But his grandfather was up there on the raised dais, seated just behind J.T., the Brethren leader.

My father was impressed. Of course he was. I would have been impressed too if I'd been there. All that red carpet and polished wood. The great organ, a hundred feet high. All that noise; all those choruses of "Amen." Maybe it was all the red in my father's memory that made him think of the Soviet May Day parades when he tried to describe it. It was making me think of the Nuremberg rallies—Hitler with all his henchmen behind him on the stage. Did my father decide that day that someday he'd be up there on that platform too? That he'd get even closer to the Brethren leader than his own grandfather?

"After the meeting," he wrote, "I was with my mother in the crowds outside the hall when J.T. came past. My mother knew him a little (he was very fond of her father) and she introduced me to him and I shook his hand. I was embarrassed, but my mother said that in future years it might mean a lot to me that I had met J.T. And she seemed to feel that some of his spirituality might rub off on me at the same time. J.T. spoke to me gravely and seriously as if I was a grown-up."

I'd watched my father preach when I was growing up. Not just in our little meeting room on Edward Avenue but in the much bigger one on Vale Avenue, where the steeply raked circular seating rose from around the central platform. I'd sit up at the back with my mother and siblings, looking down through the hats and bodies, studying the way he paced the floor when he preached, or how he gestured with his hands, or how he made his sentences rise and fall.

I particularly admired the length of my father's silences. All Brethren men knew how to pause and hold a silence—it showed that they were waiting for the Lord to guide them—but my father would pause right in the middle of a sentence and stretch out that silence so much longer than everyone else. I'd press my fingers into the soft leather of my Bible in suspense as I counted out the seconds.

There was one particular line I listened for in my father's preaching, a line that had especially beautiful rhythms. An important Brethren sister from Ireland in the early days had once said: "Let us put away our playthings, for the world is in flames," and that line, dark and poetic, was passed down among Brethren over the years. My father loved it. He wouldn't just use it once; he'd repeat it for effect. When I was six years old I heard him repeat it five times. I whispered each of the words along with him under my breath, second-guessing where he was going to put the next stress, anticipating the next long pause, and at the same time keeping a close eye on my grandfather down in the front row to see, from his expression, if my father would get away with it.

A few years ago I found myself absentmindedly mouthing that sentence, with my father's inflections, as I approached the podium of a vast hall in Heidelberg, where I was about to give a lecture on Aristotle and early ideas about evolution. My words must have been picked up by the powerful microphone pinned to my lapel, but thankfully they were drowned out by the sound of applause. When I pulled up the first slide—a striking photograph of the lagoon on Lesbos where Aristotle had once studied fish and birds—I held the silence for as long as I dared, until I could see people leaning forward in their seats. I am my father's daughter, I thought, as I began to speak, unable to suppress a smile. Had I, I wondered, worked all those years to become a writer and scholar so I could take the microphone, like my father and grandfather, and claim my seat up on the platform too?

17

In 1948, the year of my grandmother's near-death vision, the year that J.T. changed the rules about the Holy Spirit, the year that my father shook hands with J.T, my great-grandmother Ada Louise was finally released from Ballarat Asylum. Now that new drugs were controlling her epileptic fits, Brethren relatives told my great-grandfather, Hugh Wasson, it was un-Christian to keep her there. Ada Louise, sixty-nine years old, finally came out of the asylum to live in her husband's house in Adelaide, and my great-grandfather's nomadic, studious, independent life came to an end. After forty years in an asylum, Ada Louise was difficult; she talked incessantly and sang hymns at the top of her voice. It was impossible for my great-grandfather to read the Bible quietly as he had been used to doing. His health began to suffer.

His English daughters read his many airmailed letters and decided it was time they "shared the burden" of their mother. They persuaded their father to sell the house in Adelaide and buy a large house in Brighton where he could live with my grandparents and their three children. It would be big enough for him and Ada Louise to have their own wing but connected enough for Kathleen to help look after her mother.

When the unhappy couple arrived at Tilbury Docks, London, in mid-July 1953, having been cooped up for weeks reading their Bibles on the SS *Orcades,* their two daughters and their families were on the quay to meet them. Ada Louise had not seen Kathleen or Betty for nearly forty years, nor had she met her grandchildren, though she'd already memorized their names and life histories. My father, then fourteen years old, was fascinated and embarrassed by his grandmother's emotional intemperance. They all were.

"She seemed to be in a kind of ecstasy," he wrote. "She kept murmuring and sighing and stroking our faces." Then, grandly, she introduced them all to her husband, forgetting that he'd been to stay in England many times.

"Rather you than us," my father's cousin hissed at my father from behind her gloved hand.

In my mind's eye my bespectacled, snow-white-haired great-grandmother, in a black dress and matching jacket with silver em-

Ada Louise and Hugh Wasson in the early fifties

broidery, stands on the quay in a new country, surrounded by strangers, looking like a Russian dowager in exile. She is sixty-nine but looks ten years older. Her face, strikingly beautiful in pre-asylum photographs, is now deeply lined, but she still looks willful. Her face is still a little like mine.

What had she been doing all those years? What had she been allowed to read or see in that grand asylum? I like to think there might have been a garden, or at best a pretty view from her window, and a piano and someone to listen to her sing hymns sometimes without mocking her. I try not to think of her in that padded cell. I like to think that, had I been standing on the quay that day, I might have stroked *her* face or kissed her hand. But I'd probably just have been embarrassed too.

Hugh bought Ada Louise a secondhand pedal organ that they assembled in the rear drawing room of the huge Brighton house my grandparents bought with joint funds. For four hours or more every

day she played and sang the hymns she'd been taught as a child—
most often "Nearer My God to Thee" and "Almost Persuaded." She
sang slowly and with deep feeling, my father remembered, her voice
wavering and breaking from time to time as the words and music
overwhelmed her. She'd tip her head back like a wolf and aim the
hymn toward the ceiling. She insisted on having the door open so
that the rest of the house could hear her perform. My father and his
siblings would try to shut it without her hearing. But she always
opened it again.

Sometimes she was so overcome by her own playing that she'd
trot out of the room and grab any passing child or my grandmother
or the cleaning lady. "Just come and listen to *this*," she'd say, forcing
her prey into the chair next to the organ. With an audience present
she'd weep through the hymn and then, on finishing, stand, bow, and
wave royally. "Then," my father wrote, "you had to say the right things
and escape as quickly as possible before she started the next one."
When visitors began to prepare to leave she'd run to the piano and
sing, "God be with you till we meet again."

Family dinners were tense, my father told me. His father sensed
disapproval from his father-in-law over domestic and Brethren matters. They'd both been used to absolute authority in their homes. Tensions between them increased when Brethren visitors came to stay.
And there was his grandmother's unpredictability. She waited for
openings in the conversation and then told long stories that embarrassed everyone. Her two teenage grandsons enraged and disgusted
her. She told them they ate too much and too quickly, and grumbled
incessantly about their "big feet under the table." When they asked
for second helpings, she'd lean her head to one side and intone:

"To bed, to bed," said Sleepy Head,
"Tarry awhile" said Slow,
"Put on the pot" said Greedy Gut,
"We'll sup before we go."

When she was not playing the organ she was listening for the bell at the front door or the side door, the one they called the "tradesmen's entrance." As soon as she heard it, my father recalled, she'd scuttle to the door. Sometimes she got there before anyone could stop her. She began by challenging callers about the state of their souls. Did they know that they were sinners in the sight of God? Had they put their faith in the blood of the lamb? Had they taken the Lord into their heart? Sometimes she'd break out into a hymn.

One Friday she answered the door to the fishmonger. Ada Louise loathed both fish and the Roman Catholic Church in equal measure. In her long years at the Ballarat hospital, they always served fish on Friday, and as she knew this was a Catholic tradition, she considered it idolatrous. My grandmother arrived at the door to hear her mother, in a righteous passion, haranguing the stupefied fishmonger about the Virgin Mary, the Pope, and the Whore-of-Babylon Vatican. My grandmother asked him politely to wait while she steered her hyper-ventilating mother back to her room and to the organ.

I had a framed portrait of a young Ada Louise on my sitting room wall until a few years ago. Visitors would sometimes say I looked like her, and my daughters would explain she was Mummy's great-grandmother and her name was Ada Louise and she'd been locked up because she had epilepsy. "Ask Mummy," they'd say when the visitors' questions multiplied. Then I'd have to find a way of telling them just enough to satisfy their curiosity without us going into the entire Brethren story again. If we went there, I knew we'd be discussing cults for hours.

But that wasn't the only reason I took down the portrait.

"She just made me feel sad," I told my daughter Hannah when she asked where the picture of her great-great-grandmother had gone.

In truth, Ada Louise's face had come to stand for all those women who'd been shut up or locked up, not just Brethren women but those bullied or belted by men who were allowed too much power in their homes. Her face haunted me. One day when my daughters were a bit older, I told myself, I'd try to talk to them about that, about patriarchy and how dangerous unchecked male power can be. I'd talk to them about Ada Louise.

A decade later a long-running story on a famous BBC radio soap opera called *The Archers* finally prompted that conversation. Heavily pregnant Helen Archer had stabbed her controlling husband with a kitchen knife after years of isolation and mental abuse. She was arrested. The audience for the show grew to millions. There were chat rooms devoted to the story line, money being raised for support groups for victims of abuse. The whole country, including my daughters, both in their early twenties, seemed to be tuning in. But my daughters didn't need me to do any explaining when the subject came up.

"It's called coercive control, Mum," Kez said. "They've passed a law about it."

"Took them decades to listen to the campaigners, though," Hannah said, her eyes bright with anger. "Did you know that the law didn't recognize rape inside marriage until the *1970s*? Un-be-liev-a-ble."

"I know," I said, trying to be positive. "But things are better for women now."

"Mum, you've read Atwood's *The Handmaid's Tale*," Kez said. "You know we can't ever take feminist progress for granted. They'll take our freedom away again unless we protect it."

"Look at what's happening in Poland over abortion," Hannah said. "Thousands of Polish women had to take to the streets to make the politicians scrap that bill."

I knew. I'd been teaching feminist theory and writing for years. I'd given my daughters each a copy of *The Handmaid's Tale* as birthday presents during their teens. We groaned together about sexist adverts on television, talked about equal pay and equal rights, and agreed about how important it was to stand up and make a noise when you thought something was unfair. Now they were bringing me articles to read and documentaries to watch written by women of their generation. I was learning from them.

I still haven't put that photo of Ada Louise back on my wall, though, despite the hope that my daughters and their friends give me about a fairer and more just future. My great-grandmother's face still makes me feel sad.

18

By the time he turned fifteen in 1953, my father recalled, he was living an entirely divided life. When his closest school friend referred to my grandfather as "a religious maniac," my father did not challenge him. He was not an unbeliever, he insisted when I pressed him, but his relationship with God had become a mere insurance policy, just in case it was all true.

Often the insurance policy did not work, he told me, with a shudder. He had remembered a summer's day in the late forties. I'd heard this story before, but now that I remembered that he'd nearly lost his mother a little while before this, the story was all the more poignant.

One winter day, when he was around ten or eleven, he returned home from school to find the house empty. This was unusual. He had no key of his own, so he climbed over the back fence into the garden of a school friend, and the two of them played with the boy's new cap gun. When he returned to the house alone half an hour later, his hands and clothes smelling of gunpowder from the caps, there was still no one there. He stood on the front steps wondering what to do.

"As I looked up at the golden scatter of clouds in the sunset," he wrote, "a horror crept up on me. The Lord had come. The Rapture had happened. I'd been left behind. The whole world seemed to be trembling," he wrote, remembering the wind in the garden trees. All the real Christians had gone and now the Tribulation would start.

How soon? How long did he have? Should he warn the neighbor's boy? Run? Soon there'd be beasts and false prophets everywhere. Where could he hide? He was finding it difficult to breathe.

When he told me this story years later, he claimed he'd passed out on the steps leading up to the tradesmen's entrance. And I sympathized. I breathed Brethren air for a much shorter time than my fa-

My father around age ten

ther, but I still find myself suppressing a shudder when I see a particularly lurid sunset or television footage of flooding or days of rain forecast on the evening news. These were the days of rain that Ezekiel had written about when he described those strange creatures he'd seen in the rain clouds, creatures with multiple human and animal heads. Even rainbows were supposed to remind us that the Lord had for some reason postponed the wrath that was going to be unleashed on us all. We were always living on borrowed time, waiting and studying the skies for signs.

When his mother, grandmother, and sister came back from their impromptu shopping expedition, my father wrote, he recovered himself. He said nothing to them about what had happened. They had their tea just the same and he did his homework, with Grandma across the hall singing to the ceiling again. It had been a warning from God, he told himself, a warning of what was to come if he continued his secret dissenting and disobedient life.

19

"When you were a teenager," I asked my father in those last weeks of his life, "did you rebel? Did you try and run away?"

"It wasn't as tough back in the forties and fifties," he said, trying to find a comfortable position in the reclining chair. "Life in the Brethren was a good way of life, provided you were prepared to accept the privations. Very few people came in from outside. We'd *all* grown up as Brethren. It was the only life we knew. Brethren looked after you and were supportive if people were in trouble. The idea of being out in the world was frightening. You had the feeling that if you went outside the Brethren there'd be no morals at all. People would cheat you and trick you because the world outside is under the control of Satan. You'd run back into the Brethren to be safe."

I remember that terror when I was growing up too. I was constantly watching—or listening—for Satan, hearing the tapping of his hooves on the cobblestone in the streets of Brighton, looking at the children on the primary school playground and imagining the scale of the wickedness in their homes.

When I took the little path through the woods behind our house to visit my grandparents, I wouldn't be watching out for suspicious strangers, I'd be listening for Satan. I made deals with the Lord Jesus to get me to the end of the path, to the gate that led back onto the street. Usually I promised to keep looking straight ahead, rather than behind—a token of my faith—in return for protection. When I broke that promise, turning my head to the sound of a snapped twig or a bird or dog rustling through the undergrowth, I'd run, terrified, toward the gate before a slavering horned Satan could step out from behind a tree to catch me. He couldn't get me once I was back across the threshold of a Brethren house. That was the only place you were really safe.

"If you went to a family wedding which was not a Brethren wedding—it was discouraged, but it did happen sometimes in the fifties—you felt at a loss," my father continued. "You wouldn't know how to behave and you'd feel exposed and you'd be grateful to get back among Brethren."

"Didn't it just seem like everyone at the non-Brethren wedding was having a better time?" I asked him. I was haunted by the phrase he'd used: "at a loss."

"If you talked to a Christian from outside they'd use words that would jar you," he said. "Brethren have a vocabulary and a way of talking about things that becomes the truth to you. It's been worked out over many years. So if somebody else comes in and starts talking about Jesus in a way that's off-key, it makes you feel ill at ease and out of place, so you're actually quite grateful to get away from that worldly wedding and back among people who speak the same language as you."

"What kind of off-key?" I asked, though I knew exactly what he meant. People still seem off-key to me out here in the world, even though I've lived among non-Brethren more than five times longer than I lived among Brethren. It often feels like the words I've learned to speak since then don't stretch far enough, don't describe the things I feel or imagine well enough. The things that crowd the dark, for instance, or flicker at the edges of my vision, have no name.

"It wasn't just phrases or ways of speaking," my father said. "It was ways of dressing and behaving as well. If an interloper got in, say, a journalist passing himself off as a Brethren visitor, he'd break subtle rules and codes of conduct so that people would immediately know he wasn't a proper member of the Brethren. There was a real tribal sensitivity. My father used to say that when he was driving to a meeting in a strange town, he could spot the Brethren sisters walking along the road. He'd say it was the Spirit telling him, but I always used to think it was their hats."

20

When my father began to study A-level English, he became even more disoriented. He read *Hamlet, Coriolanus, Much Ado About Nothing,* Wordsworth, Keats, Housman, Coleridge, Dylan Thomas, *To the Lighthouse, Howards End,* and T. S. Eliot. And then one day his English teacher gave the class Yeats's "The Wild Swans at Coole" to study. My father was utterly bewitched.

When his teacher told my grandfather in 1957 that my father was uniquely talented and should be studying for Oxbridge, my grandfather, impressed and proud, agreed to let him sit the exams. In the fifties, Brethren young men were still allowed to go to university, though in 1961 university attendance would be banned. More than fifty years later, Brethren still have a ban on higher education. "It takes our people away from the Lord," a Brethren priest told a journalist in a rare interview in 2003.

Now my father's lies escalated. To study for the Cambridge exams, he had to lie both to his father and to his teacher. When his teacher arranged summer camps at Stratford to see Royal Shakespeare Company productions, my father had to make excuses not to go. When he was offered the lead in the annual school Shakespeare production, he had to find a reason to refuse. But he also went to his teacher's house

My father in his teens

in the evenings for extra tutorials with other members of his class despite his parents' disapproval. He lied to his parents when he made his first visit to a theater to see Paul Scofield play Hamlet. Fifty years later, he could still remember the names of the entire cast.

He heard Brethren voices perpetually as he read, he told me in a lowered voice, and then he'd summon them to show me what he heard, what surfaced in his resting mind every day, every minute. "There were the father voices," he said, "they were harsh and judgmental:

> *The mind of the flesh is death . . . the mind of the flesh is enmity against God . . . it is not subject to the law of God, neither indeed can it be. . . . He that is a friend to the world is constituted an enemy of God.*

But there were also the kinder mother voices, which came on the other side of his head:

> *When Israel was a child, then I loved him, and out of Egypt I called my son. . . .*
>
> *Take my yoke upon you, and learn from me, for I am meek and lowly in heart, and ye shall find rest to your souls. . . .*
>
> *How often would I have gathered thy children, as a hen gathers her chickens under her wings. . . .*
>
> *Come, for night is gathering quickly o'er this world's fast fleeting day. If you linger in the darkness you will surely miss your way.*

Fifty years later he could still quote those lines from Scriptures and hymns. "Those voices," he told me, "never gave up."

I heard voices too as a child, sometimes when my head tipped to a particular angle or when I was falling asleep or had just woken: loud, soft, haranguing, enticing, sometimes in English, sometimes in a language I did not recognize. They were very similar to the voices my father described, though he seems to have heard primarily Brethren mantras and Scriptures. Eventually, of course, my father would recite the mantras himself when he preached. Repetition of simplified mantras and maxims, social psychologists have proved, is one of the key methods of indoctrination; it affects the physiology of neurological pathways, particularly in teenagers, whose brains are still growing. It's a powerful form of brainwashing. And of course my father's exceptional IQ and photographic memory made it very hard to silence those voices once they got into his head.

In high school my father's Brethren voices were telling him that Yeats and Shakespeare were a frivolous waste of time, that all the apparent vistas that were opening to him were carnal and corrupt, *the pleasures of sin for a season.* He veered from one way of seeing to another. "One was graven on stone," he wrote, "the other rippled like water. One asserted, the other side sang and whispered, beguiled, suggested, asked questions, claimed nothing, resonated."

21

It wasn't all prohibition and exegesis in the Brethren in the 1950s. Before 1959, Brethren were allowed to take holidays. Brethren families converged in St. Ives in Cornwall every summer. It was where many Brethren young men selected their future wives or had them selected for them. St. Ives is where my father met my mother.

"If you looked down on Porthminster Beach from the road above on any day except the Lord's Day," my father wrote, "you'd see the holidaying Brethren immediately. There'd be a huge semicircle of perhaps sixty or seventy deck chairs set close together. The chairs kept them closed off from the rest of the beach; the area they made was bounded by the sea on its open side. 'Worldly' families were scattered over the rest of the beach, but the Brethren had no contact with them.

"Within the semicircle the older Brethren men—some of them quite distinguished in Brethren terms—spent their days on the beach discussing 'the Truth.' They had their Bibles open on their laps and they'd talk for hours. The sisters talked about their children, and some of them knitted or sewed. Some of the respected spinsters and elder wives took part in the Bible discussions, but they were restrained and tentative; most of what they said was framed as questions. Paul said: *I do not suffer a woman to teach, nor to exercise authority over a man.* So Brethren women were expected to keep their opinions to themselves. Small children played in the sand within the semicircle. Teenagers swam in the bay and played cricket or rounders. There was also tennis on the hard courts above the beach.

Brethren women at the beach

"On no-meeting nights, Brethren teenagers were allowed to gather together after their hotel and boardinghouse dinners. They met at a coffee bar called the Picnic Box. They drank coffee and sometimes ordered the specialty of the house, a very large circular plate of biscuits and exotic cheeses. Afterward, they walked together along the cliffs. Sometimes they swam at Porthminster Beach after dark. Sometimes during the week, Brethren families went to Praa Sands and Perranporth in a convoy of cars to play cricket.

"There was no swimming or beach-going on the Lord's Day. On the Lord's Day evenings, after the Gospel in the meeting room, some of the Brethren gathered on the quay and several brothers preached to the passersby. They'd have to compete with other evangelical groups—get themselves heard above the sound of the Salvation Army band. Then the teenagers would walk along the cliffs to Porthmeor Beach and sing hymns above the breaking waves at sunset. We'd usually finish with 'How Sweet the Name of Jesus Sounds' to the tune of 'Crimond,'" he remembered, "so that we could practice the descant."

Later my father said that he could remember very little about the hotels they stayed in or the interior of the St. Ives meeting room. But he remembered the beach, the golden color of the sand and the sound of the cricket ball hitting the bat, the texture of browned and bare skin, and the white of a particular swimming costume gleaming in the dark.

My father, very tall and athletic, not exactly handsome but more than usually eloquent for a seventeen-year-old, stood out from the crowd of Brethren young men. He'd fallen in love, not with my mother but with the girl in the white swimming costume. She had slipped her hand into his during one of the evening walks. She was three years older than he was and the assistant matron at a boys' private school. They had four days together before she had to leave. They swam out to the anchored raft on Porthminster Beach after dark one night and lay kissing on the fiber matting under the moon and stars. She walked with her toes turned out a little, the way that dancers sometimes do, so he called her Penguin.

She left St. Ives by train the following day, the same day that my mother arrived with her sister and parents. She and my father had been introduced on the beach, but he'd been too heartbroken to talk much. He exchanged letters with Penguin every day for months. Her letters arrived with a small penguin drawn on the back of each envelope. After Christmas she wrote to say that as they lived so far apart and their ages did not match, she thought they should "discontinue" their "friendship" and, she added, "my parents wish it." The penguin on the back of this particular envelope lay flat on its back and had an arrow in its stomach.

When my father expressed interest in my mother, the girl he'd met fleetingly at St. Ives, another Brethren girl invited them both to her birthday party. He was seventeen, my mother twenty-one. They met again at a Brethren wedding. My father invited my mother to the boat race in Putney in March. He'd won a place at Fitzwilliam Col-

lege, Cambridge, he told her. He'd be starting in September and was
going to try for the rowing team.

He remembers walking along the Thames. He remembers swans
and weeping willows and my mother's coat, which had a fine her-
ringbone pattern and a large soft collar that she turned up behind her
head. When she laughed and turned toward him, he told me, the
darkness of her hair, thickly plaited and pinned up around her head,
took his breath away. They talked about Jane Austen, Charlotte
Brontë, and Yeats, he said, but I know he would have done almost all
of the talking. Cambridge won in the boat race. It rained. On the
London–Brighton train they ordered tea and toast and talked, my
father said, as if they were already engaged to be married.

He went to Salisbury for a weekend to stay with my mother and
her parents. It was a disaster. Head in a book, he'd missed the train
and turned up very late. She had to cancel the restaurant reservation
she'd made. The following day he borrowed my grandfather's car, a
Rover that was polished every week, and took a turn too tightly,
scraping and denting the car all along the left-hand side. It was a sign,
my mother told me decades later, that she should have taken notice
of. He was going to go on crashing cars for the rest of his life.

22

My father's first letters home from Cambridge were all about rowing
and the problems he'd had getting his rowing kit washed and dried in
time for the next outing. His college crew were out on the river every
day, training in the early-morning mist.

He was going to lectures, writing essays, talking to the other undergraduates on his corridor and on his crew. In comparison to life at
home, he must have felt very much in the world, and he clearly rel-

ished it, but he also knew, as all Brethren undergraduates did, that the local Brethren were keeping a close eye on him and would be writing home to his parents with regular reports. He was expected to attend the Cambridge meeting most days of the week and several times on the Lord's Day.

My father messed up his first year at university, his cousin told me. Reports from the Cambridge brethren arrived claiming that he'd gone off the rails, that he was backsliding morally. "Backsliding" was a word I'd often heard used about Brethren young men. It seemed to cover a multitude of sins. I suspect my father's worst crimes were that he missed some meetings and had been seen going to the cinema and socializing with non-Brethren. It probably also meant he'd begun to ask questions about doctrinal matters.

Everyone back home was holding their breath. The family honor and reputation were at stake. My great-grandfather Hugh Wasson now decreed that no other young Stotts were to go to university or into any other form of higher education. My father had been corrupted and muddled, he declared. He wasn't going to risk that happening to any of his other grandchildren.

In his second year of university, now in love with my mother, my father began to attend lectures by C. S. Lewis. He read his way through all Lewis's books, but it was the final page of *Mere Christianity* that brought him to his knees one night, both metaphorically and literally, in his small room on Willis Road. The conversion was so violent that, years later, the details of the room, the wallpaper, the light through the window, the scattered pattern of the papers on his desk, had seared themselves like scorch marks onto his memory.

"Submit to death . . . ," Lewis wrote. "Submit with every fiber of your being, and you will have eternal life. Keep back nothing. . . . Look for yourself, and you will find in the long run only hatred, loneliness, despair, rage, ruin, and decay. But look for Christ and you will find Him, and with Him everything else thrown in."

"The words," my father wrote, "leapt off the page. Here was the most powerful of my new literary apostles reinforcing all the old Brethren arguments."

His defenses collapsed suddenly, he wrote, "like the walls of a sand castle swept by an incoming tide." There was that sea metaphor once more. He'd been engulfed again. He knelt down and prayed in his bedroom; he described it as a "halting, painful prayer.

"I look back on that young man and his capitulation," he wrote about himself—confirming in that one word, "capitulation," the degree of exhaustion I'd sensed in him—"I look back on that young man in that small lonely bedroom with affection and sympathy. I didn't have a chance."

It's the empathy that surprises me again. The empathy he has for his remembered, capitulating self. And mine for him.

I didn't have a chance.

A chance to do what, though? To get away? To not believe? But he had made a *choice*. He chose to follow Lewis's kindly, pleasure-taking God instead of his father's punitive one.

"I'd been brought up to believe in a transcendent God," my father wrote. "Now, with Lewis and Donne, I began to think about an *immanent* one." He quoted lines from Gerard Manley Hopkins: *The world is charged with the grandeur of God. It will flame out, like shining from shook foil.* This new God loved the world rather than shunned it.

Under Lewis's spell he went to see *Look Back in Anger* and *Waiting for Godot* at Cambridge Arts Theatre. He watched Ingmar Bergman's *The Seventh Seal* and *Wild Strawberries* at the Arts Cinema.

"Cinema stopped being furtive entertainment," he wrote. "It contained both moral instruction and metaphysical power." In Brighton during a vacation he saw Laurence Olivier in *The Entertainer*. He had "chosen" a complicated, spine-contorting middle way: He would stay in the Brethren and bring this other world into it.

23

My parents look happy in the black-and-white photographs I have of them from the 1950s. Among those packs of young Brethren in St. Ives in the apparently halcyon summers before 1959, I can see them moving gradually closer together. In the early photographs, they stand far apart, on opposite sides of a big group, he leaning up against a seaside railing, she with her stylish collar turned up against the wind; then there's a picture of them closer together in a group of four or five cousins. The women are conservatively dressed; some wear headscarves; they wear no makeup. The men look a bit

My father on the beach at St. Ives, 1956. He is on the far right.

geeky, but otherwise, if you'd been on the promenade in St. Ives that day, you wouldn't have known they were any different from anyone else.

Many ex-Brethren I've talked to describe the fifties as a golden age in Brethren life. It was only when Jim Taylor, Jr., took over as Man of God in 1959 that things went wrong. He ruined it all, they imply. He was an aberrant, a monster. He made good people do unspeakable things. But even in the fifties, I can see, there were already serious prohibitions in place:

No cinemas, theaters, circuses, music halls.
No sport halls.
No radio or television sets.
Friendships with non-Brethren—tolerated but not
    encouraged.
No trade unions.
No sex before marriage.
No trousers for women or short skirts.
No fashionable clothes.
No tabloid newspapers.
No thrillers or modern novels.
No short hair.

Within five years the prohibition list would grow four or five times this long. Within ten years it was at least twenty times as long.

Around this time, in the late fifties, my father remembered, he and my mother, now engaged, discussed whether they would stay in the Brethren. Now that the rules were getting stricter, many young people were leaving. My mother suggested they put the decision to the Lord. What she meant by this was that they should look for the answer on the scriptural verse on the Day Dawn calendar for that particular day. It's what many Brethren did. If you were going to let the Lord direct your ways, you had to be confident that you could read the signs He sent. The Day Dawn calendar was one of the ways the Lord directed the Brethren. You might as well have rolled dice, I wanted to protest, or read tea leaves or spun the roulette wheel.

He couldn't remember the exact text on the Day Dawn calendar that day, he told me, though he thought it had been about walking in the light. He and my mother decided that those particular words meant they should stay in the Brethren.

But I'm pretty certain they'd both have stayed without their consultation of the Day Dawn calendar. They were optimistic and happy. They didn't know what was ahead. And anyway, how could they leave? If my parents had left the Brethren in 1959 they'd never have seen their parents, siblings, uncles, aunts, or friends again. They would have orphaned themselves.

24

"We're in 1959," I said, looking back over my notes. I'd just seen that sense of urgency creep up on my father again. He wanted to watch the cricket match; he wanted to sleep. But he knew he was running out of time. He was an eyewitness to this strange piece of history. Very few people had seen what he had seen. He *had* to make a record before he died.

I went to fetch the tape recorder.

"Why didn't we see it coming?" he said again.

"It's easy to see it with hindsight," I said. "I'm not sure I would have guessed what was going on either. Maybe even J.T. Junior didn't know."

I adjusted his chair so he could sit up a little. My brothers had gone for a walk; my stepmother was taking a nap.

"Just half an hour," I said. "You need to conserve your energy." I closed the door. Something had made me want to draw the curtains. There'd been more snow flurries outside overnight.

"You should see the soil," I said. "The snow's dusting it like icing sugar. It's very pretty. I can see twenty or thirty lapwings from here too. Twice as many as this time last year. They'll be nesting in a month or so."

But he wasn't to be distracted. He was already back in 1959.

"That was the year that J.T. Junior seized power," he said after I pressed the record button. "It was a seismic shift in Brethren history. *Seismic.*"

All ex-Brethren describe 1959 with similarly dramatic metaphors. Sometimes they call it a coup. Whatever comparisons they use, geological or military, they mean that nothing would be the same again. There was no going back.

"It took J.T. Junior ten years," my father said, "to completely transform the Brethren into a cult. It didn't happen all at once. But when

Brethren photographed at Central Hall in 1959. Gerald Cowell is at the lectern, J.T. Junior seated immediately to his left.

he seized power it was violent and sudden. The rest was a kind of ten-year lava flow."

My parents were out of the country when the coup happened. They'd married quickly so that my mother could accompany my father to South Africa. He'd been offered a three-month summer internship in an ice cream factory in Johannesburg; they'd be staying with Brethren families, and he'd be preaching. In June 1959 they flew into a South Africa deeply scarred by a decade of apartheid. The Brethren coup took place in Central Hall, London, a month later.

Ever since James Taylor died in 1953, the hundred thousand Brethren all around the world had been waiting for the new Man of God to emerge. For six years, leadership rotated among four men, one of whom was the rather erratic J.T. Junior, James Taylor's son. When that conference at Central Hall came around every year, people half expected one of the four to take the upper hand, but summer after summer things went on much the same. Until 1959, that is. My grandfather was at the gathering, but he wasn't among the top brass up on the stage in the photo that one of the ex-Brethren sent me. Perhaps he wasn't important enough yet. Had he minded not being up there?

It was the usual vast gathering. Senior ministering brothers from South Africa, New Zealand, Australia, the United States, South America, even Iran, had flown to London. My grandfather described the events to my grandmother. She wrote about them to my father in Johannesburg.

"The question of professional associations came up again," my father said.

I was struggling to keep up. I couldn't see how any of this was important. Yet remembering the details of that 1959 gathering seemed to be agitating my father more than anything else in the story he was trying to tell me.

"Professional associations?" I said. "Why did that matter?"

"James Taylor had banned union membership ten years before," he explained, with obvious impatience. "Now Brethren were saying that if blue-collar workers weren't allowed to belong to unions, then white-collar workers—Brethren doctors, architects, chemists, and lawyers—should leave their professional associations too. But that was going to be a problem, because many of them would lose their jobs."

"Someone had to decide," I said, feeling my way.

"Yes, exactly. One of the four leaders, Gerald Cowell, took the microphone and began to make the case for a slow, staggered withdrawal from the associations. He even suggested that someone might write to the government and get some kind of special dispensation."

He asked me to adjust his pillows so that he could sit upright.

"Now, at this point," he continued, his eyes brighter than I'd seen them for days, "at this point, J.T. Junior intervened in a way that was very un-Brethren-like indeed. He came in very abruptly and said, 'Are you saying we shouldn't get out immediately?' Cowell was slightly taken aback, but he repeated his proposal.

"Taylor quoted the New Testament at him: 'Come out from among them and be separate,' he said. 'That's what it says. It doesn't say *go slowly*. Come out from among them and *be separate*. That's what it says.'

"J.T. Junior just kept hammering on about this. There were awkward pauses, and a very un-Brethren-like contretemps went on, and J.T. Junior made this sort of howl of 'Come out, come out!'"

"*Howl?*" I said. "What kind of howl? Was that normal?"

"Taylor was unpredictable," he said. "He could be aggressive. It wasn't the Brethren way, but suddenly here he was, openly defying Cowell, goading him, then howling, 'Come out, come out!' Once he'd shouted down Cowell like that, everyone knew J.T. Junior was the new leader."

Had J.T. Junior planned to take the leadership? Several ex-Brethren who lived through this period, some of whom were at Central Hall in

July 1959, have told me since my father died that they think Bruce Hales, an Australian accountant and J.T. Junior's right-hand man, was behind the coup in some way. He was the uncle of the most recent leader, also named Bruce Hales. The elder Bruce had married J.T. Junior's daughter Consuela Taylor only a year before the coup. Had he begun to work on J.T. Junior over family suppers? Had he stoked J.T. Junior's impatience with the pace of Brethren decision-making processes? The timing certainly looks right. When my parents flew back from South Africa that August, J.T. Junior was already putting draconian new rules in place. Neither of my parents could have guessed the scale of the storm they were about to enter.

During

1

Three weeks before my father died there was a lunar eclipse. A blood-red moon hung low in the sky above the mill, silvering the fields and river. He staggered outside to the riverbank, leaning on my younger brother, and they stood there watching the moon turn black. Two tall men, father and youngest son, their arms around each other, gazing at the sky.

The following day, laid out in the middle of the room under a moth-eaten gold velvet throw, he was fighting the effects of the morphine, and though he was impatient to get on with our interview, he was easily distracted. He wanted the door closed before we began. He seemed to think there might be someone out there listening. "Is that noise coming from in here?" he whispered when the whir of the tape recorder started up again.

I hadn't expected his story to be full of the minutiae of Brethren leadership conflicts. Through all the hours I recorded him that week, my father kept to a ruthlessly straight chronological line, describing each new Brethren edict, each new struggle for power, month by month, excommunication by excommunication. We both knew he was running out of time, that he couldn't afford to meander. But he only got to 1963, the year before my birth, before he was too tired to continue. He was still only twenty-five in 1963, tall and lanky, a fledgling preacher and already the father of a son.

"But how did you feel?" I'd interrupt. "What did my mother think about that? Wasn't that the month that Chris was born? Didn't you cut his umbilical cord?"

I kept trying to get him to step sideways, out from amid the Brethren patriarchy and their closed rooms and doctrinal disputes. I wanted him to tell me about the family home where my mother was having babies and sterilizing bottles, that detached four-bedroom mock-Tudor half-timbered house built opposite Hove Park, with the lilac tree in the garden, where the bush grew with the white berries that you squashed between your fingers and where our tricycles made tracks in the morning dew.

We'd lived through those dark years too, after all, and had been marked by them. But it wasn't just that I wanted to be in this story of his, it was that I was increasingly certain that the full picture, the one he couldn't bear to look at, had to include our day-to-day family life and our private dreams as well as the dramas played out in the Brethren corridors of power. It had to include the women and children as well as the men. It would only be half a story without that.

But my father had only one objective in the hours I recorded him: He wanted to understand how he and the other Brethren men of his generation had been bewitched, turned from decent, earnest, promising young people into brutal Brownshirts. He had to understand that before he could be ready to die. It struck me that even after we'd recorded five hours of that interview, he was getting the facts down but still not really understanding what they meant. I think he knew that too.

It wasn't just me he was talking to. When he woke in the night in those last days he'd open up his laptop to write to a group of eighty or so ex–Exclusive Brethren all over the world in an online forum called PEEB. The name came from a word outsiders used to describe the

Brethren: Peebs, or the PBs. The site had been set up by ex-Brethren to provide a place for escapees to get support and for ex-Brethren to talk about their experiences. It had a flashing red RESCUE button on the home page. My father had been talking to the PEEB community for six years, sometimes every day. He seemed to have become an important presence there. He'd met my stepmother there.

Now that they knew he was dying, these ex-Brethren from Australia, the U.K., and the United States gathered online to listen and to console. *They* didn't keep interrupting with the wrong questions. They knew what to say and what language to use.

One of the first things I had to do after my father died was to write to these people to tell them that he'd gone, that, yes, that *was* what his silence meant. I told them about the owl that had come for him. I told them he had died a good death with his family around him. I thanked them.

In January 2013 the PEEB website mysteriously disappeared. The ex-Brethren host, Tim Twinam, who ran the site from a log cabin in Vermont and who'd been wrestling with Brethren legal action for five years or more, suddenly wasn't answering his emails or his phone. People speculated that the Brethren had either paid him off or threatened him. His seriously ill wife, they said, had just had expensive hospital treatment, more expensive, they guessed, than he could have afforded without outside help. Even now, no one really knows what happened to make Tim Twinam shut down the site.

But all those conversations and exchanges and words my father wrote on the PEEB site didn't disappear. One member of the community sent me a transcript of everything my father had posted, retrieved from a data dump somewhere. It ran to hundreds of pages. More ex-Brethren websites and blogs sprang up after PEEBS.net closed down, my informant told me. "That's the thing about the Internet," he said. "You can close down one part and another part will grow somewhere else."

As I read the to-and-fro of daily banter in the transcript, my father's conversations with ex-Brethren from New Zealand and Australia, Germany and South Africa, I was struck by how many different voices there were. Some were irascible, others grief-stricken or furious; many were still devout Christians, while others were zealous atheists. They teased him; they sent him poetry; they wrote to tell him about what the Brethren were doing now; they told him about someone who'd escaped and was being sheltered, about what had happened in their houses in the sixties and seventies.

The PEEB community must have been, it seems to me now, like a Greek chorus in the chambers of my father's mind as he slipped away. All through those last weeks, while I had been asking my clumsy questions long after he could no longer reach for his laptop, these people were in the house, in his head, attending, a hushed, respectful presence. They helped him to face his death, but they also helped him to remember. They reminded him that his story was their story too.

2

My parents flew back to Britain from South Africa in September 1959 for the final year of my father's Cambridge English literature degree. They rented out part of a house close to the Cambridge meeting room. My father went back to his rowing, his classes, his books and essays, his Brethren undergraduate friends. My mother bought secondhand furniture, sewed curtains, washed his rowing kit, and cycled two miles every day to her new full-time job as an accountant for Spillers flour mill up near the station. They broke bread with the Cambridge Brethren at the Mawson Road meeting room on the Lord's Day.

They wouldn't have had much time alone. Every night my father's friends came to the house and sat up late talking as they'd always done, except now they talked about the Brethren families who were leaving.

At university in September 1959 my father was studying Edmund Spenser's *The Faerie Queene*. Spenser had composed the long Protestant allegorical poem in the late sixteenth century, my father wrote, "to fashion a gentleman of noble person in virtuous and gentle discipline." The gentle knight of the story, a Red Cross Knight like those of the Crusades, goes through a series of ordeals and trials. It must have been perfect reading for my father.

When I looked at the annotations in my father's hardback copy, shelved next to Mee's *The Book of Everlasting Things*, I was struck by how he'd turned the poem into a theological thinking ground for himself, by how many scriptural references he'd added in the margins, many distilled down to mere numerical references: Tim 2:2, Cor 3:5, and so on. "Can you explain the difference between the Solomonic and the Davidic codes?" my father's friend William remembers him asking one night that winter. William couldn't, but my father could. He seems to have been sharpening his rhetorical tools and gathering ammunition. He was preparing to enter the ring as a Brethren combatant. He knew he'd have to know his Scriptures inside and out if he was going to win rounds against the older Brethren.

J.T. Junior, sixty years old, was also preparing himself for a fight. He'd been waiting in the wings for thirty or forty years, biting his tongue, furious about the way his father's "new light" on the Holy Spirit had been ignored. Now that he'd assumed leadership he wasted no time in asserting his authority. He had some things to prove.

In the spring of 1960, only months after he'd taken leadership, J.T. Junior placed an absolute ban on membership of professional associations. "If you're not with me," he told the Brethren, "you're against me."

Hundreds of Brethren professionals around the world—chemists, lawyers, doctors, and architects—now "unyoked" and resigned from their professional associations. Many lost their jobs. The Brethren were now in the news. They'd be in the papers most months through-out the 1960s.

Although many Brethren were now leaving the fellowship in pro-test against the new hardline edicts, J.T. Junior remained defiant. The great winnowing had begun, he declared. It was, he said, a clear sign that the Rapture was close.

"You either had to commit yourself or get out," my father said years later when he was interviewed for a documentary about the Brethren. "It became a bit of a crusade. . . . Before, it had been a bit flabby and inconclusive. Now it was something that you could either accept or reject, something very clear-cut. People were suffering for it—giving up professional associations and losing their jobs, and giv-ing up jobs that involved entertaining clients, and so on. This is why I said there was a spirit of a crusade."

J.T. Junior spoke about the Brethren as his ranks; together, he promised, they would rout Satan on his own battleground. "We must keep in mind," he wrote, "that the Lord is a man of war." And by the time he flew to the U.K. from his home in New York in late July 1960, ready to drive his new hard-line militaristic separatism home, he was in full war mode. The timing was good: Cold War tensions were run-ning high. There were new charismatic leaders on the world stage too: Billy Graham was rallying millions to his evangelical crusades; JFK had just been nominated as a presidential candidate.

J.T. Junior had won the battle over professional associations. Now it was time to step up another gear and clean up all the Brethren households once and for all. Brethren had no business eating with non-Brethren, he declared. It was time to build some walls.

J.T. Junior gave an address on Park Street, London, in July 1960, called "The King and His Men," a speech designed to rally a new gen-eration in his crusade against Satan. My father was in the auditorium that day; his father, as a trustee of the Depot, was now sitting up on the platform.

In a series of notes I found in one of my father's files, he described

"The King and His Men" speech as the principal turning point in his own radicalization. I can see why. He was twenty-two and newly married, head of his household. He'd spent his life cowed by his father's absolute authority. He'd been following the Red Cross Knight through Spenser's *The Faerie Queene*. He was ready to become a leader and he wanted a place up on that platform for himself.

J.T. Junior took as his Scripture that day the story of King David capturing Jerusalem in 2 Samuel 5:6–10. The Lord wanted the Brethren to go to war, he told his audience, to become David's men, to take risks on the battlefield, to capture Jerusalem. Now was the time. But although he could see that the young men were ready to fight, he told them, the older Brethren in Britain were holding back, hesitating, because they were self-important, stuffy, and stuck in their ways. They didn't have the stomach to fight. They'd have to be barred from the house, he said, if they didn't commit. The young bloods—the Davids—would show them what was what. They shouldn't put up with these dithering old men anymore.

It was a clever move. J.T. Junior was marshaling the young against the patriarchs. It was the 1960s, and he was using the spirit of revolution that was already in the air to promote an extremely right-wing puritan crusade in which the young would take the lead.

For my father, imagining himself as a knight taking on the corrupt forces of Roman Catholicism, as a soldier in David's army defeating the Jebusites against all the odds, or as David himself taking on Goliath, that address, as he put it, "reset the agenda." It stirred his blood. He may have been sitting down in the auditorium with his Brethren friends while his father was up on the platform, but nothing was set in stone.

"Now," he wrote in his notes, "a sizable, and powerful, number of young Brethren began to rise up and make themselves heard. Driving the traditional Brethrenistic element in Britain onto the back foot, making them feel defensive, that was a very important part of the whole campaign. J.T. Junior persuaded us young Brethren that we'd inherited a radical tradition but the old people had turned it into a comfortable establishment. It was our job to stir them up to radicalism again."

"A great sifting is going on," J.T. Junior would repeat; sometimes he called it a "spewing." This must mean, he'd tell them again, that the Rapture was close. The Lord was moving quickly. "The Lord is cleansing his temple," he said. Time was running out. For the next eight years, every time things got difficult, J.T. Junior would tell the Brethren it was a sure sign that Satan was ramping up his assault and that, in turn, was a sure sign that the Rapture was getting ever closer.

3

When I read the transcript of J.T. Junior's "The King and His Men" speech, the rhythms of the language took me straight back into meeting, where as a very small child I listened to my father's and grandfather's voices as they rose and fell, cadences incanting and descanting. Satan was close, they'd preach; he was a trickster, always looking out for opportunities to use a wayward brother or sister to get himself inside our closed circle. The Brethren had all grown up thinking of themselves as besieged by Satan's forces, who were rallying outside the walls of the meeting room, so J.T. Junior's new rhetoric of attack rather than defense must have stirred their blood.

As a child I struggled to think of all those stocky men in their suits and hats going to war. It was even more difficult to imagine the sisters in their hats and headscarves whooshing up into the air when the Rapture came. I was always worried about how they'd keep their hats on and their skirts down.

But despite the apparent blandness of our suburban lives, according to those preachings and addresses, spectacular dramas and showdowns were always happening. J.T. Junior persuaded the Brethren that personal suffering and subjection to his absolute leadership were the only ways to fight back against Satan's growing power. The miniskirted sexual decadence of the 1960s and the sheer number of Satan's new converts out there were, he claimed, sure proof that the Rapture was fast approaching. The Lord was sending the Brethren more and more powerful signs in order to keep his precious people walking in the light when everyone else was disappearing into Satan's darkness.

My father was already primed for battle in 1960 by that heady collision of C. S. Lewis's lyricism, Edmund Spenser's Calvinism, and the Bower of Bliss–smashing Red Cross Knight's and J.T. Junior's calls to arms. When his closest Brethren friend began to consider leaving and then died suddenly, he persuaded himself it was a personal warning from the Lord.

A photograph of a group of my father's undergraduate Brethren friends taken around 1959–60. Christopher Tydeman is second from the left.

"A fortnight before his death," my shocked father wrote to his mother just after Christopher Tydeman's funeral in the summer of 1960, "Christopher was here [in Cambridge] for a weekend. He came at his own invitation. His last words to me were 'I'll see you in a fort-night's time if I'm still in fellowship.' He was upset and puzzled by recent happenings, and when he came here he was full of questions. We talked very late both Friday and Saturday evenings. I wasn't able to answer his objections, his mind was always more acute and ana-lytical than mine, but I think we both became impressed as the dis-cussion went on with the stress that is laid on action ('he that hears My words and does them'). I say we were both impressed because I don't want to give the impression that he was the questioner and I the answerer. That was not so. We helped each other on Saturday night, I think."

Christopher, still considering whether to leave, had gone to hear my father preach the following day. When my father drove him to the station, Christopher's goodbye was enigmatic: "Thank you very much for the weekend," he said. "I got my answer and it wasn't what I expected." My father wrote to his mother that he'd been searching for an explanation of those words ever since his friend's death.

Christopher wrote to my father a few days later. He'd come to a decision, he said, but he still did not reveal what it was. Then two weeks later, down in St. Ives, he slipped on a rock pool, hit his head, and died.

At the funeral, Christopher's Brethren father took his son's under-graduate friends aside and told them that he was certain the death was "not an accident." Did he mean that Christopher had killed him-self? Jumped? Or worse: Was Christopher's father telling those young men that his wavering son had been singled out by God, struck down, and made an example of?

Whatever it meant, my father changed. His letters were now full of crusading metaphors too. Gone was the pleasure-loving, hesitant young man of the Cambridge years and in his place there was a zealot, or at least the performance of one.

Later I found a tiny newspaper cutting among my father's papers entitled "Man Falls 100 Feet." The man was Christopher Tydeman.

He'd fallen from a cliff and died from his injuries, not slipped on a rock pool at all as my father had been told. Was this the beginning of a larger pattern of cover-ups, secrets, and lies around the rising number of Brethren suicides?

4

In the spring of 1960, while he was finishing his last year at Cambridge, my father went for an interview in Birmingham for a job with 3M, the Minnesota Mining and Manufacturing Company. The company had been manufacturing products such as masking tape and sandpaper in America since the beginning of the century, and now, in the early sixties, it was expanding into global markets with new products, including surgical tape and audiotape. Their success, they told my father over lunch after the interview, was rooted in treating their employees as one big family. They were looking for bright, talented ideas-people who could sell their products and help expand 3M's place in the U.K. market.

Six foot four, affable, well built, Cambridge-educated, and soberly dressed, my father must have looked and sounded impressive. He came, he told his interviewers, from a long line of traveling sales-people: His father had been a salesman for Dubarry's and Roger & Gallet, and he himself had worked in South Africa as the assistant sales manager for the brand-new sales team of Walls ice cream. The job would be perfect for him, he told my mother when they offered him the position, as 3M wouldn't require him to join a union or a professional association.

But by the time, six months later, that my father put on his suit and took himself off to the U.K. head office in Birmingham, J.T. Junior had proclaimed that Brethren should no longer eat with non-Brethren, because eating together was "an act of fellowship." The charter once again pointed to Paul's letters, 1 Corinthians 5:9–11 this time: "I have written to you in the epistle not to mix with fornicators," Paul wrote, "not altogether with the fornicators of the world, or with the avaricious and rapacious, or idolators; since then you should go out of the world. But now I have written to you, if any one called brother be fornicator, or avaricious, or idolater, or abusive, or a drunkard, or rapacious, not to mix with him; *with such a one not even to eat.*"

The Brethren fishermen who sailed in mixed crews up at Eyemouth, Port Seton, and Peterhead now had to find ways of eating separately from their crew members on tiny boats with a single cabin, or had to leave the crew. Understandably, they caused offense. Non-Brethren sailors began to refuse to sail with Brethren sailors.

When my father told his employers he could no longer eat or drink with his work colleagues or clients, they accused him of hypocrisy. He'd eaten with them during his job interview, they said. Why not now, only a few months later? He tried to explain that this was a new rule in his church; that he was simply following orders. He even tried to quote the passage from 1 Corinthians 5, but no one was interested.

It is difficult to convey the scale of the devastation that the "eating rule" caused, not just in the workplace but in Brethren homes around the world. If a Brethren husband was living with a non-Brethren wife, he could no longer eat at the same table with her. If a Brethren daughter had taken her elderly non-Brethren mother to live with her and her family, the mother would have to eat in a separate room. If a Brethren teenager did not want to join the Brethren, he or she would have to eat in another room. Brethren children had to come home from school or eat at a separate table in the school canteen to avoid being contaminated by non-Brethren children. My mother picked us all up from school at lunchtime and gave us a meal at home. When we drank the bottles of milk the school provided, the teachers had to usher us into a different part of the room from the other children. No one explained why. I suspect no one really knew how to.

Many ex-Brethren told me stories about how difficult it had been at work once the eating rule was imposed, how lonely and isolating it was. My father's closest friend during the sixties, William, agreed to meet me for lunch with his wife in a restaurant on the Essex marshes forty years after we'd last seen each other. I couldn't help feeling we were meeting out there, miles from anywhere, in an almost empty restaurant, because we needed to be sure we were not overheard. Outside the windows, the halyards of sailing boats clanged against their masts.

In 1960, William told me, when my twenty-two-year-old father was selling tape in Birmingham, William was working in a raincoat factory as a sales representative. He was also in his early twenties, also newly married. He was doing well at work, gaining trust, establishing his place in the team. But with the new eating prohibition, suddenly he could no longer socialize with his colleagues. He had to eat at a different table in the canteen and explain that this was a religious rule. He didn't dare break it in case someone saw and reported him.

His colleagues were offended and baffled, he told me. He became increasingly isolated. Every day he felt he was walking on knives, that he might be sacked at any moment. He dreaded lunch and coffee breaks and would search for excuses to get out of the office. It was impossible to concentrate on work. Soon, he said, he was lurching constantly between anxiety, insomnia, frustration, and rage. My father, working among the bright ambitious young men of 3M, must have felt the same.

William knew that what was going on was wrong, but neither he nor his wife had ever lived outside the Brethren; they could not imagine doing that. They were frightened. William had broken Brethren rules as a young child, just as I had, just as my father had. He'd hidden

Brethren-banned books like *Biggles* in the saddlebag of his bike under Brethren-approved books about bird-watching and astronomy. He'd even considered leaving altogether when he was in his twenties, but when he tried to talk to his mother about his doubts, she said sternly, "Something's wrong with you, William," and he started to wonder if perhaps she was right. In 1960, when he expressed his concerns about the eating issue in a letter to a family friend and told her he was thinking about leaving the fellowship altogether, the friend wrote back, "Are you really prepared to kill your mother?"

A cousin introduced me to an ex-Brethren woman she knew who lived near me in London. I asked her to dinner. "Ruth"—she doesn't want me to use her real name either—was seventy. She and her parents had lived through the J.T. Junior years. I asked her what had happened in her family as a result of the eating rules. She still found it difficult to talk about it, she said. Even fifty-five years later it was painful for her to remember.

She'd been the only child of a Brethren father and a non-Brethren mother. Before 1960 it hadn't been too much of a problem, she told me. She attended Sunday meetings with her father and uncle and aunts; her mother didn't. In 1960, when J.T. Junior began to enforce the new separation rules, her uncle, struggling to keep his job and comply with the new Brethren rules about professional associations, committed suicide. Ruth was fourteen. Only weeks after her uncle's death, the local Brethren told her father that if her mother didn't join the fellowship he'd either have to leave her or leave the Brethren.

Late one evening, two of the local Brethren priests came to the family's North London home. Ruth watched the whole episode from the top of the stairs. Their home was unclean, the priests said; it would contaminate the local assembly. Was Ruth's mother now ready to join the Brethren? When her mother told them she wasn't going to join, they turned to her father: Was he now going to leave his wife?

When he said no, that he wasn't going to leave her, they told him he'd have to leave the Brethren. The two priests then left.

Ruth went to bed as she was told, but the house had "an atmosphere of unbearable tension." She was woken up sometime later by frightening sounds from downstairs. She ran down the stairs just in time to rescue her mother from being strangled to death by her father. He had her on the floor with his hands around her neck. Ruth had to use all her force to pull him off.

"When he turned toward me," she said, "it was with an unrecognizing, wild look in his eyes unlike anything I'd seen before."

The next morning a doctor referred her father for psychiatric treatment. Soon after, with her mother still refusing to join the Brethren, the three of them left the fellowship altogether, leaving behind all her father's family, who would not be able to speak to them again. Her parents stayed together, Ruth said, but their marriage never really recovered.

Everywhere this new hard-line separatism was making life difficult for Brethren—sometimes unbearably so—but as my father would tell the BBC interviewer sixteen years later, there was also something exhilarating about that collective suffering. J.T. Junior kept on telling them that suffering was "the thing." Consider Christ's suffering on the cross, he'd roar at them, and you think you have it bad?

I found a picture of my father in the years he worked for 3M. He looks handsome, dressed in a well-cut suit, with several pens lined up in his top pocket. He is standing alone in some kind of conservatory, looking not down over the great view below but up, as if he is waiting for inspiration, about to preach. He looks lonely, lost in his thoughts. A single hook hangs ominously from the wooden window frame above him. It seems to be hanging there in the void of his future, as if he were snagged on it, or a puppet to it. I wondered if my mother had taken the picture. Had she seen the hook too?

My father, photographed around 1960

The choice of jobs for young Brethren men like my father narrowed dramatically in the early sixties. Almost every line of professional work was now out of reach for most of them: bankers, architects, pharmacists, teachers, engineers—they all had professional associations. Most employers would not take on an employee who refused to eat with his colleagues or clients or join a union. Married Brethren women were now not allowed to work at all.

Next, J.T. Junior banned university attendance. Being a member of a university, he declared, was like being a member of a union. Education corrupted: it nurtured the natural mind rather than the spiritual mind and it took young people away from the home and the watchful eye of their parents and other Brethren. All Brethren young men and women who were enrolled in degree programs now had to leave their universities or leave the Brethren. My father had just slipped through.

J.T. Junior's extreme rules of separation in the early sixties forced thousands of young men either to join Brethren businesses or to start up their own. They must have been relieved to leave non-Brethren jobs after all the social isolation and anxiety that the eating rule caused. This generation of young Brethren men were enterprising and resourceful. A group of cousins in Sussex set up a company that imported wood to make matchboxes decorated with Sussex scenes. Others sold fudge or honey or hardwood flooring or handcrafted kitchens. Older Brethren were expected to provide loans for these new businesses and to keep them afloat if they ran into trouble. Most flourished.

J.T. Junior, guided and advised by his son-in-law, Bruce Hales, and Bruce's brother John, now set about creating a global infrastructure for wealth creation and accumulation, all under the direct management of Brethren leaders. Later they'd work out ever-inventive ways to avoid paying taxes, including using gift aid, trusts, and campaigning for charitable status. Soon the Brethren would be very rich indeed.

5

"A ruthless gestapo had been set up to enforce Big Jim's new rules," my father told me.

"Gestapo?" I said. "Isn't that a bit extreme? Nothing in the Brethren story compares to the scale of what the Nazis did."

He was reading *The Rise and Fall of the Third Reich* again—I'd seen his copy open on his study desk.

"It's not the *scale* of what happened," he insisted, "it's the pattern. There's always a charismatic leader and a group of people who are cut off from the world. They're slowly brainwashed into thinking they're the chosen ones; that they're surrounded by evil and that if they want to save themselves they have to do exactly what they're told. It's the same pattern every time."

Later, once I started reading books on the social psychology of cults, I could see he was right. "Totalist systems," as experts called them—and that could mean the whole Maoist regime or a cult like the Exclusive Brethren—did have common patterns. They all depended, for instance, on a network of enforcers and interrogators to operate effectively.

He and other young Brethren men, my father said, had hauled themselves up onto their hind legs to turn themselves into the two-legged thug pigs of George Orwell's *Animal Farm*.

But what did that *mean*? What had he and William—and other men like them—actually done in the sixties that was so bad?

My father had not been able to face writing that part of his life story. He died trying to face it. So I wrote to William to ask, as carefully as I could, if he had interrogated other Brethren or if he remembered anything my father had told him about all of that.

It was just too painful to remember, William replied a few days later. Too shameful. It made him shudder. But he would try.

"Unlike your father," he wrote, "I was only involved with three cases. They were all men. It was normal for two Brethren to conduct the questioning. Usually it took place in the sitting room, but with the understanding that we were not to be disturbed."

I thought of fourteen-year-old Ruth watching from the top of the stairs as the black-coated priests interrogated her parents. It was easy to feel for her. Now—for the first time—I was beginning to imagine what it might have been like to be one of those priests, knocking on doors late at night, embarrassed and ashamed but not able to show it, making older men confess to having had sexual thoughts, humiliating them.

"If a confession was finally made," William wrote, "it was something quite innocuous or trivial, usually about [unfulfilled] sexual desires, at least in all the cases I was involved in. The sessions could last for two to three hours; sometimes they'd go on till quite late at night. I used to go home feeling that I was probably more guilty than the person we had humiliated."

Although there may have been many Brethren priests in the sixties who were confident that they were routing Satan, there were also men like William who felt very uncomfortable with what they were doing. I'd seen this discomfort in the body language of three Brethren priests interviewed on a documentary the BBC made in 2003; the Brethren were doing everything they could at the time to counteract bad publicity. Those three men, dressed in perfectly pressed white or pale-blue, short-sleeved cotton shirts, sat on one side of a table clutching their Bibles and answering the interviewer's questions.

They looked like rabbits caught in headlights, I thought as I watched the interview, paused it, and played it back in slow motion. Each time I replayed the scene and saw how nervous they were, the sight of them there behind the table scared me a little less. The youngest of the three, in his late thirties, seated in the middle, talked, with an attempted assurance, about how he'd been lost to the darkness but had returned to the light. But every time he tried to defend Brethren expulsions or the way they shut people up, he stuttered, hesitated, and stuttered again. His eyes darted from side to side looking for guidance from the two older men.

When the producer of the documentary gave an interview to *The Guardian,* he said the priests had threatened him: "We're rich," they said. "We'll take you to the cleaners." One of them had told him, "The devil's here. I can see him behind you."

But what had it been like for my father? I wondered. How had he felt about making these visits that William described? I wrote to the PEEB community. What was it like, I asked, to be visited by Brethren interrogators back in the sixties? Did anyone remember? And did anyone remember what it was like to be a priest?

Ten or eleven people replied to my request for information. Some wrote just a few lines, some several pages. Everyone seemed angry or upset by what they remembered. Many of them, I noticed, replied in the early hours of the morning. "You've opened up a real can of worms here," one wrote. The memories, she said, had made her shake.

The answers I received were all about having been interrogated. No one wrote about doing the interrogating. Their stories were shocking and remarkably similar. The men were called priests, not interrogators or exactors, they said. Their visits were called priestly visits, or just—rather chillingly—priestlies or PVs. The interrogation might last two hours or more; it always took place in the family sitting room; no one ate or drank anything—the priests would be contaminated if they did—and no one else was allowed in the room, even when the priests were questioning a teenage girl.

Sometimes the priests would be satisfied with a simple confession and there'd be prayers and tears and "restoration." But if there was resistance or denial, or if the sin was particularly grave, the priests would have to recommend to the "care meeting" that the sinner be "shut up" or placed "under discipline." This meant consigning them to solitary confinement in a room in their family home with no contact with any other family member, their meals left on a tray outside the bedroom door, for an unspecified period of time. The priests would continue to "visit" every few days, sometimes for weeks or months, until they felt the sinner had "come right" or was "in the clear." The priests didn't use the language of exorcism, my informants told me when I pressed them on this, but to me it seemed implicit in what they were doing. "Smell out the enemy," J.T. Junior had preached. "Chase after him and kick him."

Most of the people who replied to my questions had been teenagers in the sixties. The misdemeanors they'd been questioned about ranged from acts that the Brethren considered very serious—such as falling in love with someone outside the Brethren, or being seen going into a cinema, smoking, or even having a cup of tea with someone who wasn't Brethren—to imagined acts or thoughts. Licentious thoughts all had to be confessed to as well.

No wonder William had shuddered. No wonder he described priestly visits as a process of humiliation. And, as he had pointed out, if my father had done more priestly visits than most of these young men, it wasn't surprising that he wasn't able to talk or write about it.

It struck me that a system of surveillance and forced confession like this must have been very effective. Even when the sinner was absolved and allowed back into the fold, all the priests would now know their secrets and have seen them deeply humiliated. And, of course, every priest would have been terrified that at any moment the tables might be turned on him. Everyone was petrified into compliance.

Sometimes when a Brethren teenager was put under discipline, the whole family would be engulfed in the punishment. "Rachel" described how, when she and her two brothers were teenagers in the 1960s, they'd been "shut up" numerous times, meaning they were confined to the house and prohibited from contact with anyone. On one occasion, she and her brothers had been made to leave the family home for a month, but usually the whole family was excluded at home together. When her youngest brother, then sixteen, went to see three Brethren priests to seek counsel about something private that worried him, they circulated details about what he disclosed. He was taunted by his Brethren peers and suffered a nervous breakdown. Soon afterward, the three siblings were made to attend a Brethren meeting in which their father was told "he was not repentant enough" and they were all made to leave and be "shut up" again.

"Our priestly visits took place mainly in the evening," she wrote, "sometimes just with my dad, my parents, or all of us together, sometimes in the lounge, sometimes around the dining room table." No one drank anything because the priests weren't allowed to eat or drink with Brethren under discipline. "At one stage," she wrote, "my dad was required to write a list of all the sins he had committed. When he handed them the list, he was told it 'wasn't good enough' and he had to try harder to remember things he may have done!"

Even if people found some way to leave the Brethren, the priests could still knock on their door at any time. Several of the people who wrote to me described finding a pair of priests waiting outside their workplace, intent on getting them to come back into fellowship.

"They used to wait until my staff had gone home and show up at the business," "Philip" wrote. "Luckily I had a front vestibule in which visitors had to ring and wait for the door to be unlocked. I would just freeze in my office chair and not move or make a noise. I would hear a low rumbling of voices until they left."

The priests were, like my father, family men, raising their children, minding their grandchildren, cutting the lawn or washing the car on Saturdays. My father would come home late at night, and lie in bed next to my mother with his head full of the remembered tears and sobs and wails from the evening's confession. Worse still, he may have lain there planning new ways to exact the confession he'd failed to get. And when the last years of the sixties rolled around, I'd have been sleeping in the next room or lying awake clutching my stuffed rabbit. In the morning he'd be planning his next preaching over breakfast, while my brothers and I quarreled about which of us was to have the cream at the top of the milk bottle. He'd be searching for a Scripture to support a new disciplinary procedure while my mother cleared away the dishes or brushed out and plaited my long and unruly hair.

No wonder he lost his temper so often, and no wonder my mother had to hurry us into the sitting room so many times and lock the door. There must have been so many things he couldn't talk about. Was this why he'd beaten me so badly at the age of three? And it wasn't just my family living in a state of anxiety and terror, nor was it just my father enforcing the rules. Priestly visits and care meetings were going on not just in our little seaside town but in Brethren households all around the world. As far as I know, they are *still* going on.

There were more suicides. On Hayling Island in 1961 a couple told their twenty-year-old son, a traveling car salesman who wasn't in fellowship, that he could no longer eat with them or his sister or even come to the house. After spending several months in exile, distraught about the shame and distress he was inflicting on his parents and the prospect of never seeing them again, he gassed himself to death.

Elsie and Winnie Rhodes, two elderly unmarried Brethren sisters, ran a small egg farm on Watling Street in Staffordshire. In 1961, local Brethren told the sisters that under the new rules they'd have to leave the egg marketing board or be withdrawn from. The small red stamp of the marketing board was, Brethren told them, the sign of Satan's system. Deprived of their livelihood, the sisters quickly fell into debt. A cousin, concerned that she had not heard from them for some time, drove to the farm, but Elsie and Winnie didn't open the door. "We were shocked by what we found," she told a journalist. The farm, once a prosperous family business, had been horribly neglected. "The hen pens hadn't been cleaned out and the gates were hanging on their hinges." A few months later, in June 1962, forced to sell their small holding and terrified of the consequences, Elsie and Winnie walked together into a local lake and drowned themselves.

6

At around the same time as the Rhodes sisters' deaths, Stanley Milgram, a distinguished psychologist at Yale, began a famous series of experiments about obedience. He'd read the reports of Adolf Eichmann's trial in Jerusalem the year before. Could it be, he asked himself, that Eichmann and his million accomplices in the Holocaust were just following orders? Were Germans more than usually obedient toward authority figures? How far would a study group of Americans go in obeying an instruction if it involved harming someone else?

Milgram took forty volunteers into closed laboratory rooms. Each was told by men in white coats to inflict electric shocks on a paired "learner" in another room every time that learner made a mistake. What the volunteers didn't know was that the "learner" was being played by an actor.

Even Milgram was shaken by the results. Sixty-five percent of participants continued obeying orders, believing that they were inflicting shocks to the very highest level—450 volts—even when they heard screams of pain and even when they knew they could kill the learner with voltages of that level. Every one of the participants continued to 300 volts. The experiment has since been replicated by other teams and the results stay roughly the same.

People obey, Milgram concluded, not just because they recognize the authority of the instructor as morally right or legally based (the white coats and the laboratory conditions of his experiment), but because that authority relieves them of responsibility for what they do. We learn this kind of unthinking obedience, he pointed out, in the family, the school, and the workplace. He did not add churches to this list, though he should have.

Why had those decent young Brethren men turned into bullies? Because closed, rule-bound, discipline-focused totalist systems like the one we lived through made dissent virtually impossible. It paralyzed people. Even if men like my father knew that what they were doing was wrong, they didn't know how to oppose it. Even if they refused to comply, they couldn't stop the bullying, because they'd simply be expelled and someone else would step forward to take their place.

7

I knew there was money being made from J.T. Junior's system, but it took me some time to realize just how much or how the system actually worked. When J.T. Junior and Bruce Hales put the vast Brethren revenue-collecting system in place in the sixties, they began by setting up tax-free payments described as gifts; they channeled these through the Depot, the Brethren publishing house.

When I was growing up, my family was always talking about the Depot. Grandpa was at the Depot again. Something or other was a Depot matter. Someone had telephoned from the Depot. I knew that the Depot had something to do with the ministries, the rows of color-coded Brethren books that lined the shelves in our sitting room. I was taken to its offices once as a small child. I remember a small brick building, windowless corridors, piles of boxes, and an untidy room with desks and typewriters. It reminded me of the Stott and Sons warehouse, with its secret rooms and back staircases. I wanted to be allowed to play there, but Grandpa Stott would never have allowed that. He left me in a small side office with a Bible while he attended Depot business in another room.

Since 1931, the Stow Hill Bible and Tract Depot published volumes of Brethren ministries, the Day Dawn calendar, Darby's Bible, and various Brethren magazines, first from a shop in Wales and then from premises in Kingston upon Thames. Until the 1950s it was a bit of a wing-and-a-prayer operation, run by four part-time trustees, with various Brethren and non-Brethren employees and a Brethren manager who liked to do the editing, and some censorship, himself.

The manager's idiosyncrasies had become a thorn in the side of J.T., especially when he'd been trying to press the new Holy Spirit line in the 1950s. The manager kept editing those sections out of his printed ministries. J.T. resolved to be patient, but the cuts infuriated his son. In the last years of his father's life, J.T. Junior spent hours counting the number of cuts the Depot manager had made to his father's addresses. He couldn't understand why his father put up with this insubordination.

Immediately after J.T.'s death in 1954, my grandfather was appointed to one of the four prestigious Depot trustee positions. Within weeks, the Depot manager was sacked, no doubt by my grandfather acting under J.T. Junior's orders.

Soon after his appointment, my grandfather began to assemble an anthology of the new harder-line ideology designed for Brethren boys. He called it *The Way Everlasting*. It was first published in 1958, when my father was nineteen. My grandfather must have had his sons in mind when he planned it. It contained extracts from thirty-four Brethren senior ministering brothers, from Darby to J.T., including three by him, one by my great-grandfather Hugh Wasson, and five by Gerald Cowell. The book warned of the dangers of worldly literature, advanced education, trade unions, and all other Christians. It was an immediate success, selling eighteen thousand copies within a year of its first publication in 1958, almost twice as many as the volumes of J.T.'s ministry the Depot sold over the same period. Like Mao's *Little Red Book,* published six years later by the People's Liberation Army, the anthology was small enough to be carried in a pocket. My father's friend William, in his late teens when it came out, remembers hearing it lampooned by another Brethren boy as *Bob Stott's Bumper Book for Brethren Boys.*

If my grandfather had seen what was coming, he'd have kept his pen dry and his head down. A year after the book came out was when J.T. Junior took the leadership position. He excommunicated Gerald Cowell and all his supporters a few months later. When the Depot's four trustees met in the summer of 1960, J.T. Junior decreed that all of Cowell's writing was to be excised from Brethren printed ministries. From now on, the Depot would print approved ministries only; there'd be no more magazines, Day Dawn calendars, or books for young people. There were to be no more reprints of *The Way Everlasting.* In front of two thousand Brethren assembled in Central Hall that summer, my grandfather was forced to confess that his book was based on a "revival of the Sunday School principle" and had been judged as wrong. This was the first of what would become a wave of public confessions.

Excommunicated husbands and wives, fathers and mothers were now bringing court cases against the Brethren and writing to members of Parliament. The Methodist leaders realized that the Exclusive Brethren, the people who rented their Central Hall every summer, were a cult that split families, and canceled their contract with them. More suicides reached the press. The story of the Methodists throwing out the Brethren made it into the newspapers too.

A three-day meeting in 1962 took place in one of the conference halls of Alexandra Palace in London. The proceedings were taped, transcribed, and published. Kez found a copy I'd overlooked among my father's papers. When I opened the transcript, the cadences of the men's voices and the phrases they used struck me as so familiar that I began to sweat. *I'm a girl. I'm not allowed in here. I'll get caught.* I remembered all the times I was ushered out of our sitting room when the Brethren men came to consult with my father. My mother caught me once with my ear pressed up against the closed door and waved me out into the garden. I wasn't going to miss the chance of listening in this time. I read on.

According to the transcript, hundreds of Brethren men gathered in Alexandra Palace as usual. They'd flown in from all over the world—Sweden, New Zealand, South Africa, France, Germany, even Jamaica. I tried to reconstruct the auditorium in my mind. I knew their hats would be hanging on hooks somewhere. They'd have their Bibles on their laps. My father would be in the auditorium and my grandfather up on the stage, sitting with the three other Depot trustees right next to the Man of God and J.T. Junior's clever businessman son-in-law, Bruce Hales, his new right-hand man. It was only a year since my grandfather's public confession. He'd be trying to keep a low profile.

Alfred Gardiner, the longest-serving Depot trustee, took the microphone. They were making good progress in reprinting the hymnbooks, ministries, and translations, he told the men in the hall, but the work was slow. Mr. Hales had devised a new system that would make it possible to bring the truth to Brethren all around the world much more quickly. Gardiner explained how it was going to work: There would be a new hardbound and numbered set of full ministries. From now on every Brethren house would be required to own a full set. It would cost £10 a year for the new volumes and £60 for a complete set. Local enforcement officers would check that all households had them. Brethren were to start paying immediately.

Bruce Hales took the microphone. Reasonable, eloquent, matter-of-fact, he explained that they'd been running a successful prepayment system in Australia for a while now. It made everything so much *easier*. If every household had a full set of ministries, all Brethren, especially the young, would receive the word of the Lord as it unfolded, as it *happened*.

I do the calculations. With an estimated hundred thousand Brethren around the world in 1959, even allowing for twenty thousand defections, there must have been at least ten thousand households remaining. The vast majority of those households were in English-speaking countries—the United States, Australia, New Zealand—but even if you allow for the fact that some were non-English-speaking, that's still at least £600,000 coming into Brethren coffers immediately, with £100,000 a year to follow.

In 1962, £1 was equivalent to roughly £20 at today's values. That means that in this one-hour meeting, the Brethren agreed to pay about £12 million pounds up front with almost £2 million in annual income to follow. One of the young Brethren administrators who worked in the Depot general office during the 1960s told me about the impact of Hales's prepayment system. He doesn't want me to use his name either, so I'll call him Frank. "The effect on the finances of the Depot was dramatic," Frank wrote. "I remember going to the bank with large amounts, many tens of thousands of pounds on one occasion" (about £80K).

When I asked my father in those last days about how the Brethren money system worked, he was defensive. He was close to the end. His lucid moments lasted only twenty minutes at most. I should have been distracting him with music and poetry, I told myself, not pestering him with questions about Brethren finances, but he was so insistent about this record of his, so anxious to get it down. There were so many questions I still wanted to ask.

"By 1962," I said, going back over my notes, "the ministries seem to have become more important than the Scriptures. How did they get everyone to agree to pay so much for them?"

"We didn't see it like that," he said slowly, without even opening his eyes. "We were getting the truth straight from the Lord. We didn't mind about the money. The Lord was working fast. He was on His way."

"The Rapture was coming, you mean?" I said. "You really thought it was *that* close?"

But he was gone again, down into the morphine.

8

It became difficult to sleep at the mill in my father's last days. With death so close, we were all wired. I took snatches of sleep in the afternoon, fell asleep in front of a Bergman film or when the cricket match lagged. I'd judder awake, frightened, certain there was something in the room, something watching. I couldn't shake off the feeling that my father and I were in trouble, that someone had been listening in, someone had reported back.

At night when the old mill creaked, I'd look out across the darkened fields, where the moonlight lit up the snow, to the glow on the horizon, where the Polish night laborers were digging up potatoes under portable strip lighting. Once a pair of red eyes—fox, rabbit, weasel—flashed back at me and then were gone.

On those sleepless nights, if my brother was taking the late watch

I'd roam my father's study, looking for photographs. The tall book-shelves were piled three or four deep with dusty books; the cheap shelving sagged alarmingly under their weight. After I'd spent a few hours in there rummaging, my hands would be coated in a layer of gray dust.

One night I found three rows of color-coded Brethren ministries hidden on a low shelf beneath a set of Toni Morrison's novels, some volumes of poetry, and a hardback copy of Richard Dawkins's *The God Delusion*, its spine broken by the number of index card notes my father had tucked inside. It struck me that in this chaos of books and papers, the ministries were the only books my father had ar-ranged in any order. He had not been able to throw them away, or even box them up and store them in the attic; he just buried them under other books. He had used these volumes, I remembered, to plan his preachings back in the sixties, in the days when he had worked hard to practice his J.T. Junior voice.

I spotted an old volume of J.T. Junior's letters on that bottom shelf, letters the Man of God had written through the sixties to Brethren around the world. I remembered the New York vernacular J.T. Junior used, his deliberately provocative and brash tone, and my father's look of intense concentration, the way he always seemed to speed up when J.T. Junior's recorded voice was playing on a tape in the car. J.T. Junior's private letter-writing voice sounded just as aggressive as his spoken one. At two in the morning he seemed to be shouting in my father's darkened study just as loudly as his recorded voice had once boomed out in the car. It still made me flinch.

In the letters J.T. Junior wrote in 1962, he was furious that British Brethren were being so slow to get their houses clean. How could Brethren still be living in the same house with aged aunts who were not in fellowship, he ranted, or teenagers who wouldn't break bread? It was insufferable. The local compliance officers he'd appointed were not being nearly tough enough.

In July 1963 he was preaching in Bournemouth, hammering

home his new edicts about "natural relations"—Brethren, he insisted, needed to cauterize their family feelings. He ranted about "circumcision." He wanted Brethren to cut off their family members as if they were bits of surplus, unclean flesh. It was time to put the Lord before family relations, he wrote, time to get those houses really *clean*. But what he really seemed to be saying was that he wanted all those thousands of Brethren to put him before everyone else.

"Have you cut off the flesh?" he asked them. "Have you still the flesh in the house? Have you cut off your relatives if they are out of fellowship? That is the suffering point."

Reading J.T. Junior's letters in the mill in the early hours of the morning, I was hearing not just his American intonations but the voices of all those other ranting men too: my father, my grandfather, thumping the table, their voices rising and falling in a confused cacophony, competing to trump each other with biblical references. The women, on the other hand, those women who always sat quietly next to me in the back row of the meeting, their soft hands folded over their Bibles, were *still* not saying anything.

By 1964, the year I was born, J.T. Junior had implemented scores of new rules about homes and family life. Brethren could no longer live in the same house as non-Brethren members. Husbands had to leave non-Brethren wives. Wives had to leave non-Brethren husbands. Small assemblies were to be merged with larger ones to form "city positions" with a designated leader. Brethren could no longer work with anyone who had been "put out of fellowship." They could not live in flats unless they had a separate entrance. No televisions or radios were allowed in Brethren houses. All young children were now expected, "encouraged," to break bread.

All around the world Brethren compliance officers held care meetings to identify and take action against the unclean households in their assemblies. Frank sent me a transcript of notes he'd taken of disciplinary decisions made in six hundred separate meetings he attended in the sixties. The notes were concise, but the stories they revealed were chilling.

Under the heading "North Finchley, 1962" one note read:

> Miss Parks in a house nearly fully divided.
>
> Miss Paynter has broken communion with her sister.
>
> Mrs. Rook and daughter are still in the same house. All three cases are a great concern. Dr. Rook is nearly an invalid. He has the wireless. There is no work of God in him.

What this meant, I realized, was that poor Miss Parks had been "shut up" and was now receiving "priestly visits." She would not be allowed to return to meeting until the priests had confirmed that she had "fully divided" from the non-Brethren family members she shared a house with—almost certainly one or both of her elderly parents. Even then the priests would not be happy until they moved her out of that unclean house completely.

Miss Paynter was doing better than Miss Parks. She was no longer in contact with her non-Brethren sister but was still under close surveillance and "under discipline." She wasn't out of the woods yet.

Mrs. Rook and her daughter, Miss Rook, were still living with the invalid and radio-listening Dr. Rook. It wasn't looking good. The two women would almost certainly have to be withdrawn from unless they left that unclean house once and for all.

So many elderly women caretakers were being bullied into absolute compliance. And this was just the picture I could see from the notes from a single London care meeting. How many more thousands were there under discipline all around Britain and the world? What was to become of these poor women, tormented as they were by the fear of having to live alone, and unprotected, in Satan's system?

According to another of Frank's notes, on February 2, 1963—eleven days before my older brother was born—Miss Paynter was in trouble again. Her name comes up under the title "Cases of Concern, re: Unclean Accommodation and Other—North Finchley":

> Miss Paynter. She has come to the preachings only. She knows very little and needs teaching. The resistance has gone. She has sat behind separately all the time. She wears the token. The matter has gone on for many months. She loves the Brethren in a small way. There is a piece of an ear.

That "piece of an ear" is a reference to Amos 3:12. "Like as the shepherd rescueth out of the jaw of the lion two legs, or a piece of an ear; so shall the children of Israel be rescued that sit in Samaria in the corner of a couch, and upon the damask of a bed."

It's very difficult to grasp exactly what verses like Amos 3:12 actually mean, but the senior Brethren ministering brothers always insisted they knew. In this case, "a piece of an ear" was code for "we haven't given up; we'll get her clean yet."

"The resistance has gone" was the sentence that haunted me most of all. It reminded me of the fate of my mournful great-grandmother, the willful Ada Louise, and those blank eyes of hers.

9

My brother was born on February 13, 1963. My father delivered him and cut his umbilical cord. My parents named him Christopher after Christopher Tydeman.

When, in his dying days, I interviewed my father about life in the Brethren, he showed no interest in describing how it had felt to become a father. He struggled against the morphine to record the tiniest details of the new edicts that were coming in during the sixties, but he seemed entirely indifferent to what had been going on with his wife and children at home.

"February 1963? Wasn't that the month that Chris was born?" I asked.

"Yes, yes, it was, yes," he replied, "but the point is that you can't understand the eating issue unless you understand the direction J.T. Junior's ministry was taking in February 1963."

How had my brothers and I learned to walk, talk, run, and read in this strained, highly scrutinized, and discipline-obsessed world?

I was born twenty months after my brother, on September 24, 1964. After four years of J.T. Junior's fierce edicts, Brethren were now almost completely isolated from the world and knew little about what was going on in it. J.T. Junior, convinced that the Rapture was now only weeks or months away, was obsessed with getting Brethren houses clean in time. In February 1964, he prohibited meals in restaurants, cafés, canteens, and trains. The following month, he banned non-Brethren cleaners or mother's helpers. Brethren were no longer allowed to sit on juries. Meetings were now expected to be held every day. As part of his campaign for clean houses, he banned all pets. Brethren had to either find alternative homes for their animals or have them put down. Thousands of parents now had to find ways of explaining to their distressed children where their beloved pets had disappeared to.

In June 1964, J.T. Junior decreed that Brethren should be employing fellow Brethren whenever possible. This would reduce their contact with the outside world even further. My father, who was working as a sales rep for Chivers jams in Cambridge, gave up his job to become a partner in Stott and Sons, my grandfather's wholesale grocer's in Brighton. My parents moved from Cambridge into my grandparents' house. The move must have put pressure on my already exhausted mother. As a young Brethren wife and mother, she'd also have to attend meeting every day with her two young children, help my grandmother to keep the peace at home, and feed the many Brethren visitors who came from all over the world.

My father and grandfather would have had a good deal to discuss, because in 1964 the Brethren came under attack. Gresham Cooke, the Conservative MP for Twickenham, appalled by the stories his ex-Brethren constituents were telling him about broken families, suicides, and excommunications, put a bill to Parliament called the Family Preservation Bill. He wanted to make it illegal for family members to be separated in this way and told newspaper reporters that he also wanted to ban the leader of this destructive cult from entering the country.

When J.T. Junior arrived at meeting rooms on his usual summer tour of the U.K. in 1965, he was jeered by large crowds of protesters and cross-questioned by journalists camped outside. At Dorking, he was jostled and forced to stop preaching because he couldn't make himself heard above the chants of the protesters. He canceled an arranged meeting with Gresham Cooke and flew back to New York, furious and shocked by what he described as press harassment. When *The Sunday Times* ran an article called "Big Jim and His Profits," he threatened the paper with a libel suit. In September there were rumors that he'd been admitted to a hospital.

With J.T. Junior in and out of the hospital and being hounded by the press, Bruce Hales and his brother John took the reins; a new business-obsessed era began. Bruce was in his midthirties, an engineer and charismatic management consultant. The brothers stepped up the pace of the money-production machine by organizing invitation-only business seminars to groom young Brethren men like my father to train others, to set in place methods and procedures for tax avoidance, gift aid, and trust funds. Just like J.T. Junior, the Haleses were often rude and sarcastic to the older members of the Brethren. They quickly garnered a large following from young Brethren like my father as a result. Meanwhile they told

Brethren that J.T. Junior was very ill, worn-out, and "suffering for the testimony."

In J.T. Junior's absence, the Hales brothers consolidated Brethren assets, amalgamated small assemblies into larger ones, and ordered a program of building new meeting rooms to their own designs. These windowless buildings looked more like bunkers or bank vaults than places of religious worship. The brothers ordered Brethren who owned rental properties to liquidate these assets to provide money for the new meeting rooms or to provide mortgages to young couples like my parents looking to buy their first home. An elderly Brethren woman helped my parents buy a four-bedroom detached house near the Hove meeting room, overlooking Hove Park. The more that young Brethren families like ours became financially dependent on other Brethren, of course, the less likely it was that they'd be able to leave.

My father became one of the Hales brothers' young acolytes. He enjoyed the status and attention. He'd been helped to buy a house. Now that he was working alongside his father in the family business, the Hales brothers were treating him, not his father, as the special one. All Brethren businesses were placed under close supervision. He and his father had to fill in forms detailing profits, budgets, targets, and time sheets. He and other young businessmen would be "whisked off," he wrote on PEEB, to business seminars in a private house in London, conducted by the Hales brothers "wearing collar mics. . . . Then in the evening, we would sweep into Park Street to a meeting that Bruce Hales was taking and feel like we had inside knowledge because we had been with him all day. We were a sort of embryonic mafia."

No wonder he didn't remember much about what was going on at home. He couldn't have been there much at all. And there must have been tensions with his father about the direction the business was taking. My grandfather must have hated being overlooked and over-ruled, but he would have had to hold his tongue.

There were mutterings against the Hales brothers throughout the winter. Two men who worked at the Depot were interviewed, sacked, and withdrawn from for criticizing them. A group of ministering brothers taped one of the business seminars and took it to J.T. Junior, complaining that the new "commercial system" the brothers were promoting was against Scripture.

Then something extraordinary happened: News reached the Brethren networks in October 1965 that J.T. Junior had *withdrawn from* the Hales brothers for "bringing commerce into the assembly." This event must have struck terror into Brethren around the world. If, like my father, they were acolytes, even lowly ones, they must have expected trouble. But they also knew that if they denounced the brothers it might be even worse for them. Brethren fathers and sons, like my grandfather and father, would have been set against each other again.

A spell of expulsions of the Haleses' supporters began, followed by another wave of confessions. These group confessions had been taking place for several years. Frank described seeing people queuing up to get hold of a microphone to confess in the Islington city meeting on the night of October 1, 1964—just seven days after I was born. It was a "frenzy," he wrote. They were still queuing at eleven P.M. Now the group confessions largely concerned the Hales brothers. Rumors circulated that Bruce and his wife, Consuela, J.T. Junior's daughter, had retired to a farm in the Australian outback and that Consuela had had a nervous breakdown. The old guard were back in power. The terrified youngbloods steeled themselves for punishment or expulsion.

Single elderly women continued to bear the brunt of the power lurchings and disciplinary decisions. John and Bruce Hales had two unmarried aunts named Rhina and Eva. They'd lived together for fourteen years in a house in a suburb of Melbourne. Eva disagreed with Exclusive Brethren separation rules and so, despite her devotion to her sister, she joined the Open Brethren. When Eva went into the hospital for an operation, local Exclusive Brethren took Rhina to live with them. When Eva was discharged a few months later, Rhina was not allowed to go home to her sister or have any contact. A few days after Eva returned to her empty house, in November 1965, only a month after Bruce and John had been deposed, relatives broke into the house and found her body on the kitchen floor. She'd gassed herself to death.

Why did the Hales brothers fall from power so spectacularly? No one I've spoken to knows for sure. There's no evidence to prove one theory or another, and whichever way you look at it there was very little "of God" in this struggle for power. And that's what my Christian ex-Brethren relatives always say when the Taylor decade comes up in conversation. "Man is corrupt," they say sadly. "This was man's doing."

By the summer of 1966, J.T. Junior had restored the Hales brothers. Was he satisfied that he'd made his point, clipped their wings, or was this all part of a plot he'd devised with them? Perhaps it was a way of showing the Brethren, particularly the Haleses' acolytes, that no one was safe, that even J.T. Junior's right-hand men were dispensable. Whatever the explanation, he had secured the terrified allegiance of all the Brethren young men who once followed the Haleses. Now he began a campaign to denounce anyone who had spoken against the brothers. A new wave of public confessions followed. Across the world Brethren were forced to admit they had been guilty of vindictiveness toward the brothers during the period of their expulsion.

10

I was, I am told, the baby who cried; the baby who refused to sleep. My mother followed the instructions given to young mothers in the 1960s, which was to leave a baby to cry itself to sleep. Sometimes, she said with admiration, I took more than an hour to "go off," and she interpreted from this, as most mothers certainly did then, that if I was to stand a chance of getting on in the world, my will must be broken.

One of my very first memories is of lying in a bed in a darkened room in our house on Goldstone Crescent in Hove. I am three or four years old. In that memory I can't see the shape of the room or any of the furniture, but there's a patch of wallpaper next to the bed that has come loose. I am pulling and tugging at it, curious about the color of the wall underneath and trying not to think about the voices I'm hearing.

Most nights I heard voices when I was close to falling asleep. They were near to my ear. Some muttered and heckled and harangued; others were sweet as honey. I had no control over them.

Forty-five years later in a Cambridge college courtyard under a dark winter sky, Oliver Sacks asked me to describe them. We'd had dinner together at Kings College and shared stories about the LSD hallucinations we'd had; we talked about Darwin and ghosts and about the drug-induced vision of cobalt blue Sacks had once seen. Now, at the end of the evening, I remembered the things I saw as a child, the voices I heard, and the monsters. It always happened, I told him, when I was falling asleep or waking up.

"Patterned and repeating shapes?" he asked. "People standing by your bed? Voices with strong patterning—very distinct in sound and texture?"

"They spoke in different languages entirely sometimes," I said. "I didn't understand some of them."

"Hypnagogic and hypnopompic," he said, as if he was used to diagnosing the odd conditions of dinner companions like this all the time. "They're hallucinations that happen when you are falling asleep— hypnagogic—and when you wake up—hypnopompic." He'd had them too, he told me. And so had Vladimir Nabokov. He urged me to read Nabokov's description of them in his memoir, *Speak Memory*.

It's difficult in truth to separate the visual from the auditory hallucinations I had as I fell asleep. I saw and heard things that my brothers and parents did not seem to experience. And according to my mother, I saw things during the day too. She describes rushing into the sitting room or kitchen to find me wild-eyed and screaming, pointing at tiny bits of fluff on the carpet, as if in fear for my life, as if there were monsters approaching. My howls of alarm and despair were a complete mystery to her. I don't remember what scared me about the carpet fluff, but I do remember the voices and the monsters I saw on the curtains in my bedroom. I can still see them very clearly. I still see things. But they don't disturb me as much now that I know there is a physiological explanation and that I'm not the only one to have them.

I remember lying in bed listening to my parents' muffled conversation in a distant room, their voices rising and falling, and seeing Satan, or my idea of Satan, all horns and scales and a flashing, grinning mouth, projected on the darkened surfaces of the curtains. It was always the same set of six or seven voices I could hear talking to me, not always in a language I recognized. When I was older they reappeared in my dreams as the Committee.

By the age of three or four I had developed a perfectly workaday, familial relationship with my God. He was an older-brother God rather than a father God. He could be appealed to and he could concede, but he was unpredictable, and not always to be trusted. If you do this, I'd say, I'll do that. Sometimes he complied, other times he didn't.

I managed the terrors of my small domestic space by negotiating with this God in what I called prayers. I appreciated the company late at night, when my father's snores grew gradually louder in my parents' bedroom next door and I could hear the creaks and groans of the house as the radiators turned themselves off.

Occasionally, if the voices terrified me more than I could bear,

Rebecca
around
age four

I'd call out to my parents and my father would come in, sometimes on all fours, pretending to be a bear. I dared not tell him what I saw projected there on the curtains—the monsters with wings and claws and hooves that were both male and female, human and animal. If my father was in a good mood, he made me laugh and told me stories. If he was in a bad mood he shouted. My mother gathered talismans to protect me from the dark: She crocheted me a comfort blanket from soft blue and green wool and gave me a stuffed toy rabbit with long ears. I discovered that if I tucked a rabbit ear between my little toe and the next toe down along my right foot, the voices would stop. Eventually I'd fall sleep. And the day would begin again.

11

When I was four, my parents, alarmed at my sleeplessness and loss of weight, took me to see a doctor. Although we were not supposed to have contact with non-Brethren, doctors were an exception. Later, when the separation rules stepped up again, I was taken to see my Brethren doctor uncle, my father's sister's husband. Mostly we were not sick and we did not see doctors. But on this occasion my parents must have been alarmed. The doctor insisted that I see a specialist.

I claimed to see things at night, my parents told him. I rarely fell asleep before midnight. When my parents had been banished to the waiting room and the doctor pressed me to confide in him, I told him I saw Satan and that when I concentrated very hard I could make angels appear. He seemed to think the angels were good, but I explained that even among the angels you had to work out the good ones from the bad and that some of them had both wings and hooves. The bad ones said terrible things, I told him; they talked just like Satan. It was very hard to tell the difference. He asked the nurse to collect a urine sample; he took notes; he ordered more tests. He did not ask my parents where I might have gotten such strange ideas.

Whether these visions were hypnagogic or hypnopompic or a form of sleep paralysis, I like to think I was dreaming the whole household's tormented dreams, that I was the lightning rod through which all my family's imaginary voices and nightmares passed.

And now I think about my mother, stuck at home with tiny children, not allowed to work, having to cook for all those Brethren visitors and get her own brood up at dawn on the Lord's Day and get us washed and changed, ready for breaking bread, then come home and vacuum—again. She had a double burden: She was expected to keep both dirt and Satan out of her home. What was happening in *her* dream world?

William, my father's closest Brethren friend, remembers my mother as both a great beauty and as the woman who hoovered. In those early days of their marriage, Brethren men would stay late to discuss assembly matters over several glasses of by-then-compulsory whiskey.

"Your mother," he told me, "would get rid of us by getting the hoover out." Of course she did. She wasn't allowed to express opinions, complain, pray aloud, or preach. She'd never win an argument against my father. She'd just set him off. With the hoover on its highest setting, it could do her roaring for her.

My mother was house-proud by nature, but she was also expected to be. There was a daily routine of vacuuming, laundering, dusting, scouring, and polishing. I helped out as I grew older.

Different rooms and cupboards in our house smelled of different cleaning and polishing products: Pledge, Brasso, Dettol, coal-tar soap, and a scouring powder called Vim. I shook out wet sheets with her, folded dry sheets, swept down the staircase, scoured the bath with Vim, tipped the reconstituted potato powder called Smash and then measured water into the food mixer and stared down into the gray-white gloop until all the lumps had mixed in. But though I was happy to do all this because I loved my mother, I resented the fact that my brothers did not help and that my mother did not ask them to help. Brethren boys did not do housework. That was women's work.

Why would only my brothers inherit the family business? Why was it Stott and *Sons* and not Stott and *Daughters*? Why didn't the Spirit speak through women? Why didn't my brothers have to sweep the stairs? Why did Brethren preachers have to be men? Where in the Bible did it say that the Lord spoke only through men? It was not fair. Nothing was fair. I studied the Brethren women around me to see if any of them were angry too, but it was always impossible to tell.

I'd heard my adored grandmother talking about her mother's willfulness, heard her talk to other women about willful wives, or about how so-and-so should remember to be proud to be flesh of her husband's flesh, proud to subdue her will to his. I knew the women would never back me if I spoke out. They'd be shamed by any insurrection of mine. It would be the work of Satan in me. If the Lord wanted me to be silent and obedient like that for the rest of my life, just because I was a girl, then I wasn't sure I liked the Lord.

I'd have howled with fury if I could, but I knew there was no persuading anyone or making any difference. Years later, a male cousin who was raised in the Brethren and ran away at the age of twenty-four asked me why I supposed that out of all his ten siblings he was the only one who'd refused to believe in the Taylor system. Like me, he'd had to nurse his outrage silently and secretly. Speaking out never brought change, he told me, only trouble. "You're just a girl," my brothers would say. *Just a girl.* But it wasn't easy for the boys either.

Brethren women and girls were not supposed to have their hair cut because women's hair, J.T. Junior had decreed, was their glory. My brothers had short hair and little combs in their back pockets to keep it tidy. My hair had never been cut, so by the time I was three or four it stretched down to my waist when it was wet. Thick, heavy, and curly, it had to be combed and braided constantly. My mother would tug the comb through the endless knots.

Friday nights were hair-washing and nail-cutting nights, a family grooming that prepared us for the five or six weekend Brethren meetings, including the compulsory six A.M. meeting on the Lord's Day. My brothers and I would sit on the landing outside the bathroom waiting to be called in to have our hair washed. While I was waiting for my turn I'd untangle my long braids and run my fingers through the knots. My mother washed my brothers' hair over the sink, and they were in and out and back to play out in the garden in a few minutes. It took ten times as long to wash and rinse mine.

My hair was too long and thick for the sink, so I'd kneel over the edge of the bath with my hair coiling down onto the white enamel. My mother used a watering can to rinse the soap out. My hair was like her own: both a glory and a burden. Hers was pinned up, mine perpetually pulled back into tight plaits. Later, when J.T. Junior decided that Brethren women should display their glory, she had to take her hair out from the braided coil she wore on the top of her head, brush it out, and wear it down her back under a headscarf.

I found no photographs of me as a child wearing a headscarf. There were very few pictures of us at all. "Cameras were frowned on in the midsixties," a cousin explained. "They were supposed to be worldly and a distraction from the Lord. None of us have many photographs from that time." Years later, when I'd failed to find photographs of me as a baby, I'd told myself my parents must have not been much interested in their second baby. I'd never connected it with the camera prohibition. It explained both the absence of baby pictures and my father's later compulsion to buy expensive cameras.

When I took the kitchen scissors to my three dolls, cut off their hair, and painted their lips red with felt pens, I like to think I did it for all of the put-upon, subjected Brethren women I saw around me. My parents sent me to my room as punishment. My grandparents questioned me closely about it. "Such a good child," I overheard my grandmother say. "What could have got into her?"

Exhausted by having to get us up and dressed for dawn meetings, my mother would take afternoon naps, particularly when an elderly Brethren baker and his wife took my youngest brother out for the afternoon in their shiny gray Morris Minor to give my mother a break. They'd return him a few hours later with cake tins full of still-warm cupcakes and scones. Before taking her nap, my mother checked that the front and back doors were locked, got out some bricks or favorite toys of ours, drew the curtains, and sat in an armchair; then she closed her eyes. "Just for a few minutes," she'd say. "I'm just going to close my eyes for a few minutes." My two remaining brothers and I would play quietly in the same room until she woke up.

In the home movies my father made in the sixties and seventies, taken furtively at first and later, after we'd escaped the Brethren, openly, we children are always moving in that strange Super 8, slightly speeded-up way: running, climbing, kicking balls, riding tricycles in rich, flickering Technicolor. We are never more than a few inches away from one another. But though my brothers are usually intent on each other or the football they're chasing, and my mother is doing her best to avoid the camera, I'm gazing up at my very tall father behind it. My eyes glitter with pleasure at whatever he is saying. "Gubbey, over here," he calls to me, using my nickname, always with the

A still from one of my father's home movies, taken around 1971

emphasis on the second syllable. I turn and smile up at him. I cover my face and uncover it. My father, behind the camera, is never visible, but the sun casts him as a long shadow here and there on a lawn or carpet, and from time to time I can see him reflected back in the dark irises of my own eyes.

12

I remember my childhood as a sequence of dimly lit meetings interspersed with short bursts of noise and light when we rode tricycles or scrambled over jungle gyms with other children in the bright green of Brethren gardens. But how much time did my brothers and I actually spend in meeting? I examined my father's documents and the list of J.T. Junior edicts that he'd collected. In the mid-1960s, J.T. Junior, apparently ever more certain that the Rapture was only weeks or months away, decreed that Brethren babies should be baptised at eight days old, attend meeting immediately, and be offered the bread and wine as soon as they were weaned. If they reached out for the bread dangled in front of them as they sat on their mother's knee, this was proof that they were ready to join.

It's not just the nonsense and trickery that alarms me now—after all, how can a six-month-old baby reaching for bread be *choosing* anything but food?—but the number of hours we Brethren children spent listening to the men talk. My brothers and I—and thousands of other Brethren children of our age around the world—attended nine one-hour meetings a week before 1968, and eleven meetings a week between 1968 and 1970. That makes a total of just over three thousand hours I spent sitting absolutely still, listening to a small group of men, including my father and grandfather, preaching obscure biblical exegesis and prophesy, in voices that rose and fell and paused in strange incantatory cadences, before I was six years old. No wonder I heard voices. No wonder they never stopped.

Brethren children were expected to be quiet and well mannered in meeting. We sat in the back row with our mothers, clothes pressed, faces scrubbed, shoes polished, hair tightly braided or pinned back with clips, Bibles on laps.

While the Brethren ministering brothers talked of the nature of grace, the coming of the Lord, wells and springs, Lot and his salty wife, Sodom and Gomorrah, the Corinthians, the Pharisees, and the Laodiceans, I daydreamed as I had taught myself to do in the warehouse, imagined scenarios, turned the men and women in the room into my puppets, made them do remarkable, astonishing things. I had the Brethren brothers and sisters fly—headscarfed, suited, or hatted—across the room; sometimes I had the flying bodies crash into one another. I had them all taken up into that mansion of a thousand rooms, set them off up there together like a human cannon, and then snatched them straight back down again.

The metaphysical questions and imaginings that vexed me, just as they had vexed my father at the same age, came from my attempts to apply a child's sense to what I heard in meeting. I produced tangled things. I picked up a few sentences of the men's ministries and biblical exegesis here and there, recognizing sections of the Bible being quoted, and tried to translate a meaning for myself. I'd get a foothold for a few seconds and then slip and slide off again.

Was it the endlessly riddling and incomprehensible nature of Brethren ministry that made me yearn to open doors I was not supposed to open? Or was it all those hours I'd spent running and climbing unsupervised in the dusty and dark warren of the warehouse, all the secret back rooms I found there up staircases that seemed to appear from nowhere?

Between my parents' bedroom and the bathroom in our house on Goldstone Crescent there was a locked door. Sometimes I got a glimpse of the dark, gloriously colored interior of the room when my mother slipped in to fetch something. The curtains were always drawn shut, so the room was dark, but I could make out two beds fitted with rich purple bedcovers, matching heavily lined floor-to-ceiling curtains, and a kidney-shaped dressing table that stood in the bay window. When my mother went in there, she'd make me wait for her on the landing. When she came out again, she'd check that the handle was firmly closed behind her, then she'd lock the door and slip the key into the corner of the copper urn that stood on the landing.

After my mother disappeared into the hospital for observation in the last month of her fourth pregnancy, taking with her several bundles of sea-green wool so she could knit my dolls new coats, my grandparents, or some other Brethren couple, must have moved in to care for me and my two brothers, to cook and run the house. I remember only the certainty that now I might finally find something interesting. I looked in cupboards, under beds and loose floorboards, not only for the many things I knew my mother hid from us—cakes, marshmallows, fruit, dolls, suitcases of baby clothes—but for darker things too, things I could not imagine or name or know I was looking for.

The first time I slipped the key from the urn, eased it into the keyhole, and nudged the door of the guest room open, a long crack of light slid across the floor like the path the moon made on the sea. I could just make out the shapes of an enormous pram with two blue hoods at the far end of the room. Smocked baby clothes gleamed white against the floral purples of the bedcover. I stood on the threshold, paralyzed by the mystery of what I was seeing and by the miracle that I'd not been caught. I didn't dare enter the room but pulled the door slowly shut, letting the latch slip quietly back into its hole, locked it, and placed the key in the urn.

Soon I was slipping into the darkened room more and more often, closing the door behind me, treading quietly to avoid noisy floorboards, opening drawers in the half-light, trying out the handles of the magnificent royal blue pram hoods to see if the mechanism worked the same as the ones on my dolls' pram, or lying on the floor between the beds to watch the inverted pictures of the garden flickering across the ceiling.

One day, when I was finally brave enough to lift the latch on the wardrobe doors built into the far alcove, I thought I saw eyes looking back down at me from a tissue paper bundle on the top shelf. Something—or somebody—needed rescuing. I knew that I'd have to stand on a chair to reach the bundle, but I feared that someone downstairs might hear me. Still, there was no other way. I dragged the chair as quietly as I could across the pink carpet and wedged it between the bed and the cupboard, climbed up onto it, and stretched as high as I could toward the bundle that I was now convinced was an abandoned child. I tugged at the nearest corner, hoping to catch the bundle as it fell. But as I wobbled up there on the chair, the tissue paper parcel fell past my outstretched fingers and hit the floor with a terrible shattering sound.

I waited, pinned to the spot, listening for the sound of running feet on the stairs or a stern voice calling my name, but nothing happened. I ducked down out of sight between the bed and the cupboard to unwrap the bundle, dreading what I would find. Inside the white tissue paper I found the shattered pieces of a porcelain doll's head, her skin as white as eggshells and with the most delicate pink paint flushed across her cheekbones. A single blue eye rocked inside its broken socket. I rolled the tissue paper back around the lacy body and stuffed the bundle behind the heavy curtains. I was certain that I'd heard it whimper.

When my mother returned home from the hospital a few days later, still heavily pregnant, I lay awake, waiting for the bundle of broken pieces to be found, all through the long night when she began to howl in labor while my brothers and I lay in our beds, our pillows pulled tight over our heads, all through the sirens and blue lights of the ambulance that came for her so that she could deliver her second baby in the hospital. Though I was allowed to touch the fuzzy walnut-brown head of my new baby brother as the paramedics carried my mother down the stairs strapped into a wheelchair, I was in agony. I told myself that the tired and tight smile she gave me was because she knew about the shattered doll and was waiting for me to confess and tell her that I was sorry and that, yes, I had taken the Lord into my heart.

"I did it!" I wanted to scream at her. "I did it. I broke the doll. And I stole the key. I'm the one. It was *me*."

I knew the bundle of tissue paper wrapping the broken doll must have been found, but no one ever spoke to me about it. The whole terrible saga disappeared into the miraculous homecoming of my tiny new siblings.

13

My brothers and I understood that outside was dangerous. And all the outside people were dangerous. I'd look through my bedroom window across the road into the darkening park beyond the thick fringe of trees and imagine Satan and his people over there, scuttling about, doing wicked things.

The streets outside our meeting rooms and Brethren homes were owned by Satan and thronged with Satan's traps and snares: shop windows full of television sets with moving pictures that you tried not to look at but couldn't take your eyes off of. Hoardings on newspaper stands, cinemas with giant illuminated letters, adverts for perfume and makeup, women in miniskirts. There were snatches of music too, from open windows or café doors, rapid drumbeats and seductive melodies. The grown-ups said all these things were "worldly," and in the meeting room they preached that Satan, the enemy, used them in his battle for our souls.

Someone gave me a notebook and a pencil sharpened to a dusky point. But instead of practicing my letters, I took to sitting on the wide bedroom windowsill with my eyes fixed on the bus stop below. I was curious about the worldly people down there, what they were doing, what sins they'd committed, how dangerous they were, what they were going to do with their sin-packed worldly days. With my new pencil and notebook I began to keep detailed records of every person I saw waiting there, noting down times and dates, the buses they took, their hair color, their height, clothing, even shoe color. As I became quicker and more accurate at chronicling Satan's people, my spelling improved. Why did my father and I both keep these obsessive records, mine descriptive and his numerical?

"Gub-bey," my brothers would call. "Gub-bey, what are you doing up there. Did you get lost?"

"I'm reading," I'd call back, holding myself very still. "I'm just reading."

I was certain that one day the police would come to our house because they'd heard that there was a child there who kept records. I must have confused the police with the Brethren priests because in my imagination the men who came to the house always wore coats and black hats, not helmets. They would ask my parents if they could speak to me. I would climb the staircase solemnly to my room, slip the notebook out from under my mattress, and carry it down to the sitting room, where my parents chatted with two "police officers," exchanging surprised and admiring looks. They'd find their murderer in my notebook and shake my hand and thank me.

The grown-ups told us that inside our house and meeting room we were safe because we were the chosen ones. We'd be protected from all the terrible things that were soon to rise up and engulf all the people outside our fellowship. But I was also frightened inside the house—by my father, at the certainty that I'd be caught looking at things I shouldn't be looking at or going into rooms I was not supposed to go into. I was frightened by the things I glimpsed in the shadows. More than anything I was afraid of the increasing certainty I felt that all the horrifying things that were about to happen to all the bad people outside our house and meeting room would also engulf my brothers and me, that we'd drown, burn, be hunted down. Because we were not good. We had not separated from iniquity. We didn't seem able to.

I felt like a cuckoo in the nest, an interloper, the child who didn't fit. But then I was also often certain that none of us *did* fit. Apart from my mother, we all cheated on Brethren rules. I can't recall a single instance in which I saw my mother transgress, though I can remember times when she failed to denounce my father for *his* many transgressions, as Brethren rules required her to do. There were many times when I heard her—or thought I heard her—make a quiet tutting noise, but she never said anything. I'd seen the radio my father kept hidden in the tire compartment in the trunk of the car. I knew my brothers hid comics under their mattresses and talked with worldly boys in the park. They knew I told lies too. There were secrets and transgressions everywhere in our house, a great webwork of them. Was I supposed to tell on my father, on my brothers? Would I be punished for not telling? Was the Lord keeping a notebook about me?

Cinemas were worldly, part of Satan's system, and cameras were frowned upon, but for some reason in the sixties Brethren were allowed to film home movies discreetly and project them on portable screens or onto the wall of their sitting rooms. Because my brothers and I grew up with no television or radio and very few children's books, these flickering, oversize Technicolor versions of ourselves were especially magical. My father bought a movie camera and filmed us playing in the garden, dressing up at our grandparents' house, or picnicking with other Brethren families in public parks.

Fascinated by these moving images of myself, I began to run imaginary film sequences in my head. One of my favorites involved a car screeching to a stop in the street where I was walking with my parents and brothers. A man and woman would jump out, hardly stopping to close the car doors, and run across the road toward me. The woman would take me in her arms, kneeling on the hard tarmac, as if in prayer.

"It's her," she would sob to her husband. "I knew we'd find her. Didn't I say, if we just kept looking we'd find her? And here she is."

There was another version in which a couple snatched me from under the eyes of my parents as we walked down the street in broad daylight. Before my parents had time to protest, they bundled me into their car. They'd heard of my remarkable abilities, they said. They wanted me to come and live with them.

Was I scripting meritocratic secular versions of the Rapture? In these car-screeching dramas, I was chosen, plucked out of suburban gray obscurity, not because I had taken the Lord into my heart but because I read well or kept scrupulously detailed records of suspected criminals. In these scenarios my parents lamented my disappearance and chastised themselves for having overlooked me.

Sometimes I found clues that fueled these cuckoo-in-the-nest fantasies. In addition to the key to the locked room, my mother kept blankets inside the copper tea urn that stood on the stair landing. I'd pull over a stool, stand on it, then slip off the lid so I could look down past the strata of colored blankets into the dark depths. My mother, I came to realize, sometimes hid food there, probably to keep it out of sight of my father or us, to save it for a special occasion. One day I saw a box of sweets; another time a box of cakes. One Lord's Day I spotted five shiny red apples nested like eggs in a gray blanket. I left them alone, but found myself coming back to lift that lid every time it was safe to do so.

One day when my parents were busy entertaining Brethren visitors in the sitting room and my brothers were playing football in the garden, I thought I saw the edges of what looked like a white box down in the darkness. I stood on the stool and quietly lifted out the blankets one by one, then reached down, listening for the warning sound of doors opening downstairs. Once the box was safely on the landing carpet, I slipped off its cardboard lid, hardly daring to breathe. The box was full of tightly typed documents, but among them were also three letters written in a fine italic hand, one addressed to me and one for each of my two brothers. I replaced the box under the blankets and slipped the lid back on the urn.

I sat for a long time examining the sealed envelopes, turning them over in my hand. This discovery would reveal the secret of all secrets, I told myself; it would change my life and my brothers' lives forever. But I knew I could not take the next dangerous step alone. I could hear my heart thumping in my chest as I walked down the staircase. I found my brothers playing in the garden and brought them, protesting but obedient, up the stairs to the landing where I'd hidden the precious envelopes under the carpet. The three of us sat in a circle around them. The envelopes, I told them, contained letters from our real parents. They'd sent us instructions on how to escape and where they'd meet us. We had to open them. There wasn't much time left.

My brothers, mesmerized, nodded assent. I ripped open the envelopes, tearing the paper across the beautiful italic handwriting. But there was nothing inside. The envelopes were empty. I could not understand why. I wept with fury and disappointment. Why, I asked my brothers, would our parents have taken the trouble to write to us but not have put anything inside the envelopes? I stuffed the torn paper back in among the other papers in the box, slipped the lid on, placed it carefully back at the bottom of the urn, and replaced the folded blankets in the order I had found them. I told my brothers never to speak of the box or the letters again.

Years later my father told me that when my mother found the torn envelopes in the box some months later she was mystified. The envelopes were a present from a stamp-collecting Brethren brother. He'd bought us all first day covers, envelopes with limited special edition stamps purchased to mark the days on which we'd been born. The stamps I had torn through were collectors' items, intended to be given to us when they had accrued value with time. My mother didn't care for stamps, and the torn envelopes did not much trouble her.

Sigmund Freud, I discovered later, had written about this fantasy of mine. Some children of a particularly neurotic or imaginative sensibility, he wrote, convince themselves that they will be rescued by their "real" parents, from whom they have been stolen or kidnapped. Almost always the fantasy family is of a higher social stand-ing, so the "rescue" reveals the bastardized nature of the siblings as well as the hollow status of the "adoptive" parents. The details of the fantasy, Freud wrote, depend on the particular imaginative materi-als available to the child: a nearby manor house, local aristocracy, books, fables, and stories. Mine were made up of the strange experi-ences life in the Brethren had given me. My rescuers were "worldly" people.

My fantasies played themselves out again and again, not because I failed to love my parents, or felt they did not love me, or because I was any more unhappy or lonely or disoriented than most other chil-dren my age, but because I was certain my parents were keeping se-crets from me. I was probably daydreaming the fantasies of my parents too. Each of them, I am certain, must have longed to be plucked out of this strange world we'd washed up into.

14

Between meetings, Brethren children played noisily in the mani-cured shrubberies of large detached houses while their parents talked inside with other Brethren grown-ups. The Brethren children who hosted us in the short breaks between meetings in neighboring towns on the Lord's Day—teenagers who seemed impossibly, throat-tighteningly glamorous—played hide-and-seek with us or took our hands and led us down through fruit trees and orchards and kitchen gardens to a musty summer house where they had stashed forbidden comics under floorboards.

One long summer afternoon two or three Brethren teenagers put on a shadow theater for us in a barn, making characters with their hands behind a screen they'd stitched together from an old sheet. We were not allowed to tell.

Children kept secrets from the grown-ups. Grown-ups kept secrets from the children. We passed around Beano comics and looked out for approaching grown-ups and made up stories that didn't have any Bible people in them. We watched one another's backs. We never talked about the meetings or whether what the grown-ups preached was right or wrong.

Grown-ups, we knew, sometimes broke promises. They were not always to be trusted. When I was five, I came to understand that my father was not to be trusted.

Although large sections of the Bible were a puzzle to me, I was convinced that if I concentrated hard enough I'd be able to figure it out, and that my father's approval would surely follow. I could not work out, for instance, whether the Holy Spirit, then such an important part of our meetings, was a dove or a ghost or the ghost of a dead dove. I turned my mind to the problem in meeting or when I was trying to fall asleep at night.

One day I had an epiphany: If there was an earthly tripartite family made up of Jesus, Mary, and Joseph *down here,* there had to be a heavenly tripartite equivalent. This meant that if the son was Jesus *up there,* and God was the father, then the Holy Spirit had to be the *mother* up there. It made a blinding kind of sense to me, given the silent, birdlike, ghostly, self-effacing nature of the Brethren mothers I knew. I felt the exhilaration of intellectual discovery for the first time: The Holy Spirit, I was now certain, was Jesus's heavenly *mother.* It was the early hours of the morning. I heard the grandfather clock in the hall strike two. My brother was snoring in the bunk above me. I was too excited to sleep.

I waited until after the morning Bible reading before I knocked on my father's study door. He was sitting behind a desk in his smart work suit and tie with his Bible open in front of him. I had a question about the Holy Spirit to ask him, I said. I carefully explained the logic of the pattern I'd uncovered, drawing the diagram on a piece of Stott and Sons–headed paper. But when I told him I had been wondering if the Holy Spirit was Jesus's spiritual mother, he laughed. I was being too literal, he said. I was using the wrong part of my mind.

When I found the courage to ask the question that was keeping me awake—who or what, then, *was* the Holy Spirit?—he read me verses from 1 Corinthians 2. In this letter, he said, Paul explains to the Corinthians that certain mysteries can only be apprehended with the spiritual mind and not with the natural mind. I was using my natural mind to think about the Holy Spirit. That wasn't going to get me anywhere.

Embarrassed and disappointed beyond measure, I dared not tell him that he had evaded my question. Instead I asked him to promise not to tell anyone about our conversation. He promised. We prayed. I did not sleep that second night either. I lay in bed looking at the underside of the bunk above me, with its links of interconnected chains, rehearsing follow-up conversations with my father and with God. I could make no sense of it, but I also knew I was not stupid.

The next morning, the Lord's Day, my mother bundled all five of her scrubbed children into the car as usual, to go to the morning meeting. This austere, high-walled, windowless redbrick meeting room on the outskirts of Brighton held five hundred Brethren brothers and sisters. We sat on wooden chairs arranged in a circle, the women and children in the uppermost, outermost circles, the men on the inside. My father, then in his early thirties, had by this time perfected a declamatory, slightly mannered preaching style and was making a stir as a young ministering brother. People traveled some distance to hear him.

On this particular day he preached to an assembly of two hundred to three hundred south coast Brethren for twenty minutes on the importance of educating Brethren children about the dangers of the natural mind. His daughter, he told them, had asked a question about the Holy Spirit and he had explained to her about 1 Corinthians 2. We should not leave our children, he intoned, to languish in spiritual ignorance. We must be vigilant. My face burned red, not with embarrassment now but with outrage. People turned to smile at me. I bit my lip hard and tasted blood. I swore I would never forget that act of betrayal.

15

My mother taught me to read when I was three years old. I remember the black shapes dark against the white flash cards she used, the intense pleasure I took in deciphering the words on them before my older brother did. Though I took to reading early, he didn't. I'd snatch the cards when he looked away and hide them among my toys.

He must have hated me then. I was a little show-off. A little *girl* show-off. I didn't care. I had something to prove. There was a begat system to violate in my house; it was enshrined in the Stott and Sons logo that seemed to have been stamped onto every surface in our house—on the boxes, on the paperwork, on the key ring my father carried, on the files my mother stacked on the shelves. Boys inherited. Boys spoke. Boys had power. Girls didn't. I countered that system with will and subterfuge. Eve *stole* the forbidden fruit. If God knew everything, then he must have known she was going to do that. He could have stopped her. But he didn't. And he didn't seem to be stopping me either.

We got our reading practice with the Bible. There were hardly any other books in the house once my father threw out all the other books my parents had once owned, as he was told to do when the new edict about clean houses came in about the time I was born. From then on, my parents just had the colored rows of ministry in the sitting room and the volumes of the children's encyclopedia arranged underneath.

Every morning my brothers and I gathered around the great iron bed in my parents' bedroom to read the Bible. Each of us would read a chapter every morning. We worked our way through the books— Genesis to Ezekiel, tipping from one story to the next, from Noah's ark to Moses in the bulrushes to Joseph and Potiphar's wife to Ezekiel with the dry bones, the staccato of Leviticus giving way to the swells of Song of Solomon. Sometimes there would be pockets of iambic beauty that I couldn't get out of my head for days.

And-God-re-mem-bered-No-ah.

Job was a particular favorite of mine. Though the story made me furious with the Lord for making Job suffer such terrible things just to prove a point to Satan, the language seemed especially beautiful, particularly the bits about the whale.

"His sneezings flash light," I read from my Bible when my turn came around, "and his eyes are like the eyelids of the morning. Out of his mouth go forth flames; sparks of fire leap out: Out of his nostrils goeth smoke, as out of a boiling pot and cauldron. His breath kindleth coals, and a flame goeth out of his mouth."

I itched to correct my brothers when they hesitated over a word or got the rhythms wrong, but I was not allowed to speak after I finished my chapter. The great victory of those mornings was getting to the end of my chapter without stumbling or showing the slightest sign of self-satisfaction. Although I could sometimes see my father's joyful approval, I did not acknowledge it or meet his eye. I was not praised. Praise encouraged spiritual pride. I didn't really understand what my parents meant when they talked about spiritual pride, but I knew it was one of the worst sins of all, one I was especially prone to, it seemed. It was one of the many things I was supposed to be vigilant about.

Despite the fact that only Brethren brothers preached and sisters were silent and obedient, I imagined a dazzling Brethren future for myself. By the time I'd beaten my older brother at reading and the times table, I had decided that I'd be one of the first Brethren girls to be allowed to preach in the meeting room and in three-day meetings. I was going to be the first of the female Brethren preachers. It was my calling.

There were plenty of glorious sons in the Bible, of every shape and size. Sons who inherited. Sons who were rewarded. Sons who were nurtured and recognized. Sons forgiven. Prodigals. And there were all those son sequences: Jacob begat Esau and Esau begat . . . In contrast, most if not all of the daughters in the Scriptures, it seemed, were traded by their fathers or brothers or raped or offered as wives or as consolation prizes. There didn't seem to be much to look forward to about being a daughter in the Bible. There were no chains of begats for daughters.

So it made sense to turn myself into the son who overtook all his siblings from behind. I'd be Joseph. And Jacob. The canny, overlooked, improbable sons. The ones who beat everyone while no one was looking. Joseph was the youngest, the puniest, the least likely, and he still got to be king of Egypt. But I'd have to know the Bible better than my brothers if I was going to get anywhere. I began to memorize whole chapters and to write lists of all the books of the Bible in the right order, just as my father had done as a child.

When my brothers and I got confused about points of theology or doctrine, we couldn't untangle them because asking questions was risky. My mother, usually busy preparing food or making curtains or feeding a baby, would say, "Ask your father," and when we asked my father, if he was home—which he usually wasn't—he would launch into a long lecture that was impossible to follow. So the misunderstandings we had privately from listening to preachings in meeting turned into muddles.

Things got even more confusing when we went to school. My older brother and I were sent to Connaught Road Junior School in Hove. There were no Brethren schools in the sixties, though today Brethren children are bused long distances to expensively equipped "faith" schools where they are closely supervised, girls are segregated from boys, "science" is carefully censored, and students are taught that evolution is a false theory. But although we were schooled alongside worldly children, we were supposed to have no contact with them. We came home for lunch to comply with the Brethren eating rule. In fact, there was no danger of our making friends with worldly children, because we had no idea how to talk to them. We spoke a quaint kind of Brethren-ese—we talked about "the Lord's Day," "walking in the light," "in the arms of the Lord"—and I noticed the effect those phrases had on the other children.

The things that preoccupied and excited me and kept me from sleeping—the precise layout of the great mansion in heaven, where the angels lived in the great city, how transparent the Holy Spirit was, whether a murderer could ever be repentant enough to get taken up in the Rapture—were clearly not things the other children thought about at all. The things we heard them talk about were fascinating but incomprehensible. None of them thought they needed to explain that *The Banana Splits* and *The Monkees* and *The Tom and Jerry Show* were children's television programs or that the Seagulls were the Brighton & Hove Albion football team. I stood on the playground with my brothers, our backs pressed up against the brick wall, trying to be invisible, watching and listening.

In 1969, all the children were talking about Neil Armstrong and the first moon landing, but I had no idea what they meant. Brethren families like ours, who were forbidden to have newspapers or television sets, would not have seen the pictures of the blue-cloud-laced Earth from far away, or watched Armstrong take those strange, underwater steps onto the dusty moon. We were, of course, living on a kind of satellite planet of our own.

16

The teachers at Connaught Road Junior School were used to Brethren families and didn't put up a fight when Brethren parents stipulated what Brethren children were allowed to read or study. They probably weren't allowed to—they were expected to respect and accommodate religious differences. And why would they object? Brethren children were well behaved, obedient, hardworking, never any trouble. You hardly knew they were there except for the strange clothes they wore.

The teachers banished us from the classrooms whenever the teaching strayed into areas that conflicted with Brethren teachings. They took no chances. And in the 1960s and 1970s, when the Exclusive Brethren took their totalitarian turn, that meant we spent many of our school hours in the long corridor that ran the length of the Victorian building.

No assembly. No prayers. No classes about poetry or fiction. No science that conflicted with the creation story. No gym. No ballet. No music classes. No sports. No discussion of ethics or philosophy. The teachers handed us worksheets. We had comprehension practice, quizzes, handwriting sheets, math sheets. We were given a stack of them and a high desk and chair out in the hallway.

It was always a relief for me to be in the corridor—it was quiet after the hubbub of the classroom. I'd hear the rest of the school as if through water: fragments of teachers' voices, children singing in choir or playing flutes or the thud of feet in the gym. The air was full of the smell of poster paint and glue.

Sometimes I glimpsed my brothers farther up that hallway with heads down over a pile of worksheets. I wasn't allowed to call out to them, but if I waited long enough, one of them would sometimes sit up, look around, see me, grin, and wave. I'd wave back. The only other people we saw out there were the worldly boys who'd been sent out of class for misbehaving. They sat on chairs outside the head teacher's room, fidgeting, waiting to be called in and reprimanded. Sometimes a teacher came out to make sure I was doing what I was supposed to be doing, but eventually they felt confident that I was entirely obedient and were content to leave me be.

One day my teacher told me that when I got to the end of a particular worksheet, I could go to the library for independent reading if there was time left before the bell rang. I still don't know if she realized what she was saying. I wasn't allowed in the library, I nearly told her, and then I swallowed the words. When my classmates had library time, I would sit on a faded red plastic chair in the corridor outside the door. I'd peered in from time to time and been astonished by the fact that there were so many books in the world, that someone had thought to put them all in one room, and that they came in so many shiny colors.

"At home we only have ministries," I told my teacher once.

Her eyebrow rose just a flicker.

"That's nice," she said, and turned to another child. There had been other books in the house once, I discovered later—my mother's adored and beautifully leather-bound Jane Austen collection, my father's volumes of Shakespeare and poetry. But in 1962, when J.T. Junior ordered all Brethren households to cleanse themselves properly, my father boxed up all the books and packed them into the trunk of the car one Lord's Day. Many of them reappeared in the years after we left—he must have stashed them somewhere for safekeeping, just as the Romans buried their treasure when they evacuated Britain in the fourth century or the Catholics hid their relics under floorboards during the Reformation. But though his books came back, my mother's Jane Austens did not.

The Lord had not said it was all right for me to go into the school library, but he hadn't exactly said it wasn't either. Usually he sent a sign. I was good at looking for signs—a bird flying one way or another, the wind blowing toward me or away from me, even car license plates could be signs. He hadn't sent a sign this time. The library door was open. That, I persuaded myself, probably meant it was all right. The Lord must be showing me the way.

I headed for the far corner where the fiction shelves were. The old floorboards creaked noisily beneath my feet. The bell might ring at any moment. A teacher might usher me out. My brother might glimpse me through the door and tell our parents. But I was already in and the bell had not yet sounded. I reached up and pulled out a book.

On the cover of *The Secret Island,* a group of four children a few years older than me crouched on a cliff looking down over a sandy beach, where suspicious-looking grown-ups were unloading a row-boat. The children looked as if they were in danger but they also seemed to know what they were doing. *Mike, Peggy, and Nora were sitting in the fields, talking together,* I read. *They were very unhappy. Nora was crying, and would not stop. As they sat there, they heard a low call. "Coo'ee!"*

I read as if turned to stone, breathing in the musty smell of the book, my bare knees marked by the edges of the floorboards. Before this I had only read the Janet and John books, with my mother: *John is in the tree. Janet is in the kitchen.* And the Bible. I had read most of it by now, aloud, kneeling on the floor of my parents' bedroom. But there were very few stories about children in the Bible other than Jesus, and he didn't seem to have any brothers or sisters or go to school or play in the fields or cry. He preferred to talk to grown-ups in the temple.

Why was Nora crying in the field?

As Peggy and Mike comforted Nora, a scruffy boy appeared over the hill and stopped to ask what was wrong. His name was Jack. The children explained that they were being treated as no more than farm slaves by their aunt and uncle, that their real parents had gone missing, that they were very unhappy.

When the bell rang ten minutes later, I stuffed the book underneath a dusty red beanbag in the corner. Brethren children were not allowed to borrow library books. I would have to hide it so no one else could borrow it before I came back.

Where had the children's parents disappeared to?

Could Jack be trusted?

17

Over the next few weeks, I read the whole of *The Secret Island* without discovery, punishment, or consequence. When the bell rang I'd go to my next lesson, complete my worksheet, and head for the library, checking over my shoulder to ensure that I hadn't been seen. Would they escape to the secret island after all? When they crossed to the island would the leaky boat they'd taken stay afloat? Where would they sleep? How would they open the tins they'd stolen from the larder? What would happen when the food ran out?

Jack now occupied the place in my head where only God and my parents had been. He was on the right and they were on the left. It was easier to keep them in separate rooms. I negotiated with God but sought advice and good sense from Jack. I agreed with Jack when he told the others that sometimes grown-ups could be cruel, unfair, and plain wrong. He was right when he said that under certain circumstances it was all right to steal food. After all, as Jack said, the bad aunt and uncle wouldn't have to provide for the children anymore once they'd escaped to the secret island, so stealing a few provisions in the night couldn't exactly be wrong.

Although I read all the books in Enid Blyton's Secret series, it was *The Secret Island* that I kept coming back to. It made my heart beat faster. I was in love with Jack. He always knew what to do. He'd know how to plan for when the Tribulation came. He found the island in the lake that no one knew about. He knew where a boat was hidden. He told the other children that they could all live there together, build a cabin out of willows, and live off the land while they waited for their real parents to come and find them. And their real parents did come and find them.

Years later, when my father recited Yeats's "Lake Isle of Innisfree" again and again—incanting "*I will arise and go now, and go to Innis-free, / And a small cabin build there, of clay and wattles made*"—I'd be with Jack in the woods on the island, tying the willow branches together. "*Nine bean-rows will I have there,*" my father would declaim, lost in his own imagined refuge, "*a hive for the honey-bee,*" and I'd be lighting the candles in the woods with Jack as night fell.

At home I became stealthy. I wrote out a list of the things that Jack told the children they should take the night they ran away:

Empty tins for storing things in
Saucepan
Ax
A fine sharp knife
Sugar
Knives and forks
Books and papers for reading quietly
Ludo and dominoes
A sewing workbasket
Matches
Mixed nails and a hammer
A small magnifying glass for making fire

"On the night before they left," Blyton wrote, "they broke into the larder and took: Some tea? Yes! A tin of cocoa from the top shelf. A packet of currants and a tin of rice from the store shelf, too. A big load, a few cakes from the cake-tin!"

By the time my mother gave birth to my twin brother and sister, I had gathered a stash of stolen objects. I'd known for some time that when my parents and all the other Brethren grown-ups disappeared in the Rapture and we children got left behind, Satan's people would come looking for us. There was nothing in the Bible about what to do when that happened. We wouldn't be able to stay in the house—I'd read about Sodom and Gomorrah and the terrible things that happened there and guessed that was what would be unleashed when Armageddon started. We'd have to escape to caves in the mountains or find a boat somewhere and cook over fires we started ourselves.

There was a copse with thick woodland and hiding places just behind our house. That's where I planned to spend our first night. But now that there were two new babies in the house, things would be more difficult. I was glad that my father and one of the other Brethren priests had baptized them in the bath when they were a few days old. But I didn't know enough about baby souls to be able to say one way or the other whether my parents would be allowed to take the babies with them in the Rapture. So I'd have to be ready in case they got left behind too: powdered milk, sterilizing equipment and bottles. I made my mother show me the whole routine and how to check the temperature of the milk by squeezing a few drops onto the back of my hand.

18

Something really bad had happened. My parents were talking in hushed voices again. I listened from the back of the car. I set up my dolls in the hallway near the phone so that I could eavesdrop on the long calls my father kept making and receiving. It was the end of July 1970. I was nearly six. We had two tiny wailing babies in the house, whose cots had been put in my bedroom, and I wasn't sleeping now— not because of the noise they made when they cried but because I couldn't stop looking at them. They were so beautiful and strange. They made my heart ache.

There were five of us now, and the baby routine on top of the usual domestic routines filled up every minute of the day. I bottle-fed my baby brother while my mother fed my sister.

The house was thick with the smell of baby sick, sterilizing tablets, and Dettol. My mother had always used a lot of Dettol, but now my father was bringing home industrial-size bottles of it from the warehouse. Even through all that noise and smell and excitement I could tell that something important was happening outside the house because the phone never stopped ringing.

My mother was usually changing one baby or feeding the other or washing diapers, so my brothers and I would answer the front door when my grandfather and the other men arrived to consult with my father that summer. They disappeared into the sitting room together. My mother carried cookies and bottles of whiskey or pots of coffee in there when the Brethren men came, and when they left, my father would summon her. She'd leave me to mind the babies and close the door behind her.

In the hushed talk on the phone, the raised voices behind the closed door, and the whispered conversations between my parents, I heard the words "Aberdeen" and "Mrs. Ker" repeated again and again. I worked hard to piece together the clues, when my father glimpsed me trying to listen in while he was on the phone, he kicked the sitting room door shut. Although I failed to work out what Aberdeen meant, or what Mrs. Ker had actually done, or why everyone was so upset, I did know that it was because of Aberdeen that our lives changed forever. Aberdeen was the reason we left the Brethren and went to live in the outside world. Aberdeen turned everything upside down.

19

What actually happened at Aberdeen only took shape for me years later. I was sixteen. We'd been out of the Brethren for eight years by then and the circumstances of our leaving had been overlaid by all the dramas that had happened since. It was 1981, the day after my father had been taken to prison for embezzlement and fraud. His landlady told my mother that if my father's effects were not removed from his flat by the end of the week she'd take them to the dump. So my mother and I let ourselves into my father's impossibly messy, postdivorce flat, taking Dettol and rubber gloves, and started opening the drawers and looking in the boxes. My mother wanted to find the deeds to the house we lived in. She had to save it from the lawyers and creditors or we'd all be homeless.

On the table, I found an open file filled with yellowing newspaper clippings. The first one I pulled out was from the *Daily Express*. It was dated August 1970. There was something about the photograph under the headline that looked creepy: A very old man was sitting on a sofa with his arm around a pretty young woman. His hand seemed to be very close to her breast. She was smiling in a rather pinched uncomfortable way. The headline read "'We Are Not Ashamed,' Says Big Jim."

Big Jim, I remembered, was what journalists called J.T. Junior, the Brethren Man of God, and here—finally—was a picture of the mysterious Mrs. Ker. Philip Finn, the New York correspondent for the *Daily Express,* had interviewed J.T. Junior in his house in New York about a scandal that had just taken place over in Aberdeen in Scotland.

I did not want my mother to see the clipping or the file I'd opened. Everything was bad enough already. I was upset for her to be seeing my father's dirty and disordered flat. She hadn't found the house deeds and now she was putting everything she could find into the black bin bags and boxes we'd brought with us. I was trying not to inhale the strange smell of off milk, cheap hair oil, and the newspapers that were piled high in every corner. I stuffed the newspaper clippings into my school satchel and went to search through the boxes my mother had left for me.

Later, when we got home, and my mother went back out to work, I closed my bedroom door and nudged the chest of drawers in front of it. I tipped all the cuttings from my satchel onto the floor, found the *Daily Express* piece, and read through it slowly.

Finn had turned this scandal into an episode from Benny Hill, all nudges, winks, and smirks. He was making it silly, but it wasn't silly— it was terrible and epic. *This* was "Aberdeen." This was what my parents had been talking about eleven years earlier. This is what they'd been trying to make sense of. *This was why we left.* Finn wrote:

> Big Jim Taylor put his arm round dark-haired Mrs. Madeline Ker at his Brooklyn, New York, home tonight, kissed her lightly on the cheek and said: "I don't care what people say. She is a very, very pure person."
>
> Then the balding, silver-haired leader of the Close Brethren said: "We have never at any time done anything improper."
>
> Resting on his lap was a large leather-bound Bible, and in his right hand he held a tumbler half-full of Scotch.
>
> As we talked in the upstairs sitting room of his large detached house 32-year-old Mrs. Ker, mother of four, from Harrow, Middlesex, smiled up at him.
>
> When I arrived at his home, Big Jim was sitting in an armchair wearing only underpants.
>
> He said: "I suppose I had better put my pants on. But, quite honestly, I find it more comfortable just sitting in my underpants."
>
> Big Jim seemed quite at ease, and quite oblivious of the sensation surrounding him and Mrs. Ker and her husband during their recent visit to Nigg, Aberdeenshire.
>
> Then it was claimed that Mrs. Ker had been found in bed with him when other members of the sect walked in.
>
> It led to a furious row among members of the sect, and today Big Jim was busy sending off up to 8,000 letters "explaining" the events in Scotland.

Mrs. K and her husband Alan, a research chemist, are staying with Big Jim and his wife Irene (60).

Today Mr. Ker was not at the house, and Mr. Taylor and Mrs. Ker explained that [he] had gone to Washington on business and would be back later.

Mr. Taylor, who claims that his hold on the leadership of the Brethren is still unchallenged, said: "Absolutely nothing happened in that bedroom that Mrs. Ker and I are ashamed about.

"It is true she was laying under the sheet on the same bed as myself. But I was on one side of the bed, and she was on the other."

Whose clothes were on the floor?

Said he: "Some of the clothes were mine. I don't know who the other clothes belonged to. I didn't ask her to lie under the sheet. Mrs. K chose to lie under it of her own free will. Certainly nothing improper happened, and it is wrong to say that she was naked."

It read like the Janet and John books. Where is John? John is in the tree. Where is Janet? Janet is in the bedroom. Her clothes are on the floor. Whose clothes were on the floor? Mrs. Ker's clothes were on the floor.

None of it rang true to me. The underpants. The photograph. The stupid, lecherous preacher. By then I was taking drugs, going to concerts, reading E. M. Forster, and memorizing soliloquies from Shakespeare so I could impress my father. But I still distrusted newspapers. I regarded them as worldly and corrupting, full of lies, Satan's way of brainwashing people. And Philip Finn wasn't helping. J.T. Junior's "bedroom dealings," as Finn called them, were grubby and embarrassing, but he had no idea how much damage they were going to inflict on so many Brethren families like mine.

20

It was another thirty years or so before I discovered the full story of Aberdeen, the distressing detail that lay behind the version Philip Finn had written for the *Daily Express*.

Kez found a pamphlet among my father's papers called *If We Walk in the Light.* My father and grandfather wrote it, she said, to help Brethren assemblies decide how to act after the scandal broke. It included scores of witness statements and a transcript made by my father of J.T. Junior's last foulmouthed, rambling preachings given while he was climbing in and out of bed with Mrs. Ker. We found other witness letters archived online. There were no sexual innuendos and winks here. This was deadly serious.

In July 1970, J.T. Junior, seventy-one years old, Brethren Man of God, flew to Britain from New York to lead the summer three-day meeting and to do his usual round of preachings up and down the country. On the morning of July 23 he arrived in Aberdeen by plane and was driven from the airport to a large blue-and-white-painted bungalow called Airylea at Nigg, a southern suburb of the city next to a golf course. A local senior ministering brother named James Alex Gardiner had been given the honor of hosting him. There were several other guests, according to the witness statements: "Dr. and Mrs. Robert Gardiner of Perth, Mr. and Mrs. Jim Gray of Edinburgh, Mr. and Mrs. Edward Steedman of Falkirk, and Miss Anne Gibb of Falkirk."

One of them, Ted Steedman, recorded some of the events of that first day:

We arrived at James Gardiner's house on Thursday evening. Mr. Taylor was in bed resting and joined us about seven P.M.

He very soon paid a great deal of attention to the sisters, spoke in a crude way of their having had relations with men, and constantly asked different ones when the results would be, "When is the delivery?" He made reference to women's bras and seemed obsessed with the sisters' breasts. He made one sister after another sit on his knee, with one especially he kissed her for minutes at a time, putting his mouth over hers and sucking her in a most peculiar way, all the time fondling and caressing her body, making her husband look out the window while doing so. His tactics with other sisters he wanted was to say that they didn't like his ministry, were not with him, and so on, until they came to him. This went on till the Kers came about nine P.M. They should not have been there, but Jim insisted they stay, so that James Gardiner and his wife had to sleep in most difficult circumstances. When he had gone off to bed we found the first sister he had handled was very upset. We found in the morning she was nearly hysterical through the night.

The Kers, a young Brethren couple with four children, were from London. They'd flown to Aberdeen to hear J.T. Junior and were due to stay with other Brethren a few miles away, but had been invited to break their journey at Nigg. There's no mention of the Ker children. Presumably they'd been left at home with family in London.

By nine P.M. J.T. Junior appears to have been drunk, aroused, and frustrated by an evening of groping those poor women. And then in walked pretty Mrs. Ker. Something had been going on between them for a while, some people told me. My father's friend William told me he had seen J.T. Junior groping Mrs. Ker's breasts through a car window in a car lot outside a meeting a few weeks earlier when he'd first arrived in Britain.

J.T. Junior insisted that the Kers stay in the Gardiner's bungalow rather than in the accommodation that had been arranged for them nearby. The Gardiners had to give up their bedroom and make up a bed for themselves on the floor.

According to James Gardiner, later that evening, Alan Ker "led his wife," barefooted and in her dressing gown, through the kitchen, dining room, and living room to the room where J.T. Junior was staying at the back of the house. He returned to his bedroom alone. The following morning, Mrs. Gardiner saw Mrs. Ker leaving J.T. Junior's bedroom. All through the day, Mrs. Ker went back to the bedroom between meetings. J.T. Junior was almost an hour late for the afternoon session. James Gardiner knocked on the door of his room but got no response. Twenty minutes later Mrs. Ker came out, saying she'd had to wait until she was "released."

Alan Ker led her through to J.T. Junior's bedroom again that night, again returning to his own room alone.

So far Mrs. Ker had been described as compliant. While the other female guests had become upset by all the gropings, some even "hysterical," Madeline Ker in her dressing gown and bare feet calmly allowed herself to be led back and forth to J.T. Junior's bedroom by her husband. She was behaving in a completely *subject* way, as Brethren women were supposed to do. But, one of the witnesses said, when she was prevented from going to J.T. Junior, she became "impudent." When James Gardiner reminded her that he was the head of the house and responsible for what happened in it, she said to him, "I don't accept you as head of this house."

I was surprised how much Mrs. Ker's behavior shocked me. It was so un-Brethren-like. Here was a Brethren woman standing up to the Brethren men, just so she could go back to that lecher's bed. I'd give my right arm, I thought, to be given an hour to ask Mrs. Ker what was going on, why she'd let herself be led like that. But no one was asking Madeline Ker anything. They were just calling her names.

The following day, Saturday, Mr. Gardiner tried to barricade the route to J.T. Junior's bedroom to stop the Kers from getting through. Mr. and Mrs. Ker tried to break down the door, cracking a glass panel. Later in the day, Mrs. Ker managed to slip into the bedroom, staying there alone with J.T. Junior for some time, so that they were again late for the afternoon meetings. When she came out of the room she told her host that J.T. Junior wanted him to know that he was a "son of a bitch and a bastard."

"It is hard," Ted Steedman wrote, "to put on paper the atmosphere of madness." When J.T. Junior woke the next day, Steedman wrote, he was calm, presumably sober. He gave a good address in the morning meeting. But he started drinking again at lunchtime, Steedman recorded, "His demeanor changed, as though something came over his mind. He became nasty, almost animal-like, and his conversation unclean."

What kind of monster was this, sitting at his host's dinner table and making the women sit on his lap in turn so he could grope their breasts and suck at their mouths in front of their husbands? These were people my parents knew. People who had been to stay in our house, slept in our spare room. Good people. Eminent Brethren men. What would my father have done if he'd been there and J.T. Junior had tried to touch my mother like that?

21

J.T. Junior wasn't just climbing into bed with Mrs. Ker. He was also preaching. In the Aberdeen meeting room, where hundreds of Brethren men and women had gathered to hear him, the Jekyll and Hyde of the Airylea bungalow turned into the spitting mouth of Samuel Beckett's *Not I*. You can take almost any page of the forty-page transcript of his Aberdeen preaching at random and J.T. Junior's words and obsessions are pretty much the same, only arranged in a different order. What he says is shocking enough—the words of a man with alcoholic dementia—but so too is the mood of collective hysteria in the meeting room. Could the Brethren gathered there that day really have thought that the Holy Spirit was speaking through this man? And what was my father thinking as he transcribed this madness, which would eventually appear in the whistle-blowing pamphlet he and my grandfather put together?

[Loud laughter and stamping.]

J.T. JUNIOR: Now we must get on with this meeting here and the next address: Now we have Mr. George Terries. The next address. You never had it so good. You big boob, you. And then, the next is what? Because we're still producing [not clear]. We had the hell of a time in our house just a few minutes ago—'ell of a life. That so-and-so. But it's number two now. We got number one. That's number one, that's George Terries. Anybody know him? Anybody know George Terries? We're going to have the 'ell of a time here. I want to tell you my purpose that he's a very good factory. I'm still looking for that. George is number one . . . number two is coming but it comes slow. She's in terrific pain. You bastard! You bastard! We need a doctor here. Go to sleep, Stanley, go to sleep. We have plenty of hymns, to hell with you. We're having a very good time. You bum, you. You big bum. Scott! Bum! Scott! Bum! Scott! Bum! Scott! Bum! Scott! Bum! Now you have it. You never have it. You never had it so good. You never had it like this, you nut, you.

[Forty-second pause with bursts of laughter, shouting.]

J.T. JUNIOR: You stinking bum! You stink! Why didn't you bring some toilet paper with you? Very fine meetings.

MBT [IDENTITY OF SPEAKER UNKNOWN]: Yes, first-class.

[Pause with indistinct remarks and laughter, then shouts of laughter with cheering, whistling, and stamping.]

MBT: What I would like to know, Mr. Taylor—is this to be the pattern for all meetings?

J.T. JUNIOR: Look at that son of a bitch there.

[Pause culminating again in laughter, stamping, and whistling.]

J.T. JUNIOR: You never had it like this before. You bastard, you.

[Loud laughter, stamping, and whistling.]

I wanted to hear what the "loud laughter" sounded like. When I found the audio recording of the meeting that someone from PEEB had put online, that laughter didn't sound anxious or hysterical as I had expected. People were guffawing. J.T. Junior must have been miming and gesturing and playing the clown, because the audience sometimes laughed in the long pauses when no one was saying anything. Sometimes the laughter and whistling went on for half a minute or more.

Had they all gone mad? Was this a kind of collective hysteria, like the one that happened in the Salem witch trials? Did they think that God actually sounded like this?

J.T. Junior goaded the older men in the meeting with jokes about feces, constipation, and purging. His preoccupation with spiritual cleanliness—a lifetime of using words like "spewing" and "purging"— had turned into a sequence of grubby jokes about bottoms and bums.

J.T. JUNIOR: David, where the hell you been? Thank God for you. I thank God for you every time. You been stinking somewhere. What you been doing at?

DJD [IDENTITY OF SPEAKER UNKNOWN]: In hell.

J.T. JUNIOR: You haven't had any privilege to do that. You feeling better? Thank God for that. You feeling better, David? Thank God for that. You feeling better, David? Thank God for that. Are you feeling better, David? Thank God for that. The whole thing too. What about your intestines? Was that the trouble? To hell with them! 'ell with them. 'ell with them. You hear that, George? George! You st . . . George! Did you hear? Yes. You st . . . 'ell with the other one! 'ell with the other one! Stay awake, you boob! What do you think, we're going to get on with all these songs from Detroit? To hell with them, 'ell with them, I said. 'ell with them! You big bum, you. You never had it so good. And don't you think, don't you think you're going to go away with this stuff. You here, what's your name? Son of a bitch.

JOHN GASKIN: John Gaskin.

J.T. JUNIOR: Get up. You look like nothing. Sit down! You never had it like this before. Eric! Awake? You awake there? Well, get up and perform, Eric, get up. Get up, Eric. Get up! Eric, get up. Sit down. You never had it like this before. You stupid people here, what do you think I am? I'm a professor. Here, you, I'm not finished with you yet. You nut! Get up. I'm not finished with you yet. Well, I'll tell you this. Don't you mention any cars anymore, remember? So what the hell are you? Skunk. You never had it like this before. That son of a bitch. I was very careful using the word "son of a bitch" because I wouldn't know. I wouldn't know you have to be careful about it. Is everything all right with your bowels? You never had it so good. Stand up, Mr. Gardiner. I would like to introduce you to Nicodemus. And will you answer the question that I ask you, Nicodemus? You couldn't. Who are you? Who are you?

22

According to the witness reports, after this extraordinary afternoon meeting, J.T. Junior and Mrs. Ker disappeared off into the bedroom again. Stanley McCallum arrived for dinner. He was one of the top brass, one of J.T. Junior's right-hand men. No one dared tell him what was going on. Someone asked Mr. Ker where his wife was. He told them she was resting. An hour or two passed. Someone asked when Mrs. Ker and J.T. Junior were going to appear. They carried on waiting. Eventually McCallum said, "There is something wrong in this house," and the older men said, "Yes, there is."

James Gardiner went through to J.T. Junior's bedroom and opened the door. He found Mrs. Ker undressed and in bed with J.T. Junior, who was wearing his pajama top, which was open at the front. Gardiner called Mr. Ker and told him to get his wife out and summoned Stanley McCallum to the bedroom to witness the scene. When McCallum reprimanded J.T. Junior, J.T. Junior brazened it out: "The devil is in you," he roared, "and I have to get him out! You've been wrong all your life."

Gardiner pointed at Mrs. Ker's clothes, lying on the floor, but J.T. Junior said, "You can't prove they are her clothes." When Gardiner demanded that the Kers leave his house, J.T. Junior yelled, "She's my woman!" He tried to leave with the Kers but was prevented. Though it was long past midnight, Gardiner called the doctor who had been attending J.T. Junior for several weeks. He gave J.T. Junior a sedative injection, which sent him to sleep. The following morning, J.T. Junior's son, James the Third, heavily sedated flew his father back to New York.

By the time Stanley McCallum got back to the United States himself, J.T. Junior's spin doctors had told his local assembly that he had plotted J.T. Junior's overthrow and that he was a homosexual and a Sodomite, and had a criminal record.

In Aberdeen, Gardiner and the other shell-shocked bungalow witnesses put together their accounts and sent them to the New York assembly.

In New York, J.T. Junior's supporters, concerned about the press attention the story was getting, rang Philip Finn, and offered him an interview in J.T. Junior's house with the Kers present. It did not go well, what with the underpants and the whiskey and all. J.T. Junior did not do himself any favors. If he'd wanted sex, he told Finn, would he have spent a thousand dollars and gone all the way to *Aberdeen*? "Brooklyn," he joked, "would have been cheaper."

J.T. Junior, backed by his supporters and the Hales brothers, now spun a new defense. Over the following weeks, the story gave way to a more sophisticated and nuanced narrative: Aberdeen, Brethren were told, had been a deliberate test of loyalty—devised, designed, and orchestrated by the Lord himself to identify and expel interlopers as the Rapture approached. By this point even the Kers were repeating this story. They'd keep doing so for decades.

In a few weeks, Brethren spin doctors had turned J.T. Junior from a lecherous alcoholic bully to a martyr, prepared to jeopardize his personal honor for the Lord's Truth and to ensure a final necessary purge before the Rapture began. But then, just three months after Aberdeen, J.T. Junior died of an alcohol-related disease.

When I made my promise to my father on his deathbed that I would try to finish his book, complete the part of the story he had not been able to face, chronicle the Nazi decade he'd talked about, I started off thinking of myself as a detective solving a crime. Now that I could finally see the full abject picture of those ten years, I wasn't gathering the details just for my father anymore. I wanted to explain all of this to the child in the red cardigan I'd once been, the girl who'd done her best to understand the deranged world she was born into but who just ended up furious and confused. I wanted to tell her that someone would put the pieces of the puzzle together. I'd done that, I realized— for her, for me.

But once I assembled the facts into order, there seemed to be no easy explanation I could offer either to my father or to my younger self. There was no culprit to be caught, no handcuffs to be placed on the wrists of a single murderer or thief. The questions the story raised were like the heads of the Hydra of Greek myth: Cut off the head of one question and several others grew in its place. How had J.T. Junior managed to remain in power for so long? How had so many clever, good people been led into such a cruel system? How had men like my father allowed themselves to become exactors and interrogators, bullying people into confessing imaginary sins? And once they'd finally seen that system for what it was—a projection of an alcoholic's paranoia, delusion, and hunger for power—what did they do about it?

Aftermath

1

In the hours after Aberdeen, my father told me, the details of what had happened began to travel along telephone lines that branched throughout the world. James Gardiner telephoned my grandfather in Hove, one of many calls he made that night. He described the details of what had happened in the Airylea bungalow, the showdown, the fact that the Aberdeen assembly had withdrawn from J.T. Junior and that most other Scottish assemblies were expected to follow suit.

My grandfather, carrying the news like a grenade clutched to his heart, telephoned my father and summoned him. I imagine the two of them together in my grandfather's sitting room, under the framed text about Jehovah always watching you, my grandfather struggling to find the words for what James Gardiner had told him. Though they were shocked and disgusted by what J.T. Junior had done, they would hardly have dared to think about the scale of the trouble that was about to begin.

My father and grandfather were by now high-ranking Brethren. My grandfather was a Stow Hill Depot trustee. My father had taken meetings across Europe and North America. Whatever Stott father and son did now, whatever position they took, other Brethren—at least in the south of England—would follow. They prayed. They sought the Lord's will. And they decided that they would have to get the truth to as many Brethren across the world as they could, before any counter-stories from New York set like concrete around them all, before the Haleses supporters got hold of the Depot. The clock was ticking.

Two days later, on the afternoon of July 28, 1970, as hundreds of holiday-makers dozed in deck chairs on the Brighton seafront, 450 shocked Brethren brothers and sisters dressed in their best clothes, polished their shoes, put on their hats, and headed for the meeting room on Vale Avenue, a large new purpose-built hall with high walls and two high narrow slit windows on the northern edge of Brighton. There was only one item on the agenda for this particular meeting: Aberdeen.

After all the phone calls and the secret meetings at our house or around the corner at my grandparents' house, after the praying, the late-night lights-out conversations with their wives, this care meeting would determine how the Brighton assembly would act.

In our house my mother must have put supper on the table as usual. She and I would have run the bath, spread out the towels on the radiators, heated the milk, sterilized the bottles, bathed and fed the babies—my brother bundled on my lap, my sister on my mother's— and tucked them into their cots as we always did. My brothers kicked their ball around in the garden in the twilight. Blackbirds sang in the lilac tree. It was just like any other night.

I asked my father and, later, William to describe the final Vale Avenue showdown. Forty-five years later, they still remembered every detail.

Brethren men filed into the lower front seats of the amphitheater-shaped room. These front rows had been fitted with handheld microphones every few feet. The women took their positions in the upper outer circles, where there were no microphones. William found a seat a few rows away from my father. His wife had stayed at home, too terrified to watch the inevitable confrontation.

When everyone had settled, John Railton, the self-appointed leader of the Brighton Brethren and a J.T. Junior hard-liner, reached for his microphone and stood to denounce the rumors from Scotland. It was a conspiracy, he declared. Satan was behind it. Stanley McCallum was behind it. How could anyone dare to say such things about the Man of God? It was an aberration.

William described how my father—only thirty-two years old—rose slowly to his feet. At six foot four inches tall, he towered above everyone else. Just as he'd agreed with my grandfather, he began to tell the Aberdeen story as he'd been told it, carefully, without drama, a simple relation of the facts.

John Railton shouted him down after he'd only spoken a few sentences. Declaring him "not fit for the fellowship of God's son," he withdrew from him. When my father picked up his Bible, coat, and hat and walked toward the door, no one followed.

"I drove home," he told me, "feeling as if I was going to be hit by a mighty bolt from the sky at any moment. It was a genuine physical dread."

William was sure he was going to be sick. He was paralyzed, glued to his chair, unable to stand. He watched a man across the other side of the room stand to object to my father's expulsion. Railton withdrew from him too.

As William watched that man pick his way through the crowd toward the door, another man—my father's cousin-in-law this time—stood to protest and was withdrawn from.

Now William found his feet and gestured for the nearest microphone to be passed to him. He wanted, he said, to ask a simple question about the Man of God. He wanted some clarification.

"Can the Man of God," he asked, "do *anything*?"

Railton roared back: "The Man of God is *pure*. The man of God is pure."

Now he declared William withdrawn from too.

William remembers a group of men sitting a few seats away, including two of his brothers-in-law, turning toward him. One of them said, "Get out, you bastard," and the chant spread slowly around the room. Soon everyone was chanting:

Get—out—you—bastard. Get—out—you—bastard.

William began the long walk to the door. He told me that he looked at the contorted faces of the chanting old men, one by one, as he passed them, reminding himself that the mortgage to his house belonged to one of them.

I remembered the story he had told me about how he asked his father where his uncle had disappeared to, and his father replied, "Outside the door, son, there is only darkness."

"I have grown afraid of the dark," William had said.

Now here he was all those years later walking directly to the Vale Avenue meeting room door. There was no one outside among the parked cars waiting for him. My father and the others were gone, and no one had followed him out. He was entirely alone under that huge black sky. He told me he stood there, in the parking lot, for a long time.

He remembered, he said, every detail of the drive home through Brighton streets that night. His head spun with panicked questions. Would he ever see his parents or siblings again? Where were he and his wife going to live when their Brethren mortgage had been withdrawn and they had to sell the house? Where would they go when his Brethren employers sacked him? What if his wife didn't want to come with him?

When he reached home he told his wife he'd been withdrawn from. To his relief, she put her arms around him and said that if he had not walked out, she would have left him.

My grandfather, who was still in the Vale Avenue meeting room as the chants subsided, told my father the rest of the story.

John Railton, his blood high now that he'd expelled so many, now that he'd gotten the chanting started, took the microphone again. If

Mr. Taylor wanted to take *his* wife, Eunice, to bed, he said, he'd feel honored.

He'd miscalculated. This was the straw that broke the assembly's back. My grandfather now rose to his feet. He could not, he said into his microphone, condone what had transpired in Aberdeen. If anyone in the room agreed with him, they should join him in walking out now. Half of the people in the meeting room stood up and headed for the door. Two hundred of them.

I wish I'd seen it.

2

My father parked his car on the drive, climbed the steps, opened the front door, and told my waiting mother that he'd been withdrawn from. She showed him the bags she'd packed, told him, just as William's wife had done, that if he hadn't been withdrawn from she would have left on her own and taken the children with her. My parents must have sat in the tidy sitting room looking nervously at each other. Perhaps he poured himself a whiskey. Perhaps they prayed.

Twenty minutes or so would have passed before they heard the sound of cars, voices coming up the front steps: my grandfather, my cousins, old people, young people, in family groups or alone, William and his wife among them. I think of my mother opening the door, wondering where she'd find chairs for everyone, boiling the kettle, opening boxes of chocolate marshmallows, pouring tea, hoping the voices wouldn't wake the five children she'd spent so long trying to get to sleep. I sat at the top of the stairs out of sight, holding my stuffed rabbit, listening. My younger brother came to sit next to me, rubbing his eyes. Eventually we crept back to bed, falling asleep to the murmur of those voices downstairs.

They must have had to do head counts. Who had walked out? Who was still in there? What were they going to do now? They'd have given thanks for their release; they'd have prayed for the Lord's guidance. They agreed that to start with they'd use the smallest Brethren meeting room, on Edward Avenue, just a few streets away from our house. My grandfather still had the keys. The Lord would show them the way.

My father and my grandfather took the lead. The first thing they had to do, they said, was to get the truth about J.T. Junior out to as many people still "inside" as they could reach. They'd use the printing presses at the Depot. Two of the four Depot trustees, it seemed, were now "out," and my grandfather had the keys to the offices. Unless someone had already intercepted it, the audio recording of J.T. Junior's Aberdeen address would already be on its way to the Depot in the mail. Someone needed to get there to pick it up. Once they had the tape, they'd transcribe it, gather all the witness statements, and print a pamphlet. They'd post it out to Brethren around the world using the Depot's networks, before anyone in New York knew what was going on.

My father and grandfather couldn't have slept much over the next few weeks. Phone calls to and from Brethren around the world continued long into the night, every night. My father typed out the copies of the Aberdeen witness letters that Gardiner sent from Scotland and transcribed the bizarre, expletive-ridden, and sexualized ramblings of J.T. Junior's Aberdeen address from the tape recording when it arrived at the Depot. That tape was important. J.T. Junior was claiming he had said nothing controversial in the Aberdeen address. The tape would be proof that he was lying.

No one at home was sleeping much either. My mother was feeding and minding, washing and dressing, five young children, including three-month-old twins. She was keeping up appearances. Praying, cooking meals, sterilizing bottles, and when necessary providing beds and food for the many sleep-deprived Brethren who came to our house to consult my father. She would have listened to him relaying the news as it unfolded, keeping a close eye on the way things were going. She'd been praying for years, she told me later, that we might all be released from a system that she knew was wicked. Now it had finally happened. The Lord had taken our family through the Brethren door and out into the world. My mother seemed different to me then, excited and bright-eyed. She didn't show her happiness and relief to visitors, but she couldn't hide it from me. I was always by her side, watching.

"For most of us," my father wrote in the introduction to the pamphlet they'd decided to call *If We Walk in the Light,* "it was like waking up from a prolonged bad dream. If we were honest we had to admit that, like Agur (Proverbs 30:2), we had been 'more stupid than anyone.'"

After Aberdeen, it was not disgust or anger or outrage that my father felt most acutely, but *stupidity.* But it's not my father and his wounded pride that haunts me. It's Elsie and Winnie Rhodes walking into that pond; fourteen-year-old "Ruth" pulling her father off her half-dead mother; it's Eva turning on the gas oven in the empty house, knowing she'd never see her sister again. How many decent people had been betrayed, tortured, and tormented by this madman and his cronies and this inhuman system they'd made?

The Exclusive Brethren had turned into a cult and played out their torments *in plain sight,* in the suburbs of provincial towns all around the world. How many non-Brethren teachers, doctors, coroners, psychiatrists, lawyers, and judges must have seen glimpses of what was going on and looked away for fear of causing offense? A doctor once listened to me describe Satan as he appeared in my bedroom at night. Instead of asking me or my parents questions, he'd ordered a urine sample to be taken. A nurse at the hospital that cared for Rhina must surely have seen Eva's distress when she realized that the Brethren would not let her see her sister again. An administrator at the egg marketing board had read Elsie and Winnie Rhodes's letter in which the sisters had quoted the Scriptures as explanation for canceling their membership. He might have smiled at how batty religious people could be before he filed it away. Despite the strenuous efforts the modern Brethren make to seal off their people from any contact with the outside world, how many teachers, doctors, psychiatrists, and judges are still turning a blind eye?

3

Eight thousand Exclusive Brethren members, including the two or three hundred defectors in Brighton, walked out of their suburban meeting rooms across the world, or were withdrawn from, in July 1970 or soon after. They formed a new schism, a group with no name. Later people would call us the Non-Taylorite Exclusive Brethren. My parents and all the other adults must have been in a state of extreme shock. They would have felt lost and rudderless. They sought guidance from the Lord, as they'd always done. They'd been delivered from wrongdoing, but now they had to find their way back to the light and to the right road. After the agonies of the screw-turning years, all these families had to learn to live in a world they knew almost nothing about and had been taught to fear. They would have to take stock, repent, pray, and start again. Within two years they'd split several more times.

Though my father was soon preaching regularly in Britain and Europe to small assemblies of Non-Taylorite Exclusive Brethren, he couldn't shake off that feeling of stupidity. It frustrated him that people weren't facing up to what had happened; a year after Aberdeen he gave an address about how some Brethren were already slipping back into the old ways, into the old sectarianism.

"What made us so weak and ignorant that we allowed these things to be imposed on us?" he wrote in a Brethren address published in late 1971, "and then in many cases joined in the imposing ourselves? Even now, when our folly is manifest to all, we have still retained an unconscious tendency to condescend to other believers." He was still using the Brethren language, he was still preaching, but his certainties had begun to unravel.

In December 1971 my father gave an address on Hayling Island, along the coast to the west of Brighton, near Portsmouth. After the preaching, William told me, he and my father drove back across the South Downs after dark. A few miles from Brighton, my father took a detour and parked the car by the side of a road that looked out over the great gulf of Devil's Dyke, a dramatic notch in the Sussex Downs a few miles north of Brighton, said by local legend to have been carved by the devil when he tried to let the sea in and flood the country. He had something he wanted to say, he told William. After he had switched off the headlights and the darkness had closed around the car, he said:

"I don't think I believe anything to do with Christianity."

When William described my father's strange confession, I felt once again as if I was looking through a keyhole, seeing something I wasn't supposed to see. What did those words *mean*? My father hadn't said, "I don't believe in God"; he'd said he didn't believe "anything to do with Christianity." I wasn't sure what "anything to do with Christianity" actually meant. Perhaps he didn't know either.

"He'd just been *preaching*," William said, "preaching to hundreds of Brethren at Hayling Island. He was good. People trusted him, looked to him to take a lead. But he hadn't believed a word of what he was saying."

The fact that my father had preached without believing the words he spoke made William angry. Of course it did. Perhaps he was thinking that if my father had done this once, then he might have done it several times. How hollow was he? I considered telling William that my father had not always meant the things he said, that he'd once given a preaching in which he'd broken an important promise he'd made to me when he'd told people I had asked if the Holy Spirit was the Lord Jesus's mother. But I didn't say anything.

Instead I wanted to defend my father.

"Sometimes it takes people a while to see things," I said.

After all, hadn't this dreadful system forced so many Brethren to dissemble in order to survive? I wondered how many hundreds of Brethren children had feigned absolute belief in Brethren doctrine rather than shame their parents. After a while it was impossible to tell what was authentic and what was performed, what you believed and what you merely said you believed. You began to wonder which parts of you were true anymore.

I could picture those two still-young men, both afraid of the dark, looking down over the void, that violent slash in the landscape, trying to work out what to do and where to go, trying to be honest with each other. They must both have known what my father's words meant. They were, it seemed, going to have to go in different directions. My father's Christian beliefs—if they had ever been beliefs—were fracturing.

A few weeks later, in January 1972, William told me, he and my father both withdrew from the Edward Avenue assembly. They'd lost their faith in the Brethren, but William was still a devout Christian and my father wasn't. William and his wife had decided to join a new church. At that very last meeting, the two men stood to read out the letters they'd written explaining their decisions.

I wish that in that meeting, my mother and William's wife had stood up to have their say too, for the very first and last time. I'd like to have heard that. But they'd spent their entire lives in a fellowship in which women never spoke, so by then it must have been psychologically impossible for them to speak in a Brethren meeting. I like to think they had already cut ties with the fellowship, that they were eager to go, but I imagine they were frightened. They did not know what the world was going to be like out there.

I didn't find my father's "resignation" letter in any of the boxes.

Perhaps he hadn't kept it. But going by the preoccupations of the preachings he made around this time, it's likely that he talked about how Non-Taylorite Exclusive Brethren were gradually returning to their splitting and shunning ways and how he didn't want to be part of that, because the Lord had shown him it was wrong. He knew this was to be the last time he had the floor, so he would have taken his time over writing and delivering his last words. This was his Brethren swan song.

When he finished reading his letter, he walked out, taking my mother and all of us with him. I have no memory of the occasion, but I can still see the meeting room clearly in my mind's eye. We sat in the back row as usual, in our Lord's Day clothes, my mother at the end, next to the twins in their two strollers. When my father finished his speech, the Brethren probably launched uncomfortably into another tuneless hymn to cover the sound of our clatter and the bang of the door as we filed out after him with our hats, Bibles, and coats.

It couldn't have been easy for him. Non-Taylorite Exclusive Brethren were not as strict about separatism, so he knew we'd still be able to see all the family we were leaving behind—his parents, siblings, nieces, and nephews—but we would not be Brethren anymore. He knew the Brethren would say that my father and mother were turning their backs on the light and consigning their children to the darkness. They would be praying for us all the time, for our return and our salvation.

William told me he saw my father on only four occasions after we left the Brethren. He and his wife met us in a park for tea in 1972, a few months after leaving that last meeting, and they came to see my father playing Richard the Lionheart in a production of *The Lion in Winter* a year after that. "Your father was very good," he told me. "He had a strong stage presence." Seeing what a good actor he was, he added, had made him wonder whether he had been acting all through his Brethren life. I was thinking that too.

After that, he said, he and my father lost contact for decades. He and his wife went to live in another country, and when they finally came back to England, William tracked my father down to the Tunbridge Wells apartment where he was living after he'd been sacked from the BBC. He was shocked by the state my father was in, how unkempt he was, but they talked for hours just the same, played classical CDs together, had lunch in the local theater café. Then, decades later, he visited my father in the hospital in Bury St. Edmunds six weeks before he died.

The remaining Non-Taylorite Brethren, including my aunt, my grandparents, and a few of my father's first cousins and their families, splintered into new groups as new leaders stressed slightly different ways of separating from the world. Each new faction now came to be known by the name of its leader—the Rentons, the Frosts, the Walkers, the Strangs. They found new, ever-smaller meeting rooms and broke bread together in their own particular ways. Each of them believed they'd found the right new path and that they had returned to the light.

My grandfather, grandmother, and uncle went with the Frosts. My aunt and her husband and small children went with the Rentons. For the rest of their lives they would disagree about doctrine and practice and about the correct ways to "withdraw from iniquity." We still saw these aunts, uncles, and cousins for dinners and occasional birthday parties, but it was often awkward. I always felt they were watching me, trying to work out how worldly I was becoming. I seemed to be always saying the wrong things, giving the wrong answers to their questions.

Eventually the Brethren Frosts subdivided yet again into what they now refer to as Hard Frosts and Soft Frosts. They still shun each other. They are not allowed to attend one another's funerals or weddings. Sometimes I hear stories about trouble in the Renton ranks: A small group has risen up to defend someone who has been withdrawn from. Others take up the hard-line separatist stance. They split. More people get withdrawn from. It's that shameful Red-Tiler-Blue-Tiler story all over again.

4

Perhaps in 1972 our parents thought we were too young to understand why we'd left. My brothers were eight and five; I was seven, the twins one. Perhaps they thought we hadn't been listening when they told us that televisions and radios were wicked, that Satan was in cinemas, newspapers, pop music, theaters, that the world outside our meeting room was corrupt to the core and would corrupt us if we went anywhere near it. Perhaps they thought we'd be delighted when they installed a television set and a radio in our house and took us to the cinema.

Perhaps they'd forgotten that they'd been telling us since we were born that the Rapture was about to come and that if we had not given up our wills and desires and natural minds to the Lord, we'd be left behind when everyone we knew disappeared off the planet and the bad people would be drowned, burned, buried alive.

But we children did not cast off Brethren teachings easily or quickly. I became, in this post-Aberdeen confusion, preoccupied with sin and salvation, particularly after my parents left the Edward Avenue meeting and began to take us to a succession of local churches.

In the spring of 1972, just months after we'd walked out of the Edward Avenue meeting room for the last time, my parents started to take us to church services on Sundays. I was still expected to put on my Best Dress, but the neat pile of triangular headscarves that my mother had made for me, that I'd kept in my top drawer, disappeared altogether. We didn't have to get up in the dark anymore. We were allowed to sleep until nine o'clock on the Lord's Day. We'd go to a new church for a few weeks, shake hands, and smile, and then my parents would try another: the Baptists on Holland Road; the Methodists on Portland Road; even, eventually, the Anglicans on Nevil Avenue.

Once we were inside we recited "The Lord's Prayer" along with everyone else. The other people knew the words by heart, but we had to read them from the sheet we were given. We were supposed to memorize it, my mother said. My father didn't appear to like any of the churches. He didn't seem to think the preachers were any good. I heard him complaining about the sermons to my mother. Within a few weeks he stopped going altogether, but my mother carried on taking us to the Anglican church on Nevil Avenue. My headscarves still hadn't turned up.

The way these other people worshipped bore no relation to the way we'd done things in the Brethren. But even if I'd felt able to ask questions, I wouldn't have known where to begin, and I was pretty certain my mother didn't know the answers anyway. She looked just as bewildered as I was. These people were Christians, my mother said, just like us, but everything they did was different—the words they used for things, the places they put things, even the way they arranged their chairs. In this new world:

Churches had pulpits and altars.
The people were called congregations.
They sat in rows rather than in circles.
The women and children were allowed to sit with the men.
Some of the women wore trousers.
The men in the rows didn't preach.
Only the men in the pulpits preached, and they wore robes.
Only the very old women wore hats.
Someone invisible played organ music when we sang hymns.
People knelt to pray.
There were no headscarves.
There was a sheet of words we were supposed to follow.

Sometimes we were supposed to join in and say things all
   together.

They talked about Jesus rather than the Lord Jesus.

They read passages from the Bible that I didn't recognize.

They talked about Sunday, not the Lord's Day.

They didn't talk about Satan or the Rapture or about clean
   houses.

No one was doing any "withdrawing from iniquity."

I was pretty sure they must have a completely different God up
there. I couldn't see how *our* Lord would be happy to come in here
with all those pictures, crucifixes, and statues.

At home things were upside down too. My father announced one
Saturday afternoon, when my mother and I were polishing the brass,
that he was taking her and us three older children to the cinema to
see *Gone with the Wind*. I glanced at my mother, alarmed, but she
did not protest. It seems astonishing now, but I remember almost
nothing of the film apart from some shots of alarmed horses and the
great fire that engulfed the land around Tara, but I do remember
reaching out for my mother's hand at the moment we stepped across
the threshold into the richly colored entrance hall and, later, watching her face in profile, flickering in the light from the screen, rapt and
terrified by turns, happier I think than I'd ever seen her.

It wasn't that I believed we were now Satan's people, or that we'd
been plunged into some dark new world, or that the worldly people
we were now allowed to talk to would trick and corrupt us, rather
that someone had changed all the rules. It was like being lost in a
town where all the signs had been changed into a language I didn't
know. I remember sometimes reaching out to touch hard surfaces to
see if I was awake.

There were other vertigo-inducing changes. Our meals and domestic routines and bedtimes had always been arranged around the

times of the meeting, especially on weekends. Without meetings, our days were shaped differently. The twins were walking now, usually in different directions. My mother was grateful to have me mind them when she was busy. I carried them back into safe range when they strayed into the flower beds under the lilac tree or fed them after she carried their high chairs out into the garden. My two brothers seemed delighted by all the new things they were allowed to do: the football stickers they collected and stuck into albums, the comics my father brought home for them, and the children's programs on the television set. But they must also have been struggling to make sense of what was happening.

I found a photograph of my brother and me in 1972. We are launching a model of a hot-air balloon I'd made with a basket fashioned from matchboxes. My Tribulation-survivalist fantasies had become more elaborate. Since I'd seen a full-size hot-air balloon drift across the sky above our house, I'd begun to wonder if I could engi-

My younger brother and me photographed in the family garden in 1972

neer ways to escape flooding using flight. When my balloon model got snagged on our new television aerial, I decided the Lord had made it happen to show us his disapproval of our new television set.

My father began to bring home art films. In September 1972, for my eighth birthday present, he brought home four reels of Zeffirelli's *Romeo and Juliet*. Sword fights, chickens, medieval Verona, and velvet and satin costumes crackled and flickered through the projector and up onto the wall of our darkened sitting room. The words rose and fell, or fizzed like sparklers. But despite my father's careful explanation of the story—the star-crossed lovers and the feuding families—I couldn't follow what was happening. My brothers soon found excuses to leave the room. My mother left to put the twins to bed. Before I eventually fell asleep on the sofa, I watched my father's face caught in the light from the screen. He was transfixed, his eyes wide, just as my mother's had been in the cinema, but he was also mouthing the actor's words to himself. Did he know the words to the whole play? *How* did he know them?

When I started a new middle school that year, I was allowed to attend school assembly for the first time. Assembly was worse than church. It wasn't that I disapproved but rather that I didn't understand the language of mild sentimental Anglicanism that my teachers used. There was a lot of talk about sharing and loving your neighbor; we were expected to do a lot of clapping.

"I love God's tiny creatures," we sang, "that wander wild and free. The coral-coated ladybird, the velvet humming bee." None of the Brethren hymns that I remembered had any animals or birds in them.

When I walked the school grounds, from the gym where we did PE to the outdoor pool where we had swimming lessons to the classroom where we practiced eleven-plus exams sitting at desks arranged in neat rows, I sometimes felt as if I was walking on the moon. I failed to find a way to explain to my teachers or the other children why I didn't know the rules of rounders or netball or how to climb a rope. After years of being asked to leave the classroom for so many lessons, I still found myself waiting for a teacher to send me out. But now they didn't. Sometimes, when the classroom was very noisy, I wished they would. My teachers praised my abilities, particularly in reading and writing, in the school reports they wrote during these years, but they complained that I seemed to have a problem concentrating.

Many people assume that leaving a cult like the Brethren must be exhilarating. "You had no TV or pop music or cinema," they say, "and then you did? It must have been amazing!"

But when you see interviews with people who have recently left cults, they describe feeling bewildered and frightened; their eyes dart around, searching for points of reference, metaphors that will get somewhere close to describing the feeling of being lost, not at home, without walls.

No one, of course, shrugs off years of indoctrination in one go. Many escapees go back to the Brethren after a few weeks, not only because they miss their families—which would be reason enough—or because they didn't have the skills to get work, but because the world frightened them. You can't just *refuse to believe* that the world belongs to Satan if you've heard it repeated over and over since you were born. It's under your skin. People also describe the difficulty of making choices—moral, financial, domestic, professional, and emotional—because inside the Brethren there are virtually no choices *to* make. The language that the non-Brethren speak seems different too.

At eight years old I still did not know how to talk to the other children at school or how to bridge the void between their world and mine. I was pretty certain the Rapture was still coming—after all, no one had told me otherwise—but I had no idea who'd be taken now that my parents had started to watch television and films and go to other churches. I'd stand with my back to the wall on the playground watching the children skipping rope, singing their complicated rhymes, and I'd be conjuring Tribulation scenarios, imagining tidal waves sweeping across the tarmac, storms tearing down the playground walls and trees, the Four Horsemen galloping across rooftops, lights out and sea levels rising. "Icky wicky wai cho, chai chickenora," someone would be chanting, or a group of children would be creeping slowly across the playground, calling out, "What's the time, Mr. Wolf?" They still didn't know what was coming. But nor did I anymore.

I began to steal anxiously from the hidden boxes that my mother kept in the house, packets of crisps, Kit Kats, marshmallows in shiny silver and red foil. Concerned about the weight I was gaining, my mother took me shopping to buy me new tentlike clothes in Crimplene, bright yellows and pinks, from a new shop in Brighton called C&A. My mother was still washing my hair in the bath. It had not yet been cut, and hung down my back in two tightly braided ropes.

No one teased me much at school—they just avoided me. I was always the last to be chosen for teams, the first to stumble on the gym mat or to fall when we were supposed to leapfrog over the gym vaulting horse. My brothers didn't want me in their cricket matches. I was just a girl and I didn't run very fast.

I read my way through the piles of library books I brought home from school and from the public library along the road: Russian, Cornish, and Irish fairy tales, collections of short stories about Arthur and his knights. The girls fared far better in these stories than the girls in the Bible. Their fathers or brothers still exchanged them or married them off, or their stepmothers put them to work, but these girls often ran away, refused to do what they were told, stole keys, disguised themselves, went where they weren't supposed to go, into the west wing of the castle or down into the dungeons; they found out things they were not supposed to know. I began to write stories for my teacher about fairies, swords in stones, and snow girls.

I wasn't the only one flailing around with metaphysics and theology. My younger brother had become preoccupied with original sin.

He and I would often wait for our mother to pick us up from school outside the Booth Museum of Natural History, a strange Victorian building a few hundred yards up from the school gates. Its steps were covered with a canopy, so we could take shelter there if it was raining. The road was at the edge of a park and on the brow of one of the highest hills in Brighton, and from the steps we could look down over the whole of the town through the trees and out to sea. I was sure I could make out the curve of the earth from up there, the sea flecked with cargo ships and sailboats.

One day I noticed that during the walk home from school my little brother was flashing me dark looks. When we got to the steps of the museum and I asked him what was wrong, it all came out in a jumbled rage.

"It's all *your* fault," he said. "It's all *women's* fault. If Eve hadn't made Adam eat the apple we'd all live *forever*."

"He didn't *have* to take it," I said. It was raining, my mother was late, and my shoes were wet. There wasn't much else to say. I was speechless with rage of my own. I couldn't counter the logic of the Genesis story. We'd been taught that every word of the Bible was absolutely true, that it was the *only* truth. He'd trumped me. The Bible had trumped me.

My brother and I didn't speak for days. I was furious about being blamed for stealing his immortality, and he was furious about having had his immortality stolen. There was no easy way to settle this dispute. We'd never discussed Scriptures with my mother; that was my father's terrain. But he was hardly ever home now, and I wouldn't have asked him anyway. I'd resolved to never ask him about the Scriptures again. I went back to my Brethren Bible to check the exact words in Genesis, but there were no exact words. That was always the trouble. It all depended on what you thought the words meant. Did the Bible actually say that it was women's fault? Is that what the story of the forbidden fruit and the serpent meant? Was my brother right? Was it all my fault?

5

At home my parents started to dress differently. My mother had complied with the increasingly strict Brethren dress codes, worn the compulsory headscarf or hat and kept her hemlines long and her necklines high. But she'd also dressed us and herself in the jewel colors that she loved and that the older Brethren women disapproved of: reds and purples, cobalt blues, emerald greens, and lemon yellows. She knitted me that red cardigan with shiny brass buttons.

Now she made herself new clothes in patterned silks and satins, with shorter skirts. She bought purple boots that laced up the front. My father bought her a white leather-and-fur coat. She wore her thick black hair just the same, piled on her head and pinned prettily into place, but she no longer covered it for meeting. I watched the way the sun lingered on her curls. She still read the Bible every day, quietly to herself. She kept it near the sewing pile. My father didn't.

He began to wear well-cut suits and slacks, occasionally a cravat. He grew a beard—Brethren men were not allowed facial hair—and shaped and groomed it. He wore a musky cologne. He lost weight as dramatically as I gained weight. He was handsome and dapper. He bought audiotapes of pop music and played songs by the Seekers—"The Carnival Is Over," "Morningtown Ride"—and by Paul Simon—"Kodachrome," "Mother and Child Reunion"—in the car and in the house, very loudly.

Sometimes he played his favorite six or seven tracks over and over again. "Listen!" he'd yell at us. "Shut up for a minute and listen." Sometimes he stopped the car on a hard shoulder. "And I dreamed I was dying," sang Paul Simon, as the guitar moved to the crescendo and my father turned the volume up as high as it would go so that the whole car shook. "And I dreamed that my soul rose un-ex-pect-ed-ly." We sang too, as loud as we could, all together. Sometimes the lines and melodies seemed to have been set to repeat for days inside my head.

When my mother wasn't in the car, my father would let me climb onto the armrest between the two front seats and push my body up through the sunroof while he drove. I'd fling my arms out wide like the wings of a bird and he'd press his foot on the accelerator and turn the volume up high. "And I dreamed I was flying," I'd sing. "And I dreamed that my soul rose un-ex-pect-ed-ly. . . ." The wind took my breath away and made my braids fly out behind me.

"Go faster!" I'd shout. "Go *faster*."

In the summer of 1972, my father joined Wick Theatre Company, an amateur group based in Southwick. Three young actor siblings—Vincent, Monica, and Peter Joyce—gave him lists of music to listen to.

"He'd never heard the Beatles," Monica told me on the phone from Corsica recently. "We couldn't believe it. He'd actually never heard the Beatles! That's how shut off he'd been. How can anyone have lived through the sixties in Brighton and never heard the Beatles? I mean, he was like Rip van Winkle. He couldn't believe how beautiful everything was. . . . I made him tapes of all my favorite music, several every week."

Wick players put on three plays a year in a barn that had been converted into a theater in Southwick. Now my father would come home from the warehouse, eat the meal my mother had cooked for him alone in front of the television news, and disappear out again to a rehearsal. Sometimes he'd sweep into one of our bedrooms to play us a new song. Occasionally he'd weep in the half darkness when he played "Bridge over Troubled Water," and that would make us cry too. The smell of his aftershave would linger in the air long after he was gone.

My mother was usually too busy to listen to music or watch television. If I came downstairs after bedtime for a glass of water, I'd often find her sitting over a pile of papers and accounts laid out on the kitchen table. She didn't complain, but she didn't want to be interrupted. She was doing the books, she said. That meant, I understood later, trying to work out where all the money was going.

When my father brought Vincent home to supper, I'd never seen my parents so animated. I'd never seen them laugh so much. My mother's eyes shone. Vincent was twenty-three, straight out of film school, charming, funny, and handsome. He had a mustache. When he asked me questions about the books I was reading, I blushed violently and dropped my head, but he carried on talking to me just the same. I was nine years old. I couldn't stop looking at him. He agitated me. I was jealous when he talked to my brothers in the same way he talked to me. So it was all the more confusing when I spotted the crucifix he wore at his neck, which, I realized to my horror, almost certainly meant he was a Roman Catholic.

What was my father doing inviting papists into our house and—worse still—eating with them? Had my mother seen the crucifix too?

In the Brethren we'd been told that all worldly people were dangerous but that some were worse than others. The Open Brethren and the people who'd left the Exclusive Brethren were the absolute worst because they'd been shown the light but turned their backs on it. Next came the Roman Catholics. They were idolaters and fornicators, the people of whorish Babylon. They were spiritually corrupt and corrupting. I'd never seen a Roman Catholic up close before. That's why Vincent was so handsome and charming, I realized. Satan, they'd always told us, made very good traps. I determined to stop talking to him. Someone had to take a stand.

As my father became more hedonistic I became more puritan. My mother finally settled on the Anglican church on Blatchington Road and she took us with her most weeks. In Sunday school there was coloring to be done and quizzes about Baby Jesus. I'd never heard the Lord Jesus called Baby Jesus before. Once I asked a few questions about Satan's dominion on the earth, and the kindly young teacher looked concerned and confused. I decided it was probably best not to ask questions here either.

Someone suggested that my mother move me to a new Sunday school, called the Crusaders. This was a much more serious puritan operation, much more my line. Here we were crusaders, soldiers in some imaginary Holy Land. We wore enamel badges in the shape of shiny red shields. There were oaths to be sworn, tests to pass, prizes to be won. I won a Bible in 1974, its thin pages interleaved with black-and-white photographs of the Holy Land.

I did not, however, take easily to the evangelizing we were supposed to do in the Crusaders. Brethren had never been interested in recruiting heathens. When the old ladies who ran the Crusader classes told us we could only stop the anti-Christ if we saved souls, I had to ask who the anti-Christ was. I'd never heard Satan called the anti-Christ before. Ask me anything about the flight from Israel or David and Goliath and I could often quote chapter and verse. Ask me anything about Baby Jesus or the angel Gabriel or the anti-Christ and I was stumped.

I began to have bad dreams. The voices I'd heard as a very small child returned in a different form. They'd turned into the Committee. The dreams were always the same: I'd be in a darkened room in some kind of semi-derelict warehouse standing in front of a table with five men and one woman—a sort of Last Judgment scenario. There was a heavy metal light on a stand behind them, the kind of light used in interrogations in films.

Why, one of them would ask me wearily, had I failed to achieve my mission *again*? Had I forgotten the reason I'd been sent to Earth? Forgotten it *again*? Each time they asked, I told them, "Yes, I've forgotten." I apologized. I stuttered. I hung my head. They dismissed me, heads bent low, hands scratching out notes on forms. Then they would send me back to the waking world. This time, they'd say, *this time*, go and do what you're supposed to do. You're running out of time.

As I surfaced from those dreams, which looped like a song stuck on repeat in some forgotten anteroom of my brain, I resolved to

remember—*this* time, *this* time, I would, I could, I will *remember*—
but I'd wake damp with sweat to find that the crucial details of the
mission had slipped through my fingers again, like sand.

6

Worldly families, I discovered, were different from ours. But the
Marsdens were *very* different. I met Helen Marsden when I was nine.
She sat next to me at school. She was shy like me, but she knew how
things worked, so soon I was asking her to explain what certain
things meant and helping her with fractions and the endless practice
tests we had to do for the eleven-plus exam. She told the teacher
when one of the boys who sat behind me kept putting the ends of my
long braids in his inkpot. She asked me to tea. My mother, no doubt
relieved and nervous, agreed.

It was the summer of 1973. As we approached the house, my
mother and I were surprised by the high wooden gates, one of them
leaning off its hinges, the long, graveled drive that wound steeply up
from the road through dense woods, beech and ash trees hanging
low and dark. The vast Edwardian house appeared to be barely holding its own against the tangle of overgrown trees and shrubs. A rusty
caravan sat in the trees opposite the front door, and we could see a
bashed-up pale blue Triumph car and bicycles in the open garage at
the top of the drive.

As my mother and I stood on the top of the front steps, trying to
figure out if the elaborate bellpull actually worked, a young boy called
out from one of the gullies in the roof somewhere high above us,
warning us to get out of the way. Several tiny silk parachutes drifted
slowly down past us onto the expanse of gravel and weeds, a kitten
attached to each one. The kittens landed safely, unperturbed, as if
they were used to it. Another child, in camouflage gear, his face

blackened with mud or paint, appeared through the long under-growth, saluted us, scooped up the mewling bundles, and disap-peared back into the green.

Helen eventually appeared in the dark crack of the door. Her mother, she said, was on the phone, otherwise she'd come and say hello. My mother excused herself, relieved not to have to talk or go in. She arranged to pick me up in two hours at the bottom of the drive. At the bottom of the drive at six o'clock, she repeated. She didn't want to have to risk being asked in. I understood that. I stepped across the threshold into the unfamiliar faint smell of stale cigarette smoke and cats.

Helen's great-grandfather had been a mayor, she explained when she saw my astonishment at the size of her home. Her parents had inherited the seven-bedroom, three-bathroom Edwardian mansion in its huge grounds. It was built for a large family in the days when people had servants. It wasn't as tidy as it had once been, she added. Her parents were going to get some decorators in soon. I nodded. I'd already noticed the cracks in the ceiling and the missing tiles in the hallway floor.

The vast Marsden house—with its east and west wings, butler's pantry and lift, conservatory with broken stained-glass panels, rows of bellpulls in every room that no longer worked, cellar, cobwebs and shadows, and huge wooded grounds with derelict summerhouses and swings—became my adopted home for almost two years. Though I loved my parents, I'd often pretend that Mr. and Mrs. Marsden were the real parents I'd once dreamed about. I fit better there, I thought, than in my own home. I stayed more and more often, sometimes for several days at a time.

My mother must have been glad to see my brothers and me mak-ing friends, but she was probably even more relieved to have us out from under her feet. She'd grown up in the country. Her house-proud mother had ushered all of her children out of their spick-and-span house whenever they were not needed to help turn the handle of the drying mangle or fold up the washing. When my mother wasn't in meeting, she roamed the country lanes, climbed trees, and played alone in the woods.

Now that we were old enough to play unsupervised, my mother would send my brothers and me across the road to the park opposite when the weather was fine, passing us a picnic bag filled with crisps and bottles of orange squash and foil parcels of sandwiches. "Off you go," she'd say. "I'll have your tea on the table for five o'clock." Then she'd disappear back into the house with the twins.

My brothers would hammer their cricket stumps into the wide lawns. Local boys we knew drifted over to take up their fielding positions. I took myself off into the hedges that ran along each side of the miniature railway line to look for birds' nests or nestle into the roots of my favorite oak tree to read my books.

I preferred reading in the Marsden woods. The Marsden boys had built a rickety tree house. To reach it you had to climb a rope ladder and then cross a rope bridge. With the sun filtering through the cracks in the side of the tree house and with Helen reading her book a few feet from me, I was back in the hold of the ark again just as I had been in the warehouse, listening for the sound of gulls that meant we were approaching land.

The four Marsden children—the eldest sixteen, the youngest eight—ran as wild as the family cats. Nothing was watched here, nothing tended. Nature had been left to do its own thing. Helen's Irish mother smoked, gossiped, told stories about her life and about the elderly patients she tended in the old people's home she ran. She would tell us anything that amused or interested her. She swore sometimes. Helen's father, a solicitor, was quiet and shy. We didn't see much of him.

Toward the end of my first visit, I thought I saw Helen's mother cross herself. Then I began to notice the rosary beads and statues of the Virgin Mary, the dusty paraphernalia of the Whore of Babylon on every mantelpiece. I tried not to look. I tried to turn my head away.

The Marsdens, I realized, were Roman Catholics. Idolaters, the Brethren would call them, Romanists. I'd already eaten with them. But how *could* they be Roman Catholics? They were so kind, and they didn't talk about the Pope. But then, that was what Catholics were supposed to do, wasn't it? They *lured* you into their traps slowly. They *seduced* you. Soon you'd be lost to the Lord. I determined to be vigilant. I might bring my Crusader badge and my Bible next time I came. But even though I knew they were Roman Catholic, when Helen asked if I'd come over again I said yes. One of the cats was due to have kittens any moment, she told me, and I wasn't going to miss that.

There were at least six adult cats in the house. All summer long the children—Helen and her two brothers and older sister—discovered new litters of kittens in cavities beneath broken floorboards, in cupboards, or in the cellar. The cats were half-feral and climbed in and out of grilles in cellar walls or through broken windows, carrying their newborn kittens in their mouths. If their nests were disturbed by Helen's little brother looking for recruits for his air assaults, the mother cats would find new hiding places for their kittens. Eventually Helen and I would track them down. Then we'd work hard to keep Helen's brother from straying that way.

I slept in a spare bed in Helen's room beneath posters of Donny Osmond and David Cassidy. Helen's mother referred to it as my bed. We played billiards with Helen's brothers in the billiard room. Her older sister had a boyfriend and was rarely at home, so Helen and I would steal into her room in the west wing and pull out any one of the several drawers that were full of lacy underwear, half-used makeup, and hair rollers, which we'd borrow to curl our hair.

Sometimes when Helen's mother was reading a magazine in an armchair in the sitting room, scarcely visible, her hand would extend as I passed and she'd pull me onto her lap into a close and prolonged embrace. Helen would apologize, embarrassed. I didn't mind at all, I told her. Nobody did that in our house. But I didn't tell her that. Now that my father was always away at rehearsals, my mother was too busy running between cooking, shopping, sewing, cleaning, and doing paperwork. And we just weren't that kind of family. Everyone in our house was usually too busy rushing around or too cross about something.

If I was visiting the Marsdens over a whole weekend, I'd stay behind when the family went to church and read my book. But one Sunday, Helen asked if I'd like to come to Mass.

"You don't have to actually *take* the sacrament," she said. I had absolutely no idea what she was talking about.

"Church," Helen's mother said in her matter-of-fact voice. "We can fit you in the car if you want to come."

She said it quite casually, as if she was asking if I'd like to go bowling. She had no idea that to me being asked to go to a Catholic service was like being asked to step into a witch's oven.

"You can ring your mother to ask if you like," she said, gesturing toward the phone.

"I'd like to come," I said quickly, lowering my eyes, trying not to think of all those things the Lord had said to Satan when he tempted him in the wilderness. "I'm sure my mother won't mind."

After all, hadn't my father brought a Roman Catholic home to dinner? My mother *must* have known. So that meant Roman Catholics were all right now. And if they were all right, then going to their church must be all right too. If God didn't want me to go, he'd send me a sign before we got there, wouldn't he? I looked around carefully, watching out for significant arrangements of letters in passing-car license plates or crows flying in groups of five, but I didn't notice anything.

The air in St. Mary's Church was thick with candle smoke and incense, the light dim compared to the bright light in the Anglican church or the meeting room. There were crucifixes everywhere. Statues of Mary holding the Baby Jesus, bleeding saints, clusters of candle flames. It was beautiful and hushed. I was just looking, I told myself.

Just looking. But when the chants began and everyone spoke the words together:

Lord have Mercy.
Christ have Mercy.
Lord have Mercy.

I began to cry, overwhelmed by the music, the hymns, the chanting, the smell of the sweet smoky incense and the flickering of the candlelight. This was not a conversion comparable to the shuddering epiphany my father had experienced when he read that last page of *Mere Christianity* but it was important. I'd never been moved in a church or meeting room before. For a moment I had stopped striving to understand. I felt I'd crept into the presence of something beautiful, dark, and strange, something I recognized but could not name. My sobs shuddered up through me like an earthquake. Helen's mother passed me a tissue and squeezed my hand. "Bless you," she said.

During the summer holidays, left to make up our own games, we played with a trunk full of Barbie and Ken dolls, all missing limbs and hair. We stole whiskey from the enormous drinks cabinet in the sitting room, decked ourselves up in chiffon from the dressing-up trunk, and danced on the lawn under the stars or played hide-and-seek in the woods. Helen and I moved into the rusty caravan in the garden, making our own food, and when her brother came out to join us, we told ghost stories into the night. On Sundays, after church, the whole family ate together around the enormous dining room table scarred from the dripping plastic of a melting action man who had been set afire as he rappelled from one side of the room to the other.

We always gave thanks in our house, but the Marsdens didn't, so I was never sure when we were supposed to start eating. My father usually went on for a long time when he gave thanks; his voice would go up and down and you could hear him trying to remember all the things we should be grateful for—that the Lord had shown us the way through something or other, that He had delivered someone or other from danger, that someone else had seen the error of their ways—and I'd be squinting through closed eyelids at my brothers to make sure they hadn't been given bigger portions than me or up at the painting of the milkmaid in her cobalt-blue apron to check that the milk was still pouring from her jug. Now that my father hardly ever came home for dinner, my mother asked my brothers to give thanks. And because they didn't know what to say, they'd repeat something they learned at school, which wasn't right at all, something like "for what we are about to receive may we be truly thankful." I'd see my mother wince, but she didn't seem to know what to tell them to say instead. We were all embarrassed. I was glad that the Marsdens didn't give thanks.

7

My father and I were both "adopted" by Catholic families after we left the Brethren. I was nine; my father was thirty-four. I found the Marsdens, and at the Wick Theatre Company my father found the Joyces.

"Your father came out of nowhere," Vincent Joyce said when I tracked him down and went to see him at his home in Hove. "None of us had met anyone like him."

I wanted to tell Vincent what he had meant to me, that he was one of the first grown-up worldly people I'd ever met, but I was afraid I wouldn't be able to explain why that was important and how beautiful and dangerous he'd seemed to me then. Instead I asked him what my father, who had only been out of the Brethren for a few months, had been like when they first met.

"He acted as though he didn't have much time left," Vincent said. "He wanted to stay up all night. He wanted everything *now*."

I remembered the feeling I'd had when I entered the school library for the first time and reached for that copy of *The Secret Island,* certain I was going to be caught. I could hear the sound of the clock ticking, the minute hand juddering round toward the number twelve, when the bell would ring and I'd have to put the book down and go to my next class. I understood why my father might have wanted to stay up all night with these new friends of his. Later I'd wanted to stay up all night with mine.

"He was so tall," Vincent said. "He had a kind of spell. I mean, if you were at a party with him, you'd want to be in his part of the room."

Vincent knew that my father had been in a religious group, knew he'd been a preacher, but they hadn't talked about that.

"Your father wanted to talk about films," he said, "filmmaking, the theater. He'd read more books and poetry than any of us. We talked a lot about poetry. Oh, and Bergman. Often until the early hours of the morning."

I'd noticed the line of books about Ingmar Bergman on Vincent's bookshelf as soon as I walked into his sitting room. Vincent had been twenty-three years old when he met my father. He'd just left film school. If Vincent showed my father a Bergman film or two, they *would* have been up all night talking, because my father would have had so many questions.

Bergman knew about puritanism. His father had been a Lutheran preacher. All his life he'd been coming back to the metaphysical questions that had vexed him as a child. He made films about them. He wanted to know what it felt like for someone to lose their faith. What the silence was like that follows the disappearance of God. What it felt like if you kept on talking to God but he stopped answering.

My father must have been amazed to discover that this Swedish film director understood some of what he was experiencing himself. I wondered if he'd cried in front of Vincent when they watched Bergman films together, just as he had always cried with me when we watched them ten years later.

As Vincent talked, my head flickered with Bergman stills: waves breaking against rocky outcrops, a tree bending in the wind, gray skies like gaping voids. Then I was back in a summer picnic that I'd forgotten. Vincent was there, my mother and father, and all of us children, others too. We were up on a hill above Devil's Dyke. I was lying in the sun on a picnic blanket, my head leaning against my father's chest, listening to him practice his lines for *The Night of the Iguana*. Vincent was playing football with my brothers, my mother walking in the distance with the twins. I could hear my father's heart beating in his chest, woven in with muffled lines from the play, and behind that a kind of distant whooshing like the waves breaking on a pebble beach inside him. I fell asleep. When I opened my eyes my father was gone. Dark clouds were passing across the sun. I cried out with a sudden sense of terror, as if I would fall and fall down the steep sides of the dyke and be swallowed up by the void of land beneath and the sky above. Then I saw my father standing a few hundred yards away—alone—looking down there too. He turned and smiled and waved, and the world turned right-side up again.

My father auditioned for every play the Wick Theatre Company put on in those two years that he was a member, I reminded Vincent. And if he didn't get a part, he signed up to do the sound effects or help Vincent build the sets.

The Lion in Winter, October 1972
The Night of the Iguana, March 1973
Othello, July 1973

When I looked closely at the parts he'd played in those two years, it struck me how closely they reflected the different stages of my fa-

My father playing Reverend Shannon in *The Night of the Iguana*, 1973

ther's Brethren years. He was the crusader prince in *The Lion in Winter*, then the defrocked priest in *The Night of the Iguana* and the duped Cassio in *Othello*.

But as I listened to Vincent talk about the stage sets he built and how they all dreaded the visits of the fire and safety officer and how good my father's sound effects were, I realized how absurd it was to think that the parts my father was given were somehow chosen for him. If those plays helped my father to understand some things for the first time, he was lucky. That was all it amounted to. It was a fluke that he washed up there, with the Joyces, at the Wick Theatre Company, just as it was a fluke that Helen Marsden had been told to take the desk next to mine. The fact that both families were Catholic was a coincidence too.

I still want to believe, however, that someone designed and built decompression chambers for my father and me. There are counselors now who specialize in treating ex–cult members after they've experienced long periods of mind control. One counselor told me it sometimes takes him years to get his clients to return to normal levels of skepticism. He has to keep reminding them that there are many different ways of looking at things; he has to help them to think for themselves again. They used to call this process "deprogramming." But when I think of dancing under the stars with the Marsden children, and the music tapes the Joyce siblings made for my father, I wouldn't call it deprogramming, I'd call it decompression. We'd been a very long way down to the bottom of some kind of sea. There was no easy way back up without getting the bends.

8

I may have resolved my problems with Catholics, but my growing body posed other kinds of metaphysical questions. It both fascinated and tormented me as, of course, it does many teenage girls. I put on weight. The body I'd always taken for granted as continuous with myself, that had once run, climbed, and jumped, entirely unconscious of its movement through space, turned into a body that bled, fell, stumbled, and burned with embarrassment. I was ten and my period had started. I was shy. When strangers or teachers spoke to me, I blushed so that my face throbbed with heat, my skin stretched taut as if it—as if I—might split open.

But it was more complicated than that. In the Brethren we'd been told that flesh was blackened by sin, but also that flesh would be left behind, thrown off like an old coat, when the Rapture came. Brethren talked about sin all the time: how much we had, how much more the worldly people had, and how lucky we were that the Lord was going to take it all away. My periods, the blood and the abjection of those sanitary towels, only compounded my sense of my own sin. I wanted to throw my body off.

I once watched one of my father's beautiful Brethren cousins pass a strawberry in her mouth to her new husband as she sat at a table across from me at a family gathering. They thought no one had seen them. But I had. The passing of that strawberry between two mouths was one of the most shocking, daring, and beautiful things I'd ever seen. That afternoon the cousin took me onto her knee, wrapped her warm arms about me, and told me there was no getting clean on this earth. My soul was black as black and *always would be*. We had crucified the Lord and there was no undoing that. Only the Lord could undo that. I had to give myself up to Him entirely if I wanted to be clean, if I wanted to be saved from all that sin. I had to welcome him into my heart.

Though I had never believed I was good enough to go up in the Rapture, I always took for granted that my "me" was merely "housed" in the body that looked back at me from the mirror. I did not call this inside "me" a soul. Brethren never talked much about souls. But it had preexisted my body, and it would outlive it. Now that we'd left the Brethren, it seemed my soul would be stuck here forever in this ungainly body of mine.

Since I'd left the Brethren, human bodies had come to seem especially strange to me. As I watched the twins sit and crawl and then haul themselves up onto their legs and take their first steps, they often looked to me like monkeys. I started to notice eyebrows and nasal hair on grown-ups. My mother had one brown eye and one green one. Why would I never be able to grow a beard like my father? Why did humans have flat faces and not pointy ones like dogs? Why did I have tiny hairs on the back of my middle finger and on my big toes?

I'd often heard Brethren preachers talk about an especially wicked man who'd gone around saying that humans had once been monkeys. Charles Darwin was sent to earth by Satan, they said, to lead men away from God by putting evil ideas in their heads. It had always seemed a strange and beautiful idea to me, one I couldn't cast off. Though they told us it was heresy of the worst order, the idea that humans had once been monkeys seemed no stranger to me than some of the things that happened in the Bible: Lot's wife getting turned into a pillar of salt, Ezekiel making people out of dry bones, or God making Eve from one of Adam's ribs.

I must have been about six when I first looked up Darwin in the children's encyclopedia. I wanted to know what the monkey man might actually have looked like. I didn't want to get caught, so I waited until my parents were busy with Brethren guests in the dining room before I slipped into the empty sitting room. I climbed on a chair, eased down the volume marked with *D* onto the table, and spread out the closely printed pages with my palms.

But there was no entry on Darwin in the *D* volume, just the sharp stubs of excised pages where it should have been. These were the volumes my father had described in his memoir, the ones that my grandfather had ordered and censored with a razor blade.

Four years later, at the age of ten or eleven and no longer under Brethren rules or scrutiny, I went looking for Darwin again, this time in the school library's encyclopedias. If this secret had been so carefully kept from me, I thought, it must be of unique importance. I was determined to find out for myself what this mouthpiece of Satan had really said. I found the entry and the photographs of the kindly looking bearded man, who, with all that eyebrow and beard hair, looked more like a monkey than any man I'd seen. I read about natural selection, the survival of the fittest, and evolution.

This was no flash of light on the road to Damascus, no conversion to some new kind of religion. There was so much I didn't fully understand. But strange images began to form in my daydreams. We'd been tiny water creatures once, Darwin said, long before we were monkeys. We swam in a warm sea that had once covered the entire earth. Had we once been lizards and birds too?

The idea that we were all animals moving and changing infinitely slowly through time into ever more fantastic forms seemed both astonishing and beautiful to me, whether it was true or not. I began to think about the strange mirrorings and differences between the shape of my fingernails and those of my brothers, the curves of our noses, the tiny flaps of skin between my outstretched fingers, my ghostly similarity to my willful great-grandmother. I imagined my body with fur or scales, my mouth tentacled like coral, my arms as feathered wings.

Even if I didn't properly understand how natural selection worked, the world of flowing and endless forms that Darwin described made a dazzling counterpoint to the rule-bound, black-and-white, Manichaean, sin-obsessed, flesh-loathing world of the Brethren. Darwin's version of a world in infinitely slow flux became a kind of poem that I'd keep coming back to for the next forty years. In this version of the world, nothing had purpose or design. Nothing drove or judged us. It was neither cruel nor kind, neither good nor bad. But it was a kind of miracle.

I now sometimes stopped at the Booth Museum of Natural History on my way to the sports field on Tuesday afternoons. I'd climb the stairs where I once sheltered from the rain and go inside. The museum was usually empty. Glass-fronted display cases, banked five or six high, stretched all the way to the ceiling on every side. Bare floorboards made my footsteps echo.

Behind the glass, birds were pinioned into tableaux against life-like reconstructions of their natural habitats. Life looked both beautiful and bloody in those marshes, mountains, and sand dunes: An eagle pulled out the innards of a lamb while the lamb's mother looked on; a vulture pecked out the eyes of a still-alive rabbit. There were slaughtered animals everywhere, throats ripped out, eyes open, gazing up at pitiless painted skies. It turned my stomach, but I also found it shudderingly beautiful.

Notices around the museum walls explained that Edward Thomas Booth, a rich Victorian recluse, had set out to shoot, stuff, and display a specimen of every bird in the British Isles. He died before he finished his project, but he'd still managed to collect hundreds of species. Once he realized he'd never be able to shoot one of every kind single-handedly, he recruited gamekeepers and game wardens all around the country to kill the birds he didn't have and to mail him the dead specimens.

A sailor from the lightship *Newarp* in the North Sea sent him all the wings taken from the migrating birds that had collided with the ship's light or gotten caught in the rigging. The list he sent Booth was a kind of poetry, I thought: *Lark 520, Starling 348, Stormy Petrel 45, Brown Linnet 15, Greenfinch 21, Brambling 6, Fieldfare 2, Fork-Tailed Petrel 1, Knot 2, Blackbird 20, Redwing 13, Chaffinch 15, Tree Sparrow 3, Rook 2, Snipe 1, Kittiwake 1.* The parcel the post-man delivered that day must have been enormous. I tried to imagine what 520 lark wings would have looked like: all those different shapes and colors and feather patterns, all those different birds.

The blood and guts and empty eye sockets of Booth's tableaux seemed to confirm something that I already half knew: that life was bloody, and that you had to watch your back or there'd be claws on you. But though Booth tried to fix all those birds, lock them into his boxes, take them out of time, I now knew too, in a crude and stum-bling kind of way, that everything was on the move, turning into something else, even if we couldn't actually see it with our human eyes. Even Booth couldn't stop that.

9

Though we'd left the Brethren, my parents kept hearing news about the bad things that were still happening in "the Jims," as they and my grandparents now called the Taylorite Brethren. The Taylor system hadn't stopped, of course, with J.T. Junior's death. Jim Symington, a pig farmer from North Dakota, took over as leader when J.T. Junior died. They called him the Elect Vessel now, rather than the Man of

God. Thousands of people were still in the Jims, including some of our aunts and uncles and cousins. From what I could tell, they were having unspeakable things done to them and were doing unspeakable things to one another. People were still being forced to confess to terrible things; there'd been more suicides.

"He has a sister who's still in the Jims," I heard people say to my grandparents, and they all looked sad and cross. My mother's brother was still in the Jims. One of my father's favorite cousins was in the Jims too. Those families had just disappeared from the landscape of our daily lives as if they'd been rubbed out.

I was nine when I first heard my parents speak of the Andover tragedy. We were in the car, coming back from somewhere. I was thinking about the clunky shoes my mother had just bought me for school. My father was driving erratically, talking fast to my mother with his voice raised, and thumping the steering wheel from time to time. When I heard him talking about an ax, I leaned forward a little so I could hear better without drawing attention to myself. I'd read about axes in the fairy tales I borrowed from the school library. The woodcutter in "Little Red Riding Hood" had an ax. He cut off the wolf's head with it.

People were dead, Brethren people. My parents knew them. But it was the ax I was interested in. And the feet. My father said the postman had seen Roger Panes's feet through the letter box. Did that mean he was hanging from something, his feet swinging in midair in the hallway? I imagined those feet with socks, then with polished boots. For weeks afterward I thought about those feet and the ax and the postman with his forehead pressed against the letter box, looking in, but I was unable to put the pieces of the puzzle together. And they were always mixed up with those clunky school shoes I hated.

I found several newspaper clippings among my father's papers in his study a few months later.

"Brethren Drove Man to Suicide," one headline read. I slipped the clippings into my school bag. Once I was back in my bedroom and with the door closed I laid them out on the floor. I tried to figure the mystery out as if it was one of the comprehension exercises they made us do at school.

The postman had not been a postman after all. He'd been a telephone operator. A relative had tried to ring the Paneses' house several times but had failed to get through so they rang the telephone operator to report a fault on the line. Someone from the telephone company went to the house, and when no one answered he knelt down, pushed the flap of the letter box open, and saw those hanging feet. He called the police. The police went to the house and knocked the door down.

Detective Chief Inspector Stanley Atkinson and his officers found a man in blood-spattered pajamas hanging by an electric cord attached to the banisters in the hall. Upstairs they found Mrs. Panes dead, lying in a double bed in a bedroom. The newspaper said she had "severe head injuries." In my mind the Paneses' house kept turning into one of the cottages in the woods in the fairy tales I was reading. I imagined bowls of hot porridge on the kitchen table, a cage with a child in it, a wolf dressed as an old woman. But this was a real town called Andover; it had policemen and telephone exchanges. It wasn't a fairy tale at all.

The policemen found three children "with similar injuries" in other bedrooms, lying in blood-soaked beds. In another bedroom they found a bloodstained ax with a seven-and-a-half-inch blade. They found Bibles by the side of all the beds and by the telephone in the hall. That didn't surprise me. You'd always have Bibles by the bed and by the telephone in the hall. You'd have them in other places in the house too.

Blood on the walls, blood on the floor, blood on the hanging man's pajamas and on his bare feet.

Roger Panes left a note. He wrote:

There's never been such a wicked man. This house will have to be left empty or bulldozed. You go to the Brethren. I trust

they will take you in. Cry to God for mercy for you all and the
dear children. The Lord is coming very soon.

When he finished writing those words, he folded up the paper, put it in the pocket of his trousers, then folded the trousers and placed them on the chair by the bed that had not been slept in. Then he went downstairs for the ax.

You go to the Brethren. I trust they will take you in.

The police went to the local Brethren meeting room and found the name of a Mr. Fennell, the Brethren leader in Andover, written on the board outside the door. They went to Mr. Fennell's house to ask him some questions.

"Roger Panes," Mr. Fennell told the police, "was shut up during November 1973, because of the way he treated another member of the Brethren over a minor technical offense and shut up that person willfully."

Roger Panes had been "shut up" because he'd "shut up" someone else. That made complete sense to me, but the journalists didn't seem to understand it. They tried to explain "shutting up" to their readers, but they didn't do a very good job. If I was the journalist, I would have told my readers that if someone didn't abide by Brethren rules, they were like lepers. The Bible laid out very clear rules about lepers. They had to stay in their homes, isolated, until one of the priests, like my father, decided they would no longer infect the rest of the assembly. Sometimes it would take days, sometimes weeks to get such a man clean again. Sometimes the shut-up person got sick.

"What was this minor technical offense that Panes had 'committed,' according to your statement?" the judge asked Mr. Fennell at the inquest.

"He shut up that person wrongly," Fennell said. "That was not right. It was contrary to the accepted code and violations of the divine principles involved in the Brethren."

Back then—when I was nine—the story had woven itself into my nightmares. But now, reading the story again, I had different questions: Did the judge ask about what had driven Panes to murder? Or did he decide it was best not to pry? Did he tell himself that he had a duty to respect religious practice—however extreme—in the name of freedom of belief that had so long been enshrined in the British way?

The police, still searching for motives, interviewed the family doctor. Roger Panes had been ill for a while, the GP told them, checking his files. On February 21, 1974, eleven days before the murders, he took an overdose and was rushed to the hospital. When a busy emergency room doctor spoke to Mrs. Panes about her husband's mental health, she said the whole business was "between him and God." Roger Panes was sent home.

No one, not the family doctor or the hospital staff, thought to ask Roger Panes what had been going on. Roger Panes was religious. No one wanted to interfere. It must have been easier to look away.

Throughout that winter, Roger Panes would have sat on his bed listening to the sound of his children playing on the other side of the unlocked door: Graham, seven; Angela, six; and four-year-old Adrian. He would have been able to tell the time by the coming and going of his wife's car as she took the children to meeting or to school. He would have heard her telling them to hurry up, straighten out their clothes, keep their voices down. He might have heard her crying. Daddy wasn't well, she might have said, as she placed his food on a tray outside his door again. Once a week or so he would have heard different cars on the gravel outside the house as a pair of ministering brothers arrived to interrogate him. Consigned to silence for so long, he must have been startled by the sound of his own voice.

There's never been such a wicked man, he wrote. They'd never get that house clean again. *The house will have to be left empty or bulldozed.*

At the inquest, a hundred Brethren turned out to fill the gallery in their hats and suits, carrying their Bibles. They'd been told to give a show of strength, a testimony of their faith. But someone must also have known that by occupying all those seats, they'd keep most of the journalists out.

When my father thumped his fist on the steering wheel that day, it was because the Roger Panes story had broken. After the Andover tragedy we understood that there was no rescuing our family members and others who were still with the Jims. They might as well have been living on the other side of a great wall. They'd have to find their way out by themselves.

10

When I think of the life my father lived after Aberdeen, it reminds me of the whirlpool I used to watch in the plughole of the bath as a very small child, that spiraling tunnel I feared would suck me down with it into the darkness. My father had been running from it— whatever the "it" was—all his life; now he was running like the frantic Tristram Shandy, leaping in and out of windows, stacking the chips, staying up all night: *faster, faster, before Death catches you.* When Death caught you, and he would, there'd be a reckoning. You'd be in trouble.

"If he'd let your mother keep control of the money after Aberdeen," one of the cousins told me, "things might have been different." Her husband corrected her. "Your mother couldn't have stopped him," he said. "No one could have stopped him. After Aberdeen, your father was a different man."

"He had a kind of excess about him," Vincent Joyce said. While most people would come to Wick parties with a single bottle of wine, my father would bring a whole case. When Vincent told him about a new camera that had just come out that he knew he'd never be able to afford, my father went and bought it for him. If the whole cast went out for dinner after a performance, my father would foot the entire bill.

It must have been that hands-in-the-sweet-jar thing, I wanted to say. He must have felt that unless he could cram as many sweets as possible into his mouth all at once, someone was going to take the jar away from him. I knew what that felt like. I often felt the urge to grab everything, eat everything, read everything—*quick now, be quick, they're coming*—before someone came and took the book or the sweets away and then you'd be in trouble again.

My father was like that at home too. Two years after we left the Brethren he decided it was time we moved to a much bigger house. Although my mother agreed, she did not think we could afford to buy a house as big and showy as the one he settled on. But he bought it anyway. It had five bedrooms, an acre of land, a carved-oak drinks bar as big as anything you might see in a small pub, a sweeping drive, and a double garage. That was important because my father had started buying cars.

Vincent told me that the first time he visited us in our new house up on the hill there were two Jaguars parked in the front drive, next to the large emerald-green Ford Cortina Estate my father had just bought my mother. My father told Vincent he couldn't decide which Jaguar model to buy so he'd brought them both home to test-drive. He handed Vincent the keys and asked him to make the decision. One of the cars, Vincent remembered, had dual fuel tanks. He'd never seen a car with dual tanks before.

One of my father's cousins told me that my father had several car accidents through the 1970s. He parked one of his cars in the driveway outside our new house without properly engaging the hand brake, and it rolled off down the slope and into the back of a parked car on the road; another time he drove into the back of a parked truck as he was returning home from a rehearsal. He must have been drinking, I thought, remembering the empty bottles of Scotch I'd seen in the trunk of the car.

My cousin lowered her voice to a whisper:

"Sometimes I wondered if he'd been trying to . . . you know."

She meant, I realized, *trying to kill himself.*

It had never occurred to me before. He'd had so many accidents, so many near misses, more than most people had in a lifetime. He was also visiting another woman and not telling my mother about it. I discovered this new secret of my father's by accident when I was eleven. When I wasn't needed at home, I'd taken to walking. It was an excuse to get out of the noisy new house full of quarrels and television, my mother's lists of chores, and my father's irritations. Even in this new world he'd found, he was still losing his temper at home. I would walk through the woods beyond the park or along the muddy track that began at the end of the cul-de-sac that curled around the back of our house and find a spot to sit and read.

The path followed a wooded ridge between suburban gardens and high fences. At one point a solid fence had been replaced with chicken wire, and from a bench there I could look down onto several back gardens and across a pretty little estate—box-shaped new houses built around a green. I liked watching the people coming and going down there, neighbors talking over garden walls, children kicking balls around, women hanging out washing, men lighting barbecues as dusk fell. I liked knowing they couldn't see me. Sometimes I took my father's binoculars.

One Saturday afternoon, when my father was supposed to be away on a business trip and I'd slipped away to the bench on the high path, I looked up from my book to see my father's Jaguar drive into view and park among the cars around the green. I put my book away, leaned forward to see better through the gap in the fence, pressed the binoculars to my eyes, adjusted the focus. A smiling woman stepped out of the car with two children. My father climbed out of the other side with bags of shopping; neighbors looked up from their hedge-cutting or car-cleaning and waved. He called back, made a joke that I could not hear. They laughed.

What I had seen was interesting and strange, but it didn't occur to me to tell anyone, nor did I know how to interpret it. It was just another secret to be added to the others I had kept for my father. There was the radio I knew he kept hidden in the back of the car in the days when radios were banned, the forbidden newspapers I saw him reading, the cinema tickets I found, the promise he broke. This new mystery wove through our new life in our new house like a red ribbon. I did not know what it meant, but I cherished it. It was my secret. I began to look for reasons to slip out again, to return to my watch post. I kept the binoculars by the back door next to my wellies.

Our big house with its huge windows and garden seemed to be waiting for something. At night, when I lay awake long after my brothers had fallen asleep, it sometimes felt to me as if the walls had become very thin, as if we might all blow away in the slightest wind.

11

The tipping point of my parents' now-struggling marriage was not my mother's discovery of the woman I'd seen through the binoculars—my mother didn't know about her yet—or my father's disappearance into the world of theater and art, or the vast sums of money he was spending. It was the trip we took across Europe in the summer of 1975.

It was the year Margaret Thatcher became Leader of the Opposition, the year that the Yorkshire Ripper began his hammer attacks, the year the IRA bombed the Green Park tube station. I was ten, nearly eleven, my older brother twelve, my younger brother nine, and the twins five. My father had rented a Dormobile, a shiny brand-new tank of a vehicle. He took us to see it in the showroom, demonstrating to my mother the seats that folded down to make beds, the tent that attached to the side, the roof that tipped up to make bunk beds in the roof, the stove and the fridge and all the clever storage spaces. It was, I thought, beautiful. It had everything. It was perfect.

It proved to be the chamber in which my parents played out the last scenes of their marriage, up front in the driving seat, with us children crammed together with the luggage in the back. There were no grand outbursts, only the slow burn of anger: my father slamming doors, the electric crackle of sighs, dark looks, and sharp intakes of breath. We were on the road for three weeks—from Calais down through France and Switzerland to Italy and back up.

The day we left I pulled off a flake of nail that had come loose on my right big toe. By the time we reached Calais my toe had swelled and reddened. By Paris it was oozing pus. My mother found pink Germolene antiseptic cream in the first-aid kit she'd brought, but in the heat the cream just melted and ran off.

My father's obsession with covering distances in record times overwhelmed him again, just as it had overwhelmed Tristram Shandy. Every day after breakfast we five children took our seats in the back, crushed into the tiny foam sofas that became beds at night, two striped seats that faced each other. My father drove through most of the daylight hours without ever stopping for more than a toilet break.

In the absence of air-conditioning, the temperature in the vehicle rose the farther south we went. My bare thighs stuck to the seat; my toe throbbed and pulsed. The windows steamed up. We soon tired of I Spy. My brothers settled into games of cards. We read books for as long as we could before the car sickness took over.

French fields slid by beyond the edge of the motorway, beyond the net curtains that were tied into bows, then Italian fields, birds, steeples of churches built high on hills, vineyards. I was ill. My skin crawled, and I had to pull a blanket around myself as the thermometer in the back of the Dormobile climbed higher. When we stopped, my mother prepared little bowls of warm water for me, with two capfuls of disinfectant, to soak my foot in.

I remember very little of the towns we visited—a flash of the twisting streets of Milan, a shop in a Swiss town that sold cuckoo clocks, the horses in St. Mark's square in Venice, rearing black shapes against a deep blue sky. My father kept a piece of paper on his sun visor on which he recorded daily tallies of the distances we'd covered and the times he'd clocked up. We covered 350 miles one day, 500 miles another. We stayed in campsites on the edges of famous cities, where we'd arrive at nightfall. He would have driven for longer each day if he could, but he knew we had to pitch the tent before dark. My mother would cook up a meal from a packet and put us to bed.

Each day there were more campsites and more nightfalls and more records broken. My mother, dressed in pretty summer dresses she'd made for the trip, gripped the seat or the car door as we drove, her knuckles white, her face gray. Then I was sick and the back of the car smelled of vomit and Dettol. My father tried to engage us with stories and history about the cities we drove through, and when he had to battle to make himself heard over the sound of our squabbling, he'd yell and shout and occasionally thump the steering wheel. Then he'd drive faster and my mother would grip the handle of the door even tighter.

During the J.T. Junior years my mother covered the seats of public toilets with carefully arranged layers of toilet paper before she'd let us use them. It was what her mother had taught her. Generally, it was better not to use them at all, she'd say, unless you were really desperate. In France the campsite toilets were often muddy holes in sheds. You were supposed to put your feet on each side of the hole and squat. She made us wash our hands again and again. But we still got "runny tummy," as she called it, and then my father complained about having to stop all the time to find toilets.

The swelling in my toe had spread to my entire foot. By the time we reached the Alps I was limping. On the San Bernardino Pass I put my swollen foot deep into the white compacted snow by the side of the road. I thought it might go on forever, burn a hole through to the other side of the earth. I was seeing things now; the clouds made faces and animals above me like the ones, I thought, that Ezekiel had seen. I stayed there, staring up at the peak of the mountain, my entire leg immersed deep in the ice for a long time, praying for something—and *to* something—I couldn't name.

My father was already drafting the letter he'd give to my mother a few weeks after we returned to England. Wouldn't they both be happier living apart? Hadn't the holiday proved that? After all that trouble they'd had in the Jims, he wrote, their marriage didn't stand much of a chance. He'd start looking for a flat as soon as he could.

12

Our mother sat us all down around the kitchen table before school and told us that our father wouldn't be living with us anymore. He would live nearby, and he'd visit and take us out for the day. She was very matter-of-fact about it. Everything would go on much the same, she said, although we would probably have to move out of the big house into a smaller one sometime soon.

I would have liked to denounce my father, but I didn't know where to start. He left my mother to manage everything; he went to live somewhere else; he had another family no one knew about; there were all those broken promises, all those secrets and lies. Instead, I excommunicated him. I withdrew from him. I told my brothers to tell him, when he called to take us all out for the day over the coming weeks, that I was doing my homework. I disappeared to my room and closed the door or went to Helen's house and stayed as long as I could. It was more than a year before I spoke to him again.

By the time the estate agents came to put a FOR SALE sign outside the big house a few months later, my mother had found us a three-story terraced house near the seafront in Hove, with five bedrooms, where she could take in language students as lodgers to help pay our school fees. We kids all shared two rooms up in the attic; my mother took the bedroom with the dangerous, about-to-crack-open ceiling on the middle floor. That left two respectable rooms for "paying guests," as my mother called them. These guests began to arrive as soon as my mother was sure the paint on their bedroom walls was dry.

The floorboards were rickety and my mother did not have enough money to buy new carpets or to pay a man to cut and lay the rolls of carpet she'd brought from the big house. She set up the sewing machine on the kitchen table at night to cut smaller curtains from the larger ones. A couple of our first guests, a middle-aged Swedish builder and his wife, alarmed by the forking ravines my mother had shown them in her bedroom ceiling, found a local plasterer to fix it.

The sea was so close we could hear the waves breaking on the shingle beach at night. Seagulls screeched like ghosts on the roof above our beds. On stormy nights the wind howled in the chimneys and rattled the windows.

When I wasn't needed at home or staying at the Marsdens' house, I walked miles along the promenade, to the lagoon with the little boats, through the derelict buildings and rusting metal of the harbor at Shoreham, down across the mass of gray mudflats that the sea left behind when the tide was out. From deep under the mud, wormlike creatures had cast up sand coils, as if they'd sloughed off their skins. In the rock pools that the sea had gouged out around the edges of the concrete groynes, there were crabs and tiny red sea anemones and seaweeds with beautiful names like bladder wrack and mermaid's purse. I brought home shiny streamers of it and hung them on the wall in our attic bedroom.

In 1976, the first year we lived in the new house, a heat wave turned everything to sweat and seemed to bring the hot sky down around us. Plagues of ladybugs covered the white hotel façades along the seafront. The buildings undulated and flickered. They looked as if they were bleeding. When I walked across the garden to bring in the washing, ladybugs crunched under my heavy school shoes. They'd fly out of drawers, heavy, beautiful, lumbering things. I found them in my clothes and in my shoes. We had to keep the doors and windows shut to keep them out.

I read the Narnia books through that long summer holiday and Laura Ingalls Wilder's *Little House on the Prairie* and *The Long Winter*. I wrote stories for the twins in which they built boats when floodwaters engulfed their town, or built log cabins to live out a long winter, or found ingenious ways of escaping monsters made of ice or seaweed. We watched episodes of *Robinson Crusoe* together on the television every morning. My fantasies of flight to a mysterious is-land opened up again. Now in my daydreams Jack and I would be weaving cabins and tree houses from young branches and twigs on a desert island. When Crusoe fixed his eyes on the horizon and blew into his conch shell in the hope that someone would reply, it was my mouth he blew through. I still imagined that a voice might reply from somewhere Out There.

That autumn someone told my grandfather that my father had gone on holiday with "another woman" only months after leaving my mother. My grandfather summoned my father and challenged him: "What on *airth* were you thinking?"

Perhaps my grandfather expected my father to repent, perhaps he even thought he could force his giant son to his knees and into prayer as he'd done years before, but my father didn't back down. Instead, now six foot four and twenty stone, educated and articulate, he shouted back, thumped his fists, raised his voice louder. He told my grandfather that he was going to live his life exactly as he chose, that my grandfa-ther had no right, no *right* to admonish him. He could go to hell.

Between them that day my father and grandfather whipped up a tempest that drove my grandmother running from the house. While my poor grandfather was in mid-invective, midsentence, mid-competition with his wayward son for the loudest, most outraged denunciation, he ruptured a plaque in his heart and fell to the ground clutching his chest. The paramedics who arrived half an hour later failed to revive him.

That was the autumn my father killed my grandfather.

That's not what anyone actually said, of course, but it's what my father believed and what he thought other people were thinking. He'd never been able to forgive himself, he told me a few weeks before he died.

Kezia had been right to get me to use the word "Aftermath." These were violent aftershocks, earth shudders and rifts, occurring not along a natural geological fault line but along a human-made one. I think of the paramedics trying to resuscitate my grandfather; my grandmother weeping and praying; my father looking on, ashen, the words he'd used to denounce his father circling around and around in his brain.

No one told us children until much later about the row that killed our grandfather. How could they? He had had a heart attack, they said. He'd gone to be with the Lord, our grandmother said. Coming so soon after my father's disappearance and in the muddied wake of Aberdeen, my grandfather's death left me winded and afraid. Where had he gone? Was he with the Lord Jesus? Why were they putting his body into the ground? What would happen to his body when the Rapture came? Why was my father crying? I'd never seen him cry before. Brethren didn't cry about death. It was supposed to be something to be glad about. The dead person was with the Lord.

At the Marsdens' dinner table in the weeks following my grandfather's death, something—a thought, an image, a question—would set me off into shuddering, gasping sobs and I'd run for the refuge of the caravan. Eventually Helen's mother told me enough was enough. My grandfather had gone to a better place, she said. He was with Jesus. He was in heaven with the angels.

"But how do you *know*," I wailed. Not knowing where my grandfather had gone tormented me. Was he really in heaven? He had believed in the Lord, I knew that, but he hadn't always been kind or good or right. Had he been good enough to get a place in heaven? Or was he in hell being burned forever and ever? If he was in heaven, would my grandmother be able to find him when she went up there in the Rapture? The mansion that the Lord Jesus made had a thousand rooms. Where would she begin to look?

None of us knew for certain where my grandfather had gone, Mrs. Marsden said firmly, and it wasn't for any of us *to* know. We'd find out in good time.

No one had ever talked like that in the Brethren. They'd have shot those panicked questions of mine down with the artillery fire of scriptural quotation. It was all right not to know, Mrs. Marsden said. This was obvious to her but astonishing to me to hear it said in plain words like that. If it was true it meant I didn't have to try to map the rooms in the heavenly mansion anymore or figure out who went where or understand the degree of transparency of the Holy Spirit. There were things I would never figure out, Mrs. Marsden said, no matter how hard I read my Bible. I was suddenly exhausted. I slept for twelve hours that night.

Would it have helped my father to confess to someone? Would it have eased his mind if he'd been shut up by Brethren priests until he came right with the Lord? Although his new acting friends would have told him his father's death was not his fault, he had to live with the guilt, muddle his way through it, or distract himself. He found consolation at the roulette table.

My brothers knew about the casino before I did, though they didn't know what it was or what my father did there. After my grandfather's death, after I'd seen my father cry, I sometimes agreed to come with him when he took my siblings out for the day, but my brothers were still seeing much more of him than I was. He'd bought season tickets for Brighton and Hove Albion, so on many Saturdays during the football season he picked them up and they were gone for a few hours. Sometimes he took all five of us to a park or a carnival. Occasionally on the way back he parked the car on a certain street and left us there for an hour or so while he went off to what he would call "a business meeting." My younger brother whispered that he was "getting money" someplace called Sergeant Yorks. It was a secret, he said. He was going to get enough money to take us all to America. My father had new secrets, and I was curious. But the windows at Sergeant Yorks were too high to see anything through.

Years later he told me that my father had promised him a day of treats for his twelfth birthday. This would have been March 1978. My brother put on his favorite shirt and trousers and washed and brushed his hair carefully. My father arrived two hours late. Once they were in the car, he told my brother that first he had to make a trip to Sergeant Yorks, but as it was my brother's birthday, he was going to give him all the money he won. They shook hands. He wouldn't be long, he said, after he'd parked the car in the usual spot; just a few turns of the wheel, then they'd get going.

Two hours later he returned to the car, deflated and stony-faced.

"I guess it just isn't your lucky day, son," he told my brother, slamming the door hard and jamming the car into gear before taking him home.

"Poor fella," my brother said, when he told me this story, and of course he meant my father, not himself.

We continued to be baffled by our father's many derelictions right up till his End Days, but they fascinated us too. His behavior was often so outrageous that we struggled to get people to believe us, or they looked shocked and upset, so most of the time we just passed those stories among ourselves. Perhaps we thought that if we told them enough times, one of us might finally understand him.

13

I started at a new school just a few months after my grandfather died. I'd done well enough at the eleven-plus exams to win a full scholarship to a selective independent girls' school, housed in a grand building on a hill with a library on the very top floor that looked out over the sea. My school fees, uniform, and books would all be paid for until I finished my A levels. My mother was both proud and relieved. My father had fallen behind with my brothers' school fees, so she'd had to take on more accountancy work and more language students as paying guests to try to keep up with the payments.

Helen telephoned to tell me she was going to the private Catholic girls' school over on the other side of Brighton. We'd be separated. At least she'd get to wear that lovely blue uniform, I told her, trying not to cry. My new uniform was a horrible bottle green. We'd still see each other just as much, wouldn't we? I asked. And though she told me we'd be best friends forever, we both knew that those different-colored uniforms would change everything. Brighton and Hove High School girls didn't mix with the girls from St. Mary's. There wasn't any animosity between the schools; it was just that they were worlds apart.

My mother took me to have my hair cut for the first time the day we went to buy my new uniform. The hairdresser put me in the chair and cranked it up. She examined the two thick ropes of braids I'd worn down my back since I was a very small child. Was I *sure*? I nodded. My mother nodded. The hairdresser still hung back.

"I can do it myself," I said, as my mother flashed me a look that said: *Mind your manners*. I showed the hairdresser where I wanted the braids cut, somewhere around my shoulders, but it was my mother she looked at when she attempted the first scissor-sawing cut into my hair. The scissors wouldn't cut. The braid was too thick. That made my mother laugh, and then we were all laughing. The hairdresser went to fetch a bigger pair of scissors from the high shelf. And then it was done; the braids unraveled and my curls were trimmed into a shoulder-length bob. It looked good, I thought, and for weeks I was running my fingers through it, stealing glances in shop windows, wondering why I hadn't just done it myself years before.

I grew tired of the foggy, upside-down, vertigoed dream world I'd lived in since Aberdeen. I began to crave facts, certainties, and meanings, walls that didn't crumble and give way when I pressed against them. Brighton and Hove High School for Girls was a gift for a child with a head full of difficult questions. It had been set up by two suffragist sisters in the latter part of the nineteenth century to teach girls the full range of academic subjects including those—such as Greek and Latin and rhetoric—that had traditionally been taught only to boys. Most of my new teachers were skeptical of orthodoxies; many of them had traveled widely and read in several languages; some of them were mavericks and misfits.

My history teacher, for instance, would write out difficult questions about the Corn Laws or the First Reform Act on the blackboard and then answer them, sometimes giving the answers a right-wing spin, sometimes a left-wing spin. She'd take up a position, argue it, and then provoke us to disagree with her and to put together an alternative case. I was a shy and awkward teenager, but in these classes, mesmerized, I forgot myself, ignored the blood rising to my cheeks, and spoke. Sometimes she praised me, no matter how much I blushed and stuttered out my answer.

"Put that in your essay," she'd say. "Then argue the opposite position. Make me think you believe both sides are true. Then show me why you think one side is more credible than the other." Credible. Plausible. Nonorthodox. Empirical. The new words I was learning in these lessons brought my questions into sharper focus.

"Take nothing on trust," she would tell the class. "You have to make up your own minds as you go along, make them up as best you can. To do that you must be able to see several sides at once."

Questions, she'd write out in looping letters on the blackboard, *are sometimes more important than answers.*

She didn't know I'd spent the first years of my life among fundamentalist Christians, of course. I was just one of the scores of young women she taught. We all had histories.

"The Bible is an old book written by human beings," she said once, and I began to sweat, the heat rising up through my body to my face. "It's been translated from one language to another to another. I'm not saying it isn't important, just that it was written in a particular time and place by particular people. Never trust anyone who tells you that they know exactly what it means."

I remembered listening to my father talking about the *current* truth, the new light, the truth that was being unfolded to the Brethren alone by the Lord at that particular moment. If J.T. Junior told them that the Lord had sent him new light, they believed him. He had so much power. Someone like J.T. Junior could wipe out all previous truths with a new light truth.

It wasn't just Mrs. Marsden and my teachers who gave me answers—inadvertently, perhaps—to some of the questions that vexed me. Over the next few years, I gravitated toward a succession of outliers: musicians, poets, and people my mother would have called hippies. They didn't lecture me or tell me what I should be thinking. They asked me questions, exciting ones. They taught me to formulate more interesting questions than the theological ones that had always bothered me. They helped me find my way back to my beyond-the-pale father, and then I'd begin to ask him some of those questions too. They taught me how to argue back when I didn't agree with something.

When our Renton Brethren aunt and uncle invited me to spend a week of my summer holiday with my three girl cousins, one still very young and the other two close to my own age, I accepted. I was fourteen. I liked my cousins. The Rentons, I knew, were not like the Jims. My cousins had explained all that to me once when I saw them at our grandparents'. They believed lots of the same things as the Jims, but they weren't so strict. They weren't supposed to eat at the same table with people outside their fellowship, I knew, but because I was family and not grown-up yet, they probably wouldn't worry about that. They were Christians, I told myself, trying to quell a sense of dread.

They were good people, my blood; they couldn't do me any harm. My mother packed my Bible in my suitcase. When she dropped me off at the station, she told me that if my aunt and uncle asked me to go with them to meeting I should probably go.

Life in the Rentons, it turned out, was much more permissive than in the Taylorite Exclusive Brethren, but it was still austere. My aunt and uncle and cousins attended meeting several times a week; they had no radio, television, or pop music; my uncle and aunt gave thanks just as we had done, and their talk always looped back, as I expected, to the Lord and the Scriptures. When we were alone, my two older cousins asked about the music I liked and the television programs I watched and the boys I knew. I was, they told me, so very lucky not to be in any kind of Brethren anymore.

At every meal we ate together, my kindly aunt and uncle cross-questioned me about my belief and my knowledge of the Bible, as I knew they would. With my cousins listening nervously, my half-formed answers seemed shabby things. While I might have been able to defend a position about the impact of laissez-faire economics or the degree to which the Great Depression contributed to the rise of fascism, my new rhetorical skills and facts counted for nothing here.

I wasn't at all sure what I *did* think about most of the things my aunt and uncle asked about. None of my school friends were interested in God or the Bible or the nature of sin or grace or redemption, so though I often thought about those things, I did not talk to anyone about them. I had wanted to. They still mattered to me. But now that I was actually being cross-questioned, I couldn't produce the certainties and opinions my aunt and uncle wanted from me. My head swam. I began to change the subject every time I saw it veer back toward the Lord and to me.

I managed only one small, rather inept act of insurrection that week. When my uncle asked whether my science teachers had managed to persuade me that I'd once been a monkey, I told him I thought he was quite wrong about all of that, and that what Darwin thought was a lot more complicated. Of course my aunt and uncle had a set of polished counterarguments about the age of the earth and the seven days of creation. I did not know enough to be able to refute them, but my history teacher, I told myself as I retreated from the table, would have called it "a good start." Though I had better things to do with my time than defend Darwin's ideas against creationists, and though I had no intention of returning to the subject with my aunt and uncle, I knew I was going to have to read more books if I was to understand how natural selection worked. I wasn't going to let myself flounder around like that again.

The elderly Renton Brethren assembly that my aunt's family attended in West London was very small. The men talked in just the same way I remembered, standing to speak in spasmodic flurries as the Spirit moved in and around the room and in and out of them, unfolding the nuances of the current truth. The women were still silent, sitting in rows at the back in their bows and hats, hands folded in their laps; the Spirit did not speak through Renton Brethren women either, and that still enraged me. The hymn-singing sounded the same. But I was no longer anxious to follow the angels-on-a-pinhead exegeses, and although I was struck by the fervor of their devotion, their absolutism and hard lines frightened me.

Something shifted inside my head in that Renton Brethren meeting room. If the apostle Paul thought that women should be completely subject to the rules of men, if he thought the Spirit was too good for them, then Paul was *wrong*. Hadn't he been just a man, after all? A particular man in a particular place at a particular time? Hadn't he had flaws and prejudices like all human beings?

What would I have been like, I wondered now, if my parents had joined the Renton Brethren? Or if they'd stayed in the Jims? How would I have swallowed my rage and sense of injustice, avoided looking at all those contradictions? And what future would there have been for me as a Brethren woman? My two teenage cousins were not supposed to marry outside the Brethren. If they did, they'd drive a wedge between themselves and their parents. But, they told me, there were no boys in their meeting young enough for either of them to marry. They were going to become old maids, they wailed, eyes wide. Did I know, they said again, how lucky I was?

14

I had a responsibility to do something with this freedom of mine, then, I told myself on my return. I needed to do something reckless and brave. When my younger brother, then thirteen, told me he'd been inside the squatters' house on the other side of the road while I was away, that there were drug dealers living there who had the most amazing record collection, I told him he *had* to take me there.

Whenever we drove past the squatters' house, my mother tutted at the unkempt garden, at the peeling paint and the tattered curtains hanging at the windows. I heard neighbors say it was a disgrace. The police should break in, they said, throw those dreadful people out and board the place up with those metal grilles they used. No one in the neighboring Sackville Gardens, they said, would stand for that sort of thing on their street.

So my brother and I hung about on the pavement outside trying to look inconspicuous for a while before we slipped down the side passage into the overgrown garden at the back of the squat. By the time we pushed through the long grass and shrubs, we were covered in cuckoo spittle, pollen, and cobwebs. My brother knocked three times before a man in his midthirties with a mustache and shiny eyes appeared at a hatch in the boarded-up kitchen window. He looked like a picture of a leprechaun I'd seen once in a collection of Irish fairy tales.

"That's Chris," my brother whispered. "The other one's Alan."

"Who've you brought with you today, little man?" Chris said as he shoved the door open with his shoulder. It was a joke, of course. My brother at the age of thirteen was six foot one. He was a handsome blond giant of a boy.

"This is my sister," my brother said.

"Hello, sister," Chris said. "Do you have a name?"

There was something slow about the way Chris moved that made me think of the caterpillar on the toadstool from *Alice's Adventures in Wonderland*. Alan, whom we met later, was tall and mercurial. He had grown his straight hair long on one side to cover his face entirely. On the other it was shaved. I'd seen the punks all over Brighton with their red, blue, and green Mohawk spikes. It was always hard not to stare at them. I tried not to stare at Alan.

My mother's house was pristine, threadbare, and brightly colored; theirs had broken sofas, marijuana plants, and chessboards. Books and records were scattered on the floor and piled high against the walls. Through cracks in doors I glimpsed mattresses pushed up into the corners of rooms, under more bookshelves and plants. Dust hung in the air where the sun slanted in. Soon my brother and I were visiting every few days, to return a book or pick up a new music tape they'd made for us. We'd slip down the side passage and into the garden, push through the overgrown shrubs and knock on the boarded-up back window. Once we were inside, time moved differently.

Chris and Alan's friends came and went to and from the house—artists, musicians, and filmmakers. They picked up work when they needed to, in a music shop or bar or café, for a few hours every week. My mother would have called them dropouts. The Brethren would have called them Satan's foot soldiers. They sold cannabis resin in cellophane parcels, which meant, someone told me, they were definitely drug dealers. But they kept their promises. And they were kind.

I used the money I earned from my Saturday job at the news-agent's to buy charity-shop long silk floral dresses like those worn by the women I'd seen at the squat. I wore them with oversize sweaters and strings of beads. I lost weight. In the summer I wore Indian leather sandals or sometimes went barefoot. In the winter I wore Doc Marten boots. I bought joss sticks for my room.

At school I made friends with a beautiful Malaysian new girl. She'd noticed the henna I started using to color my hair. She said that in her country they made henna patterns on their hands. She was Hindu, and when I asked what that meant she said no one had asked her that since she'd come to Britain. She explained what her family practiced and why and told me why it was good to be a Hindu. She didn't know any Hindus in Britain. She and her brother and mother were living with their grandmother, who was Christian.

Why was she living with her grandmother? I asked. Her father had died, she said. Before they left Malaysia her little brother lit the funeral pyre they burned him on. Why had it been her brother who had done that? I wanted to ask. Why didn't they let her do it? Did Hindus consider her "just a girl" too? But when she talked about the funeral pyre her eyes were full of tears, so I changed the subject.

In the last weeks of the summer of 1979, when I had just turned fifteen, if my mother was out at her new job working as an accountant in a neighboring town and the twins were busy or playing with friends, my brother and I would slip across to Chris and Alan's smoky living room. Over there in the half-light I didn't worry about blushing or stammering. No one noticed. We'd perch up against beanbags or cushions and play chess or backgammon, but mostly we were there, like everyone else, to listen to music. Alan played Kraftwerk and Roxy Music and Joy Division. Chris played Bowie, Lou Reed, and Iggy Pop. I liked the music Chris played best. We drank tea, took occasional nervous drags from the joints people passed around, and listened to Chris and Alan argue about the new albums they brought home and played loud on their huge speakers.

"Did you feel anything *this* time?" my brother would ask as we crossed the road back to our house for dinner. And I'd shake my head. Neither of us dared inhale, so although I sometimes felt light-headed and heavy-limbed, I knew that, like him, I was never really stoned. It was LSD I wanted to take. I'd been asking Chris about the things he'd seen when he was tripping. But he said LSD wasn't good for people who had bad dreams. It was meditation I needed, he said, not acid. I was only fifteen. I was much too young to take LSD, he said.

"When I'm sixteen, then?" I asked. But he just laughed and shook his head.

He gave me a leaflet for a meditation course. I walked to the Old Salvation Army Hall one Saturday afternoon after work, found the administrator for the adult education section, and signed up for twelve weeks of Sunday afternoon classes, paying for them with my savings. When that course came to an end, I signed up for a communication class run by the same teachers. I sat cross-legged in a darkened room opposite my cross-legged partner while we repeated the phrase "All cows eat grass." All language was inherently empty, the instructor explained, but we could learn to communicate deep and complex thoughts and feelings through apparently meaningless phrases.

For thirty minutes my partner would repeat the words "All cows eat grass" to me. Then for thirty minutes I'd say it to him. In between our weekly sessions we were supposed to practice this technique—locking eyes with strangers at bus stops, in queues and cafés—"It's cold today," I'd say intensely. "Is the bus delayed?" What I was really saying in my mind was "Isn't life fascinating?" or "I understand your pain."

Now I practiced making eye contact with every customer who bought sweets or newspapers at the newsagent where I worked, particularly the ones who were shy or in a rush. "That's twenty-seven pence change," I'd say, smiling, projecting love, thinking of those cows eating grass. Every encounter, my meditation teachers reminded me, was sacred. Every man and woman on the other side of my counter had a deep secret place I was supposed to reach.

I was embarrassed at first, but I stopped blushing when I saw the powerful effects my newly fierce attention had on people. The most misanthropic of my customers now found excuses to linger at the counter and talk. I began to extend the range of my questions. That shirt's a good color on you—is blue your favorite? Why do you buy that particular newspaper rather than that one? Are you reading anything interesting? Have you ever memorized any poetry?

At the squat, Chris began to ask questions about my father.

"Why roulette?" he asked as he showed me how to roll the joint that everyone especially admired, the one that forked in the middle and was made of six long Rizla papers. "I mean, is there something about a roulette wheel that's different from slot machines?"

I was so spellbound by the question that I missed seeing the way he made the fork in the middle of the joint.

"Was there a connection," he asked, "between your father losing his belief in God and starting to gamble?"

"I don't know," I said, thinking about the tallies of black and red numbers I'd seen scattered on scraps of paper around the car. How would anyone know?

"He has a number system," I said, crumbling the resin down the middle of the long trough of tobacco cradled in Chris's hand.

"If he really thinks he can predict what number is going to come up next," Chris said, "that's *amazing*. I mean, if he does—and your father is smart, right?—then he believes humans can predict the future. Does he think he still has a hotline to God?"

"I don't know what he thinks," I said. "I haven't asked him about that." I hadn't really asked him about anything.

"Would he *mind* you asking?" Chris said as he showed me how to make the little twist of paper at the end to keep the tobacco and the weed in. "I mean, could you ask him questions like that?"

15

They'd put *Macbeth* onto the O-level syllabus, I told my father on the phone the next time he called. Could he take me to see it? The teachers said we were supposed to see at least one performance if we could.

He'd seen Anthony Hopkins play Macbeth in 1972, and Helen Mirren play Lady Macbeth in 1975, but the very best *Macbeth* performance *ever staged,* he said, with his usual maddening hyperbole, was the Ian McKellen–Judi Dench Royal Shakespeare Company production, which he'd now seen four times. It was on at the Young Vic again. Good thing I'd mentioned it. He'd get us tickets.

I'd once dreamed of railing at my father for his broken promises, for the fact that he'd made life so hard for my mother, but now I wanted more than anything to know if he thought the future was knowable. As soon as I got into the car he put on a tape of the Hollies' "The Air That I Breathe" and I had had to bite my lip so that I wouldn't cry. Chris and Alan would have said that the Hollies were trite, but I didn't care. I was sure he'd put on that song just for me.

In my mind, I was up on the armrest again, my body through the sunroof, my arms outstretched like a bird, the wind whipping my braids against my face.

Before, I'd always been in the backseat with the twins. Now I had the front passenger seat all to myself and the run of the glove compartment, where my father kept his precious tapes.

"Have you still got 'Kodachrome'?" I said coolly as I rummaged through it. " 'Mother and Child Reunion'?"

We'd set off late, so soon he was driving at ninety miles an hour up a crowded A23 toward London. Even as the rain began, he was overtaking all the other cars, his foot pressed down hard on the accelerator.

For the first twenty minutes or so I put on all the old songs my father had played repeatedly in the upside-down days after we left the Brethren: "Bridge over Troubled Water," "Morningtown Ride," "Sinner Man": *Sinner Man, where you gonna run to?* I told myself he must be remembering all the same things I did from those days, but Chris's voice was in my head now: *None of us really know what's going on inside other people, right?* Perhaps Chris was right. We were all dreamers; life was a dream.

I was relieved when, somewhere north of Crawley, my father began to slow down a little and lecture me about the play. How much did I know about *Macbeth*? he began, but he wasn't really interested in my answer. He wanted to tell me about everything he had in the *Macbeth* drawer in the filing cabinet in his brain: every interpretation Wilson Knight had ever made of the play, the connection to the Scottish witchcraft trials, what hubris meant, what the tragic flaw meant in relation to the play, Shakespeare's obsession with sin and blood and stains and the relationship between the stains and puritanism.

"If Macbeth had refused the call of the witches," I asked him, desperate to stop the flood of his talk, "if he'd *not* actually killed Duncan, would Birnam Wood have come to Dunsinane?"

My father stopped talking. He smiled.

"Interesting question," he said. He was thinking.

Then he turned the music down and began to recite Yeats's "Leda and the Swan" slowly, assuming I was keeping up, getting his inference, understanding how the complex poem answered the question I'd asked.

As he reached the lines *"A shudder in the loins engenders there,"* his voice began to break. The rain was now hammering the windscreen in great lashing strokes. *"The broken wall, the burning roof and tower . . ."*

The wipers screeched across the glass because the rubber had perished and he hadn't bothered to replace it. We were swerving toward the side of the road, and he was still beating out the rhythm on the steering wheel:

"And-Ag-a-mem-non-dead."

Suddenly we were in a ditch, white fog lights and red hazard lights refracting and splitting through the rainwater, the long rising and falling of truck horns as they swerved around us.

While we sat waiting for the tow truck, the rain running like a dark river over the car, he started up his monologue about Yeats's gyres, by way of explaining how the poem answered my question. His talk spiraled out and spiraled back just as his preaching had. You just had to keep up, concentrate.

I might have been furious with him for nearly getting us killed, for making us miss the play, for lecturing me, but I wasn't. I had my father to myself, and I wanted to understand about the gyres, and the patterns the rain made on the windows in the dark were so beautiful.

"Yeats believed," he said, "that time was like a necklace of intersecting spirals."

He tried to draw the shape in the air with his huge hands, but he couldn't make it work, so he reached into the inside pocket of his jacket, and sketched the pattern on the back of a betting slip:

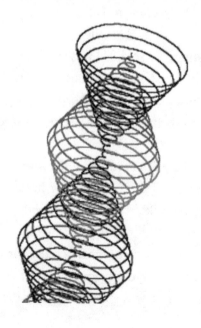

"The spirals of the new gyre start to spool outward here," he said, adding arrows to his diagram, circling the axis points with his red pen, "just as the last gyre is coming down into its end. See? Each new gyre of history starts with a kind of violent annunciation at an axis point: Zeus turned into a swan; he seduced Leda. That's there at the axis, here, and then the gyres open out: Leda gave birth to Helen; then Helen's beauty brought the Trojan wars into being. It spirals out and out—see, until everyone's caught up in it. Then a new axis point opens inside the gyre here—see? The angel Gabriel visited Mary. That's another collision between man and god, of course; Mary gave birth to Jesus and Jesus ended up crucified and before you know it, two millennia of Christianity have come into being. It spins out and out, and this time the burning walls are monasteries and abbeys and country churches. . . ."

I'm thinking of the wings beating above the two staggering girls, Mary and Leda, already pregnant, already incubating, feathers everywhere.

"History spirals out from moments of violence like that," my father continued.

"It was rape," I said. "Not seduction."

"What?"

"You said Zeus seduced Leda. He didn't—he raped her."

"History isn't *kind,*" he said, as though I was being sentimental. "It's violent and unstoppable; it builds to bloody crescendos." He was beating out the rhythm on the steering wheel again:

"And-Ag-a-mem-non-dead."

We're all caught up in history, I thought, like the girl caught in the swan god's bill.

The tow truck arrived and pulled us out of the ditch and we got going again, and an hour later, when my father parked and managed to persuade the ushers to let us creep into the back of the theater, we caught McKellen doing his "Tomorrow and Tomorrow and Tomorrow" speech. Now I began to see it all more clearly: the gyres and the witches and the whole relentless unraveling. Macbeth knew exactly what he was doing. Even if he suspected there'd be a price to pay for his apparent invincibility, for seeing out his course, he just *didn't know how to stop*. He turned himself into his own private gyre. My father was doing that too. He didn't know how to stop either.

"I am in blood stepped in so far," Macbeth mutters to himself, "that, should I wade no more, returning were as tedious as go o'er."

He imagined himself wading through a river of blood. He was up to his thighs in it. But it was too far to go back, so he told himself he might as well just keep going, let the gyre run its course because he couldn't stop it.

My father must have felt that way too, I thought, when he looked at the debt collection letters that he piled up unopened on his desk, when he looked at the pattern of numbers he'd discovered. Neither he nor Macbeth knew what lay ahead, but they knew it had to run its course.

Did my father think the future was knowable? I still didn't know, but I could understand why he might have wanted to believe that it was. He thought it was all going to come right. That with that One Big Win at roulette he'd be redeemed, lifted off the earth as it crashed and burned into the thunder and lightning, earthquakes, and plague of the Tribulation.

16

Through the winter of 1980 my father drove me to see plays in London, in Bristol, and in small theaters along the south coast. We talked about music, morality, Bergman, and Shakespeare, his gambling system, his new diet, the books I was reading. But I still couldn't find a way of putting into words the questions about God and free will that

Did he think the universe was ordered and that he had found a way of reading it? When he described his intricate system, he behaved as if he was sharing a great confidence, an alchemical formula, the secret of the philosopher's stone. If he could predict numbers, I wanted to ask him, then why couldn't he predict other things?

I found another column of numbers in the back of his notebook. It was a list of his winnings and losings. I ran my fingers down those columns. He was, of course, losing *so* much more than he was winning. So the system wasn't working after all. How, I longed to ask him, could he know one thing—that he was losing vast amounts of money—and still believe another—that his system was infallible?

I had to come to the casino with him, he told me. He had to *show* me how the system worked; then I'd see for myself. He picked me up from school one afternoon when I knew I wouldn't be missed. I had brought a change of clothes in my sports bag, as we'd agreed, clothes that would make me look older than my fifteen years. "None of that hippie stuff," my father had said. "Something smart."

The doorman called my father by his first name, shook his hand, refused the £10 "tip" my father offered him, a bribe that, I guessed, was supposed to make him overlook the fact that I was underage. The red-velvet-upholstered alcoves, mirrors, and dim light inside made the interior seem a place of perpetual midnight. A group of men in expensive suits sat at the bar with cocktails. Four or five older men were playing roulette shadowed by glamorous, much younger women with loud laughs who didn't play; a croupier saluted my father ostentatiously. My father fetched a high stool for me and placed it in the corner of the room so I could use the high shelf there to keep a list of the winning numbers. He took out a roll of £50 notes from his inside pocket.

The way my father moved around the roulette table, sliding colored chips from the pile in front of him to the numbered squares, slipping backward and forward from his chips to the roulette wheel, was different from the way the other players moved. He looked like he could make these moves in his sleep. The others cheered when they won. He was silent. He was rapt, his eyes shining.

The numbers were stacking up in the patterns again, he told me, glancing at the list I was keeping. Could I see? There was the red seven, a black thirteen, two red nineteens. Opposite me, in the half-light, an old woman in a white fur coat pushed £50 notes down a hole in the roulette table with one hand, very slowly, passing her chips from square to square with the other hand, as if she was moving underwater.

When my father won, he collected his winnings from a hatch at the back of the room in rolls of notes held together with red elastic bands, but instead of leaving he bought more chips and started feeding the notes straight down the hole again. It would take me fifty hours to earn a single one of those notes in the newsagent's shop, I whispered, as he leaned over me to check the list of numbers again, but he was already back to the roulette table dance. Soon he seemed to have forgotten I was there at all.

I began to visit him after school in the new, smaller flat he'd taken near the Stott and Sons warehouse. I could walk there on my way home. It smelled of cigarette smoke, old newspapers, off milk, socks, and kitchen rubbish. I washed up. I cleaned. I made a pile of his dirty clothes and left notes telling him to take his clothes to the launderette with diagrams about how to get there and how much change he'd need to take with him. I threw the mountains of newspapers in the bin, making sure to cut out the crosswords first. He liked doing crosswords when he couldn't sleep.

He took me to see a performance of Ibsen's *The Wild Duck* at the National Theatre in London. I was sixteen. In the car, he explained Ibsen's idea of the "life lie" with great care and attention. Life lies, he said, were the lies people told themselves to make life bearable.

The Ekdal family in *The Wild Duck,* he explained—father, mother, teenage daughter, grandfather—were poor but happy. They keep going, he said, because they have delusions. The grandfather thinks he's a great hunter. The father is convinced he's making an invention that will make him famous and pay off all the family debts. The daughter thinks her father is a great man. These were their life lies.

"So Ibsen," said my father, "sends in a visitor, Gregers, an old friend of the father's. Gregers exposes all their life lies, and tells them a few more things they would rather not have known. Then Ibsen makes us watch what happens next. It's not good, of course," he said. "But that's the point: Ibsen isn't sure we should make people see how deluded they are."

How could my father see intricately complex patterns in the black and red numbers of his columns but not have seen his own life lie reflected back in Ibsen's mirror that evening?

"I just need one big win," he told me again as we drove back through the night. He'd begun to rant about how the new partners at Stott and Sons were fleecing the business. "Just one big win will make everything come right."

17

My mother noticed the whited-out entries on the check stubs and the ragged holes in the income and outgoings ledgers. Though my parents had separated, she was still working in the Stott and Sons office down at the warehouse. She must have guessed that the stubs had something to do with the pattern of my father's afternoon disappearances, but she could not have known the scale of what would unravel when the partners decided to bring in specialist accountants to take a closer look at the books.

It took the partners, the accountants, and the police several weeks to gather the evidence needed for my father to be charged. He'd been embezzling money for years, fiddling the books to pay for his gambling. For some reason he stopped trying to cover his tracks in the last months of 1980. Did he want to be caught? Did he want someone to make it all stop?

The police investigation was secret, but my father must have sensed the walls closing in. He hadn't been sleeping for some time; he complained of stomach pains; empty bottles of whiskey rolled around in the trunk of the car and under the passenger seat; he kept boxes of antacid tablets in the glove compartment and took seven or eight at a time; his skin looked gray.

There'd been another suicide. Anna Napthine, a young Brethren wife and mother, had hanged herself in London. My father collected the newspaper reports and added them to his file.

"They've learned *nothing* since the Andover tragedy," he said, passing me the clippings. "The journalists don't get it, of course," he added. "They never do."

He'd had to ask around about Anna Napthine, he told me. He'd phoned some ex-Brethren to find out what happened.

Jim Symington, the Elect Vessel, had decided that there was a backlog of sins that now had to be "cleared" if the Brethren were going to get clean enough for the Lord. He'd gone over the old tapes of meetings to identify people who'd been troublemakers or who'd asked difficult questions back in the sixties and seventies. Hundreds of sinners had not been properly disciplined the first time around, he told the Brethren, so priests must root out these people in their local meetings and put them under seven days of "assembly discipline" to get them properly *clean*.

London Brethren, my father said, put Anna Napthine on their list. Years before she'd "confessed" to adultery, but had not been "shut up," so now they told her it was time for her to get properly right with the Lord. They had shut her up for much longer than the now-statutory seven days, though no one knew why.

In her bedroom, isolated from her family for weeks, tormented by her own thoughts and the visits of the priests, Anna Napthine got sick. Her husband took their two young children to the local park one afternoon, and when they came back to the house they found Anna's body hanging from a ceiling joist.

"They're completely *unshameable*," my father said.

Symington, my father told me, preached about the suicide in a ministry meeting in Australia the following day. He told the Brethren that Satan had used Anna Napthine as a weapon to stop them from doing the Lord's work: "The devil urged her to do that to counter the Lord's demand for a review and an adjustment of defective assembly administration."

My father looked stricken and depleted.

"How many more?" he asked.

That winter of 1981, after he was arrested, charged with embezzlement and fraud, and released on bail pending trial, my father played me the Bergman faith trilogy: *Through a Glass Darkly, Winter Light,* and *The Silence*. He sat on the floor of his flat, among the discarded newspapers, drinking his way through another bottle of whiskey, pausing and replaying scenes to puzzle out their meanings to me, and to himself.

In *Winter Light,* a priest who has lost his faith gives Communion to the last two or three remaining members of the congregation of his remote Lutheran church in midwinter. Although he goes through the rituals and preparations, he's tormented by God's silence, God's failure to say something back.

We watched the light move around the empty church up on the screen, slanting in through windows, lighting the priest's tormented face as he gave his sermon or collapsed in exhaustion in the vestry. We watched him berate and entreat God, perhaps trying to provoke him into sending some kind of sign. In one shot, the priest stands looking out at the snow falling across the fields, his face lit up. This is all there is, Bergman seemed to be saying, just the light on the snow. But look how beautiful it is. We are too busy fretting about the next world to see this one in all its strange beauty.

When a tortured young man—the father of a young family—comes to talk to him about God, the priest stops just short of telling him that there is no God. The young man disappears into the snow and is later found hanged. The priest, racked with guilt, takes Communion just the same.

We watched *The Silence* the same afternoon. It was even more haunting and incomprehensible, scored by the sound of clock hands ticking and fans whirring. Two sisters and a ten-year-old boy, traveling across Europe on the brink of war, wall up in a two-room apartment in a semi-derelict central European hotel. The elder woman is dying, self-medicating with vodka and cigarettes, and trying to finish a manuscript. The child, whose mother is the younger sister, goes wandering in the corridors of the hotel. He meets a troupe of Spanish dwarfs and stares out the window as a lone tank rolls down the road at night.

"No one *says* anything," my father said. "That's the thing. Everyone's locked into the silence. Everyone's trapped. They're all talking into a void."

Especially the boy wandering the corridors, I thought. Especially him.

I remembered the boy my father had once been, the boy who collapsed on the steps of his house when he thought his mother and sister were taken in the Rapture and he'd been left behind, the boy counting the Bible letters in the meeting, longing for time to himself, hectored by the father voices he heard in his head and beguiled by the mother voices. But when the silence finally came it engulfed him.

"I've met a boy," I told my father, just weeks before his court case. We were sitting in his flat. I could still smell the smoke from the previous night's bonfire in my hair. I had twenty minutes to get back to school for my afternoon history class, and because my father was in a hurry to show me *Through a Glass Darkly* he didn't ask me any questions about the boy. We watched the film and I missed my history class.

I'd met the boy at a bonfire party a couple of weeks before. In the summers, my friends and I roamed the seafront promenades like flocks of birds gathering on wires. Emma lived on the next street and her parents took in language students too, but they were much younger and wilder than the ones who boarded with us. They invited us to parties on the beach, where they gathered in large numbers around a bonfire after dark. We'd bring our friends. That night we were sitting on old blankets thrown over the pebbles, drinking cheap white wine, smoking weed, talking about university applications. I'd missed too much school, I told them. My teachers must have predicted very low grades for me. I'd had four university rejections out of five. Someone was telling me I should think about signing up for a kibbutz instead.

I'd been watching the boy over on the other side of the flames playing his guitar, his enormous brown leather jacket pulled around his hunched body, his long fingers picking out chords. He wrote his own songs and music, I heard someone say; he was in a band. His name was Tom.

A week later, Tom walked me home from another bonfire party. We sat on a bench looking out over the ocean, the full moon making a road across the water to us. Seagulls drifted overhead like ghosts. We stayed there talking until a line of pink gradually widened along the horizon and the sea slowly disgorged the great fireball of the sun. He told me he was leaving home. His parents didn't understand him. They were philistines, he said, and I asked him if he knew who the Philistines were. When he said he didn't, I explained, and then he kissed me. My father was about to go to prison, I said, watching his dark eyes open wide. When I crept back into the house after dawn, I was relieved to find I'd not been missed.

18

I was afraid of what my father might do in the days leading up to the court case, I told Tom. Especially with Marsha and her children away on summer holiday and him staying in their house all by himself. Marsha had been my father's girlfriend once. Now she was just his friend. My father was not well. He'd asked me to stay with him there, to keep him company, now that my exams were finished. My mother didn't think it was a good idea, but who else was going to go?

I packed a bag. My mother drove me to the edge of that leafy estate where my father's onetime girlfriend still lived with her teenage children. She made me promise to call her if I needed her.

"Just keep it ordinary," Tom said. "Just use your instinct. Watch films. Keep him talking. Call me."

There were books he wanted to talk to my father about, he said. He'd come over. I told him it was probably better if he didn't.

This was the house I'd watched from my seat up on the hill. I'd never been inside. My father had often invited me to meet Marsha. I'd like her, he said. She was smart, and she knew all sorts of things about books and music and films. But I refused. I didn't want to meet the family I'd seen through my binoculars. I didn't want those neighbors to see me getting out of my father's car, walking along the path that he'd walked with them. I didn't want to put myself into that world.

But now I was inside. There were pictures of Marsha with her ex-husband and children. There were pictures on every wall, babies, portraits, holidays. There were photos of my father with her and with her children and their friends. Those were her books on the shelves, that was her music collection next to the record player.

That week my father drank from the moment he woke until the moment he fell asleep on the sofa twelve hours later. He'd bought a case of whiskey. He woke in the night and paced the house, clutching one of his battery-operated radios. When he started talking about killing himself—how he was fit for nothing, how he was so ashamed, how he'd never forgiven himself for killing his father, for leaving my mother—I made more tea, gave him films to watch, or talked about anything and everything that came into my head.

Tom tapped on the window one night and I invited him in. He and I sat at the top of the stairs, my father asleep downstairs on the sofa under the rug I'd pulled up over him. When Tom saw the check-list I'd made of things to hide from my father—the knives in the kitchen, the painkillers in the medicine cabinet, the keys to the car—he told me I was being overdramatic. I think you mean "melo-dramatic," I said.

A week later, my father was given a twelve-month prison sen-tence that would, my mother told us, probably be reduced to three months. There'd be no more running for him now, I told Tom. He was safe. He had a new Iron Room, I said, and then I had to explain what an Iron Room was. Tom asked why anyone would want to build a church from corrugated iron. I told him it was complicated and that one day I'd explain. My father would be fine, I repeated. He'd have books and pens and paper. He could finish that play he'd started writing.

Why would they call a prison Wormwood Scrubs? I asked Tom, but he wasn't much interested in what I knew about the Bible, so I didn't tell him that Wormwood was the name of the star in the Book of Revelation that blazed like a torch, fell from the sky, and poisoned all the rivers and springs. The waters turned bitter and many people died. Falling stars, comets, and poisoned waters were all signs that the End Times were coming.

It was July. School had finished. I was in love. My father was in prison and he was safe. And York University had offered me a place to study English literature.

The largest bundle of the letters Kez found in the envelope my father had labeled PRISON LETTERS were from Tom. During my father's time in prison, Tom and I were walking the streets of Brighton at night, sneaking into the back of gigs so we didn't have to pay, lying under the stars on the beach in the early hours of the morning talking about books, God, music, swimming at midnight, waiting for our A-level results. Through all of that, Tom, who'd met my father only once before the court case, wrote to him every day he was in prison. And my father wrote back. That surprised me. They wrote to each other about T. S. Eliot, about Camus and Sartre, about transcendentalism. Tom told my father not to worry about my silence—that, though I wasn't writing to him, I was thinking of him. I was busy, he wrote, with all the various part-time jobs I had: "two pubs and a shop . . . She often talks of you."

I *was* busy, and in love. But the reason I didn't write to my father in prison was that I'd had enough and I was furious with him. Not because he'd shamed the family—that hardly seemed important— but because it seemed to me that he'd played straight into the Brethrens' hands. I knew that the news of his prison sentence would be traveling down Brethren networks. The Jims would be using him to tell the same old story: Look what happens when you leave. Look what happens when Satan gets hold of you. They'd be using my father's story to frighten more teenagers into compliance. Look what happened to Roger Stott. *Outside the door, son, there is only darkness.* My father had written the Brethren the perfect morality—or immorality—tale, and there was no undoing it.

I needed new air. In August, Tom wrote to my father to tell him that my A-level results had been unexpectedly good. York had confirmed my place. Classes started in the middle of September, just two weeks after my father's release date. I had, he wrote, already started packing.

19

When people asked me about what happened to my father after prison, I told them how he landed himself a job at the BBC. For ten years he worked as a researcher for religious programs and then he was promoted, and made three brilliant films. He interviewed George Steiner and various eminent bishops for his first film, *A Brief History of Hell*, I'd tell them proudly. He even met the Pope. He worked with Susan Sontag on his second film, *Just an Illness*, which was about illness and ideas of divine punishment. In his last film, *The Isle Is Full of Noises*, he used poems by Yeats and Heaney and Hughes to show how ancient spirits and gods haunt our landscapes.

And I'd be thinking: He never let up, did he? He'd spent all his post-Brethren years trying to figure out what had happened to him—in his memoir, his plays, his poetry, the books he read, and then in his BBC films.

When I listened to myself describing my father's postprison years like that, it sounded like a redemption song: the lost man who gets back on his feet and makes something of himself. But his life was more complicated than that. There were other sides to it; there always are. I tried to avoid telling the story about how he continued to steal or borrow from my brothers and me and his friends so that he could keep returning to the roulette wheel, that he'd been sacked from the BBC for financial irregularities, that he was still gambling online on his deathbed.

We all knew how that particular part of his life story was going to play out. So I didn't tell people that he and I were estranged on and off over the years, that I'd stopped talking to him when he came out of prison and I went off to university, and again when he conned money out of family members and lied to cover his tracks. But, I remembered now, the silences between us never lasted for long.

He'd say the gyres were still opening up and that we were all caught up in them, especially him, and that he couldn't help himself, but I don't see it that way. To me the world is made up of delicate branching webs and networks. That way of seeing comes, I think, from reading Darwin and George Eliot in my second year of university and, when I fell pregnant, thinking of the child growing inside my womb and that miraculous network of neural pathways forming both in his new brain and my older one. We *were* all "netted together," just as Darwin had said. Everything we did had an effect on the people around us.

I thought of those networks again when, decades later, I found my sixteen-year-old daughter Hannah crying outside a temple in Jaipur. She'd seen me praying at the Hindu shrine, she said, and, because I'd brought up my children in a secular way, my prayers had felt to her like a kind of betrayal.

"Does that mean you believe in God?" she asked, her eyes swollen and dark. I cursed myself. I should have talked with them more about God and religion and souls, I thought. We talked about other difficult subjects like love and sex easily enough. I'd told myself it was best to leave them to puzzle out their own beliefs about God, not for me to tell them what I thought, but the truth is I probably wouldn't have known what to say.

A woman had said to me once, I told Hannah on the bus to Push-kar, that there were some mysteries we'd never figure out. I saw mysteries everywhere now that I was older, not just about God but in the science I read about—in pure math, in animal behavior, in studies of consciousness and the mind and memory. The more we find out, the more mysteries we seem to discover, I said. I was thinking of my mother greeting the moon. "Hello, moon," she'd say as she closed the curtains on the night, "there you are again."

When I lost myself praying in the temple in Jaipur, I told Hannah, it was because in India I felt that mystery of who we are and where we've come from and where we are going like a fire in my blood.

"I look at you," I said, "and I think about all the voices and questions in your head, and your brother's head, and your sister's head, and the thousands of miles of neural pathways you have between you, and that's a miracle too. There are things we'll never know."

"You taught us that," she said, and we were both crying now. "You taught us that it was okay not to know."

When our Muslim guide asked if we wanted to join the Hindu ceremony on the banks of the holy lake at Pushkar to mark New Year's Eve, it was Hannah who volunteered first. She wanted to sit and watch the sun set on the last day over the holy lake with all those people, she said. And when the setting sun made a burnished road across the lake and the lake birds rose all together as the temple bells began to ring out, and the drumming began, I told her it reminded me of the night of my first kiss. She laughed. It made her think, she said, of how little we are.

When I think of my father now I often think of two jars. The first was made of transparent plastic. It sat on a shelf in my son's attic room at Christmas twenty years ago, a treasured, closely guarded jar, half-full of brightly colored cellophane-wrapped sweets. Jacob had vacated his bedroom, begrudgingly, for his grandfather's visit. Though he liked Dodge, as we all called him by then, and thought of him as a bit of a legendary scoundrel, he didn't much want to give up his room, especially at Christmas.

In the days leading up to Christmas, my father quickly filled my son's room with the detritus that he always scattered around himself: newspapers, empty wine bottles, notebooks full of columns of numbers. I dared not look. I knew how this would end up. My son would be outraged, despite the fact that at the age of twelve he was, like his grandfather, a detritus-scattering boy, his room on a normal day full of abandoned clothes and the tangled wires of computer equipment. So I steeled myself when he came to find me in the kitchen on Christmas morning, beckoned me to follow him upstairs to his room, and gestured through the half-open door with an expression of both horror and intense admiration.

There, among the old newspapers and discarded clothes, amid a scattering of sweets and empty wrappers, was the sweet jar, now filled with bright yellow liquid.

"Someone's been sleeping in my bed," Jacob said, reciting the words from *Goldilocks and the Three Bears,* his eyes shining. "Someone's been peeing in my sweet jar and they've filled it right up."

We closed the door quietly and took ourselves back downstairs to the kitchen, where my father was holding forth about Yeats or Dylan Thomas again. My then-husband glanced up from basting the turkey with a look of exasperation.

Through the eating of the turkey and the paper hats and the toasts and the exchanging of gifts, Jacob returned again and again to the candy jar. He came to tell me it was *still there.* The next day, after we drove my father to the station and said our goodbyes and he told Jacob that he'd send him Seamus Heaney's new collection, my son and I went back up the stairs to the attic bedroom together. The jar was now on its original shelf, the sweets back inside. We stood there, he and I, staring at the jar that was now misting up with condensation:

"Good old Dodge," Jacob said. "Sound. Nice work."

And of course I wanted to say something about how a man might steal, embezzle, and betray, and you'd still want to be in his part of the room, that a man might be both *sublime* and *abject* and, I thought, if Jacob asked me what that meant, I'd say that my father could be downstairs talking about Yeats or free will and upstairs peeing in his grandson's sweet jar. But I knew there was no way I could explain that yet. Jacob would have to figure some of those things out for himself. We high-fived instead.

The second jar was the same shape and size as Jacob's sweet jar but made of opaque red plastic. The woman at reception at Cambridge Crematorium asked me to sign for it as she passed it across the desk. It had my father's name on it and the date of his cremation. The red of the plastic was dark, somewhere between blood and wine, the texture slightly mottled.

"That's him?" I said. "That's all of him?"

Had they really managed to get all of him in there: his bones, sinews, bile, arms, legs, and that scar that ran from his ear to his Adam's apple?

"They removed your father's pacemaker first, of course," the receptionist said, checking her files, as if she thought I was complaining of being shortchanged. Did I want to take that away with me too?

No, that's not it, I wanted to say. It's just that he was so *big*. He'd stand in my kitchen reciting poetry or explaining why Poliakoff was the second-greatest playwright currently writing for British television, or describing the pattern growing in the columns of numbers he'd made, and it would be so hard to get around him, he took up so much space. I'd ask him to sit on a chair so I could cook or get to a baby and he *would* sit, but then he'd spring back up again to reoccupy the middle of the room.

Instead I signed the form she gave me to say I'd taken the ashes but not the pacemaker.

It was raining. I put the red jar on the passenger seat of my car and turned the ignition so that the wipers cleared the windscreen. We sat there together, he and I, in the cemetery parking lot, while I waited for the rain—and my own sobs—to subside. Now there was only the red jar with the lid screwed tight.

"Say something back," I said. "Just say *something*."

There was only the sound of the rain on the roof, the windscreen wipers screeching against the glass, and the caw of a crow from a nearby tree.

But I hadn't tuned in. I wasn't listening:

"Yeats, you see," my father was saying, "believed that time was a necklace of interlinked spirals." And he's drawing the gyres on his betting slip, circling the axis points with his red pen—"See?"—and he's slipping seamlessly from Leda and the swan to the angel appearing to Mary and on to the Crucifixion.

"Sooner or later," he's saying, "the burning walls of Troy become the burning walls of our monasteries and abbeys and country churches. . . ."

And I'm saying, "Does that mean you still believe in God?"

20

I haven't seen a Brethren family now for several years. There are forty-five thousand of them around the world, but they keep to themselves; they blend in. So I was surprised when Kez found an assembly last summer in rural Norfolk just a few miles away from the house I'd rented in Norwich.

I had read Mark Cocker's *Crow Country* and bought myself a pair of binoculars so that I could go off on weekends to the marshes and broads; sometimes Kez came with me. It was summer, the wrong time of year for the great rook displays, the Strumpshaw Fen bird-watchers told me, but if I was patient I'd see bitterns, marsh harriers, and kingfishers instead.

I spent several Sundays listening out for the mating boom of the bittern on the marshes but failed to hear it, so I decided to go farther north, out of the Yare Valley and up onto the Broads. Kez said she'd join me.

A few days later she rang to say that if we left really early on Sunday morning we could park outside the Brethren meeting room in Salhouse and watch them all go in to break bread before we went off to find the bitterns. She'd found the Norfolk Brethren meeting rooms on Google Maps a few weeks before—there were only two: a small one in Salhouse and one huge one in Rackheath.

"It's perfectly legal," she said, when I protested. "The meeting room is right next to the station. We wouldn't be trespassing."

"But we'd never see over the wall," I said.

"This one seems to be made of some kind of metal with gaps," she said, "with shrubs along the inside. You can see through in places. I've checked on Google Street View."

We drove through the streets of an eerily empty Norwich at five A.M., heading north. A thick blanket of fog hung across the fields, pooling in pockets in the lower ground. When a young fox crossed the road in front of us, the fog curled around it like currents in a river.

As we approached Salhouse down a farm track called Muck Lane, floodlights on the horizon lit up the morning sky. That was the parking lot of the meeting room, I told Kez. I remembered the lights at the Vale Avenue meeting room in the early morning. They'd hurt my eyes when my father lifted me out of the car half-asleep.

The meeting room was a dark wooden building with blacked-out windows. It stood in a sea of tarmac built on fenced-off land adjacent to the station car lot. Once we'd parked, we peered through the chain-link fence between our parking lot and theirs. The lot was full. We were too late. The Salhouse Brethren were already breaking bread. They must have started at 5:30, I told Kez; that was half an hour earlier than the time we broke bread when I was growing up.

While we waited for them to come out, Kez pulled up the previous night's episode of *The Archers* on her phone and played it through the car speakers. I turned off the engine to listen. Helen Archer was in prison awaiting trial for having stabbed her abusive husband. She'd just had her baby. We both wanted to know if she was all right. Kez passed me the binoculars.

Eventually the meeting room doors swung open. Twenty or thirty men and boys came out first, each of them dressed in a dazzlingly white shirt and black trousers. The effect of all those white shirts against the dark building was startling, like the foam on the top of a wave that was moving in my direction. Behind them, women in brightly colored headscarves tied at the backs of their necks ushered small children toward cars. One of the women, spotting our car, walked straight toward us and peered through the metal fence.

I gasped and reached for the button to lock the car doors. Kez laughed.

"She can't see us through the glass, remember," she said. "It's tinted."

The woman glared at our darkened windows. We looked at her. After a few seconds she turned and climbed into her car. Kez grabbed my hand. "I won't let them get you," she said. We both laughed.

We waited for the last of the cars to leave and then drove slowly through the village suburbs in the fog. Clusters of Brethren men and boys carrying Bibles came into view and then were gone. Soon the big cars and the men in white shirts disappeared completely. We were alone in the dawn on the outskirts of Salhouse.

"Now it's time for the bitterns," Kez said, pouring coffee from a flask and unwrapping the sandwiches we were supposed to save till lunch.

As we walked the path around Salhouse Broad, passing the binoculars between us, scanning for reed buntings and listening out for the elusive bitterns, the little girl in the red cardigan kept appearing in my mind's eye. I wondered if there were girls like her in meeting rooms now, sitting in the back row among the women, trying to work out how transparent the Spirit was, and if those girls sometimes wondered, as I had, why the women didn't just stand up and stamp their feet and shout.

It was a summer's morning; bird-watchers and walkers were gathering; all around us giant oaks and elms puffed up their colossal greens into blue sky. Cuckoos called from distant fields. We saw a kingfisher flash past and a pair of herons take to the air together, but still we didn't hear the bitterns.

My children grew up very differently from me: my son, Jacob, born in my second year at university, was raised in a commune of intellectuals and writers; my daughters, Hannah and Kez, are not afraid to ask questions or speak up or take to the streets together to demonstrate about the refugee crisis. The gyre is not inexorable. They've been raised to love this world of ours. They do not believe in absolute good or absolute evil. They'll fight to protect this fleeting life and one another and to make the world more just and kind.

My aftermath has been slow, which is why, I think, I have spent so much time reading in libraries and talking about literature in university seminar rooms, writing books about Darwin and teaching classes on feminism. The Iron Room of my father's world swung open to the skies when, at the age of ten, he was allowed to keep Arthur Mee's *The Book of Everlasting Things*. Since that first burst of joy and terror I felt when I reached for the turquoise spine of the school library copy of *The Secret Island* or tracked down Darwin in the school encyclopedia, I have spent much of my life in libraries: Cambridge University Library, the English Faculty Library, Cambridge Zoology Library, and now the British Library. I read erratically sometimes, veering from poetry to science to history to fiction until I find myself caught up in something. It might be seventeenth-century glassmaking, or Darwin's barnacles, or what happened to Londinium after the Romans left it derelict, or the hunting patterns of peregrines.

I haven't had that dream about the Committee for a while, but I'm certain they'll be back. Next time I'll have a few things to say. For fifty years they've summoned me back to their Iron Room to hector me with questions about why I've failed to do what I was sent here to do. . . . Have I forgotten *again*?

Next time I'll take a few paces across the room and grasp the iron handles of that heavy interrogating light of theirs with both hands. The beam will sweep across the room, shadows contracting and stretching until I have them all pinioned in its glare.

"I don't have to remember what I was sent here to do," I'll say, "because I wasn't sent here *to do anything*."

I'll borrow some phrases from V. S. Ramachandran's book on consciousness.

"My brain is made up of atoms forged billions of years ago in the heart of countless far-flung stars," I'll say. "Those particles drifted for eons and light-years out there in the universe until gravity and change brought them together in my skull to form the tangle of atoms that make up my brain. Now I can wonder about the gods, or life after death, or consciousness and where we've all come from and where we might be going to, and I can sit outside under the stars talking with my children and their friends and wonder about my ability to wonder. You'll never build an Iron Room strong enough or big enough or dark enough to stop that. There'll always be a crack where the light gets in."

I went to fetch my children—Kezia who was then twelve, Hannah fourteen, and Jacob twenty-three—so that they could say their good-byes to their grandfather. He had not spoken for days, I told them. He hadn't opened his eyes or moved. Even when I had read him the whole of *Four Quartets,* his favorite poem, his face did not flicker. His breathing was shallow. "He's our tribal leader," Jacob said. "I can't imagine him not being there."

Up on the fens, the snow was falling again; the setting sun cast a red glow across the white fields. We drove slowly up the lane following the line of the river, until the pink tower of the mill came into view over the brow of an incline. My brother and stepmother were cooking dinner in honor of our visit, an elaborate cassoulet from one of my father's recipes. The sitting room in the mill tower where my father lay was warm and fragrant, the table laid out with candles and open bottles of wine.

But when the children took their positions around his reclining chair and Jacob called his name—"Dodge," he said softly—his voice cracking with tears, my father's eyes opened. I took Kez's hand.

"I'm sorry I can't talk now," he whispered, struggling to catch his breath, "but in a little while I'll unfurl my wings and then fly a little, you'll see." Then he disappeared back under the morphine.

It was the last thing he said.

Four days later the owl began its slow ghostly flight down the riverbank toward him.

Acknowledgments

Many people have helped me to write this book. Ex-Brethren have checked facts, tracked down source material, provided photographs, notes, and diaries; explained obscure Brethren doctrine; or told me their family stories. Most of these people, several of whom appear with substitute names in the book, have chosen to stay anonymous. For many of my informants, remembering was difficult. Their determination to answer my questions despite that difficulty kept me going when the task of finishing this book occasionally seemed impossible. I particularly thank "Frank," "Ruth," and "William." They became a chorus in my head as I wrote, just as they had been for my father.

I am grateful to Ian McKay for his friendship, encouragement, patience, and the speed with which he checked my account against his records, archives, and his digitalized ministries during the two years of the book's evolution. Thank you also to Graham Johnson of the Christian Brethren collection at Manchester University Library, who provided archive material.

The trustees of the International Retreat for Writers at Hawthornden Castle gave me a monthlong fellowship to finish the book and they turned a blind eye on my occasional excursions to remote graveyards and fishing villages. Thank you to Hamish Robinson for an early-morning drive to the local GP surgery after the wasps attacked.

To my friends Tiffany Atkinson and Petra Rau, who were also my readers and who, like so many of my colleagues at the University of East Anglia, take risks with form and breach disciplinary boundaries in endlessly inventive ways. Tiffany helped me to understand embarrassment and even, occasionally, to find pleasure in it.

I thank Alex Stein for her twelve-week course on the Social Psychology of Cults and Totalitarianism taught at the Mary Ward Centre in London, and to the group of people in the class that summer. Most had children in cults or had lived in cult communities. I am grateful for their stories and for the reading Alex gave us—books and essays from Hannah Arendt to Peter Lipton, and extracts from Alex's own work on brainwashing all helped me to understand the Brethren as a cult and to see how cults work.

Don Paterson convinced me it was time to begin, showed me both how to start and, after a duration, how to end.

I thank Rebecca Carter, my agent at Janklow & Nesbit, for seeing what I couldn't yet see and for her unique insights and instincts along the way. I am grateful to my very brilliant editors—Helen Garnons-Williams of Fourth Estate and Cindy Spiegel of Spiegel & Grau—for understanding what the book might be, and for challenging me through every draft to go further and find answers to questions I did not yet know how to formulate. Thank you too to Robert Lacey of Fourth Estate and Annie Chagnot and Kelly Chian of Spiegel and Grau for putting the book through such scrupulous and eagle-eyed copyediting and into production.

My thanks go to my grown-up children, Hannah, Kezia, and Jacob, for reminding me why this book mattered. Kezia chivvied and challenged as I wrote and was often ahead of me with the torch finding the way. Jacob and Hannah read and improved drafts. I could not have written this memoir without my brother Benjamin, who is one of the kindest and wisest men I've ever known. And finally my thanks go to my father, for leaving me such a complex and rich inheritance; and to my mother, for keeping the family ship afloat in the often mighty turbulence he left in his wake.

Select Bibliography

ARCHIVES OF BRETHREN MATERIALS

Christian Brethren Archive, John Rylands University Library of Manchester University

www.mybrethren.org

Archive of materials on the Plymouth Brethren: www.brethrenarchive.org /archive/

BOOKS ABOUT THE BRETHREN

Adams, Norman. *Goodbye, Beloved Brethren.* Aberdeen: Impulse Publications Ltd., 1972.

Bachelard, Michael. *Behind the Exclusive Brethren.* Carlton North, Vic.: Scribe Publications, 2008.

Bailey, Michael, and Guy Redden, eds. *Mediating Faiths: Religion and Socio-Cultural Change in the Twenty-First Century.* Farnham: Ashgate, 2011.

Baylis, Robert H. *My People: The Story of Those Christians Sometimes Called Plymouth Brethren.* Wheaton, Ill.: H. Shaw, 1997.

Cutler Grace, Margaret. "Diary Account of J.T. Junior Edicts." Papers of Margaret Grace Cutler, Box 141, Christian Brethren Archive, John Rylands University Library of Manchester University, 1959–70.

Dickson, Neil T. R. *Brethren in Scotland 1838–2000.* Milton Keynes: Paternoster Press, 2002.

Dronsfield, W. R. "The Brethren After 1870." Christian Brethren Archive, John Rylands University Library of Manchester University, Neil Dickson Collection, Box 115, 2009.

Goodall, Felicity. *A Question of Conscience: Conscientious Objection in the Two World Wars.* Stroud: Sutton, 1997.

Ironside, H.A. *A Historical Sketch of the Brethren Movement.* Neptune, N.J.: Loizeaux Bros., 1985.

Napoleon, Noel. *The History of the Brethren*, 2 vols. Denver: W.F. Knapp, 1936.

Neatby, William Blair. *A History of the Plymouth Brethren*, 2nd edition. London: Hodder & Stoughton, 1902.

Newton, Ken and Chan, Andrew. *The Brethren Movement Worldwide: Key Information 2011.* Lockerbie: OPAL Trust for International Brethren Conference on Mission, 2011.

Pickering, Henry. *Chief Men Among the Brethren.* Neptune N.J.: Loizeaux Bros., 1996.

Rowdon, Harold H. *Who Are the Brethren and Does It Matter?* Exeter: Paternoster Press, 1986.

Shuff, Roger N. *Searching for the True Church: Brethren and Evangelicals in Mid-Twentieth-Century England.* Milton Keynes: Paternoster Press, 2005.

Scotland, N. "Encountering the Exclusive Brethren: A Late Twentieth-Century Cult." *European Journal of Theology*, Vol. VI (1997), pp. 157–167.

Tonts, M. "The Exclusive Brethren and an Australian Rural Community." *Journal of Rural Studies*, Vol. XVII, pp. 309–322.   date ?

Wilson, B. R. "The Exclusive Brethren: A Case Study in the Evolution of a Sectarian Ideology," *Patterns of Sectarianism: Organisation and Ideology in Social and Religious Movements.* London: Heinemann, 1967.

Wilson, Elisabeth. " 'The Eyes of the Authorities Are Upon Us': The Brethren and World War I." *BAHNR*, Vol. III (2014), pp. 2–17.

Memoirs

Arnott, Anne. *The Brethren: An Autobiography of a Plymouth Brethren Childhood.* London: Hodder & Stoughton, 1970.

Bell, James. *The Exclusive Sinner.* London: AuthorHouse, 2014.

Field, Marion. *Don't Call Me Sister!* Woking: Petra, 1993.

Field, Marion. *Shut Up Sarah.* Godalming: Highland, 1996.

Gosse, Edmund. *Father and Son: A Story of Two Temperaments*, ed. Michael Newton. Oxford: Oxford University Press, 2004.

Thomas, Ngaire. *Behind Closed Doors: A Startling Story of Exclusive Brethren Life.* Auckland: Random House, 2005.

Virtue, Noel. *Once a Brethren Boy.* Auckland, N.Z.: Vintage, 1995.

Wood, Christine. *Exclusive By-Path: The Autobiography of a Pilgrim.* Evesham: James, 1976.

Notes

RECKONING

29   *In 2009 an Australian investigative journalist* See Michael Bachelard, *Behind the Exclusive Brethren* (Scribe, 2009).

29   *Australian Prime minister Kevin Rudd once described* Philip Cooney, "Brethren Still a Cult in Rudd's Book," *The Sydney Morning Herald,* August 23, 2007.

30   *"We have to get a hatred"* Bachelard, *Behind the Exclusive Brethren,* p. 3.

30   *"That's in hand," one British* Billy Kenber and Alexi Mostrous, "Extreme Sect Secures £13m Tax Breaks," *The Times,* March 17, 2015.

BEFORE

40   *The Bible didn't specify* Carl E. Olson, "Five Myths About the Rapture," *Crisis* (Morley, 2003), pp. 28–33. Although it is understood that about 50 percent of contemporary Americans believe in the idea of the Rapture, there was no common notion of a pretribulation Rapture before the eighteenth century. Olson writes: "Vague notions had been considered by the Puritan preachers Increase (1639–1723) and Cotton Mather (1663–1728), and the late 18th-century Baptist minister Morgan Edwards, but it was John Nelson Darby who solidified the belief in the 1830s and placed it into a larger theological framework."

41   *He wrote to the rest* Norman Adams, *Goodbye, Beloved Brethren* (Glasgow: 1972), pp. 31–32.

41   *In 1869 the newspaper editor James Grant* James Grant, "The Religious Tendencies of the Times," *Sword and Trowel,* June 1869.

43   *To keep them out* Ian Smith, *Tin Tabernacles: Corrugated Iron Mission Halls, Churches and Chapels of Britain* (Salisbury: Camrose Organisation, 2004), and Alasdair Ogilvie, *Tin Tabernacles and Others* (Photo-Stroud, 2009).

44   *"Satan is the god of this world"* John Nelson Darby, *Collected Writings*, vol. 41; cited in Bachelard, *Behind the Exclusive Brethren*, p. 21.

50   *In the seventeenth century* See Brian P. Levack, *Witch-Hunting in Scotland: Law, Politics and Religion* (New York: Routledge, 2007). For all my information on Eyemouth, I relied on Peter Aitchison and John Hume Robertson, *Children of the Sea: The Story of the Eyemouth Disaster* (East Lothian: Tuckwell Press, 2001).

58   *Within four years he'd be* "Scotch Bankrupts," *Glasgow Herald,* August 26, 1885.

61   *Tens of thousands of Lowland cottars* Tim Devine, *The Scottish Nation 1700 to 2007* (Penguin revised edition, 2012), and Peter Aitchison and Andrew Cassell, *The Lowland Clearances: Scotland's Silent Revolution 1760–1830* (Birllin, 2016).

61   *Joining a nonconformist church* Callum Brown, "Protest in the Pews: Interpreting Presbyterianism and Society in Fracture during the Scottish Economic Revolution," in T. M. Devine, ed., *Conflict and Stability in Scottish Society, 1700–1850* (Edinburgh: John Donald, 1990).

66   *All this excommunication* For Brethren accounts of the Glanton division, see two pamphlets in particular: D. L. Higgins, *The Glanton Crisis Explained* (London: G. Morrish, c. 1915), sets out the London position; W.T.P. Wolston, *"Hear the Right": Plain Facts Regarding Alnwick and Glanton, Edinburgh and London* (privately printed, 1908), sets out a defense of the Alnwick Brethren. Both can be found on the website of archive materials Brethrenarchive.org

67   *During the later years* Napoleon Noel, *The History of the Brethren* (Denver: W. F. Knapp, 1936), 40ff.

85   *One third of those women died* Peter Bladin, *A Century of Prejudice and Progress: A Paradigm of Epilepsy in a Developing Society: Medical and Social Aspects: Victoria, Australia, 1835–1950* (Epilepsy Australia, 2001), and M. J. Eadie and Peter Bladin, *A Disease Once Sacred: A History of the Medical Understanding of Epilepsy* (Eastleigh: John Libbey, 2001).

109 *it affects the physiology* Kathleen Taylor, *Brainwashing: The Science of Thought Control* (Oxford: Oxford University Press, 2004), p. 126.

DURING

127   *His seriously ill wife* Bachelard, *Behind the Exclusive Brethren,*
       pp. 272–285.

130   *"You either had to commit"* "Doctrine That Divides," *Anno Domini*
       (BBC Everyman, Peter France, dir., 1976).

130   *"We must keep in mind"* J.T. Junior, *Letters* vol. 2, p. 324.

131   *It was the 1960s* Roger Shuff, *Searching for the True Church: Brethren
       and Evangelicals in Mid-Twentieth-Century England* (Milton Keynes:
       Paternoster, 2005).

134   *Or worse: Was Christopher's father* Quoted from a letter in the author's
       possession.

143   *"We're rich," they said* Stephen Bates, "Secretive Sect Softens Ban on
       Outside Contact," *The Guardian*, March 15, 2003.

144   *"Smell out the enemy"* J.T. Junior, *Readings at Nostrand Avenue and
       Other Ministry,* vol. 1 (1970), p. 2.

145   *When he handed them the list* Email in author's possession.

146   *I would hear a low rumbling* Email in author's possession.

147   *"We were shocked by what we found"* Gerard Kemp, "Brethren Drove
       Them to Suicide," *Daily Mail*, July 24, 1962.

148   *He did not add churches* Stanley Milgram, "Behavioural Study of Obe-
       dience," *Journal of Abnormal and Social Psychology* 67, no. 4 (1963),
       pp. 371–378.

150   *My father's friend William* Robert Stott, ed., *The Way Everlasting*
       (Kingston on Thames: Stow Hill Bible and Tract Depot, 1958).

151   *Kez found a copy* "Notes of a Meeting in Connection with Stow Hill
       Depot held at Alexandra Palace, London," July 12, 1962. A copy can be
       found at: www.brethrenarchive.org.archive/later-exclusivism/raven
       -section/taylorite/notes-of-a-meeting-in-connection-with-stow-hill
       -depot.

152   *"I remember going to the bank"* Manuscript in author's possession.

155   *"Have you cut off the flesh?"* J.T. Junior, *The Service of Song and Other
       Ministry: Notes from Meetings at Bournemouth, Haywards Heath and
       Croydon* (1963), vol. 25 of *The Ministry of J. Taylor Jr* (Kingston on
       Thames: Stow Hill Bible and Tract Depot, 1964), p. 91.

157   *Miss Paynter. She has come* Unpublished manuscript of "Notes
       Taken from Meetings 1957–1970"; document in the author's
       possession.

159   *Meanwhile they told Brethren* Alan Clarke, *The Compliance Officer*, unpublished manuscript in author's possession, p. 138.

161   *The terrified youngbloods* Clarke, *The Compliance Officer*, p. 138.

185   *There were no Brethren schools in the sixties* Bachelard, *Behind the Exclusive Brethren*, pp. 215–245.

195   *"Big Jim Taylor put his arm round"* www.discourses.org.uk/History/ TheAberdeenIncident.pdf

197   *This was deadly serious* This account is assembled from two documents: witness statements assembled in Robert Stott, *If We Walk in the Light* (Stow Hill) and a letter written by Ted Steedman: see transcript online at wikipeebia.com/wp-content/uploads/2013/02/Steedman _letter.pdf.

197   *"We arrived at James Gardiner's house"* Steedman letter, p. 2.

199   *Twenty minutes later* Steedman letter, p. 3.

200   *"It is hard"* Steedman letter, p. 3.

200   *"He became nasty"* Steedman letter, p. 3.

201   *[Loud laughter and stamping.]* Stott, *If We Walk in the Light*, p. 3.

202   *J.T. Junior: David, where the hell* Stott, *If We Walk in the Light*, p. 3. Nicodemus is a Pharisee who helped prepare Jesus's body for burial. I have no idea why J.T. Junior is invoking him here or referring to "Eric" as Nicodemus.

205   *They'd keep doing so* In 1987 the Brethren brought a lawsuit against the author and publishers of a book about the Brethren published in the Hague, in which the Kers testified to the good character of J.T. Junior. Their testimony is online at wikipeebia.com/wp-content/uploads/ 2013/02/Kertestimony.pdf

AFTERMATH

216   *"What made us so weak and ignorant* Roger Stott, ministry in the author's possession.

248   *Once I was back in my bedroom* Martin McGregor, *The Town That God Forgot* (lulu.com, 2011) and "Father Ostracised by Sect Axed Family to Death," *Daily Telegraph*, March 21, 1974.

285   *He told the Brethren that Satan* J. H. Symington and Wilbert J. Seed, *Ministry of J. H. Symington* (Minneapolis: 1981), vol. 95, pp. 134–135.

Photo Credits and Permissions

page 165   Rebecca at around age 4, from photograph in family possession.

page 170   Rebecca at eight, still from family film footage in author's possession.

page 224   Rebecca and brother in garden, from photograph in author's possession

page 242   Roger as Reverend Shannon in *Night of the Iguana*, 1972, from photograph in author's possession.

page 276   A diagram of Yeats's Gyre, courtesy of Neil Mann.

page 279   Rebecca as teenager cutting her father's hair, from photograph in author's possession.

About the Author

REBECCA STOTT is a professor of English literature and creative writing at the University of East Anglia. She is the author of *Darwin's Ghosts: The Secret History of Evolution,* the novels *The Coral Thief* and the national bestseller *Ghostwalk,* and a biography, *Darwin and the Barnacle.* She is a regular contributor to BBC Radio and lives in Norwich, England.